When Lewis Diuguid's mother implored ~~~~~ accurate and valid picture of black men, neither suspected that he would do this through a vivid memoir of his remarkable father. This social and historical memoir takes you into the long and good life of "Doc" Diuguid, scientist, inventor, manufacturer, citizen, mentor and untiring fighter for justice. He passed on to his son his talent for observing and recording detail so there is a sense of rich life on every page. Doc was a teacher of his values: integrity, responsibility, care, accuracy, compassion and appreciation of life. Readers of all ages may be inspired by Doc as I have been.

Peggy McIntosh, Ph.D.,
Founder of the National SEED Project (Seeking Educational Equity & Diversity), Former Associate Director Wellesley Centers for Women

Lewis Diuguid once again shares the painful, sharp details of how racism shapes family, community and U.S. society. This time, this award-winning journalist takes us on the incredible journeys of his father Dr. Lincoln I. Diuguid, illuminating a beautiful life of resistance, dignity, and deep, undying commitment to support, love and nurture the black men in his life. Despite the impactful narratives that guide readers through historical connections to today's anti-black violence and ever-present onslaught of systemic racial hatred, Lewis Diuguid's smooth, fast-flowing writing makes this book an easy read. Diuguid takes readers across time and space, sharing intimate details of his own family stories, immortalizing a man we should all be familiar with, and in the process, reminding of the permanence of race and racism in the U.S. *Our Fathers* forces readers to rethink history, challenges what we think we know about the U.S., and ultimately reminds us that our very salvation as a country lies with how we look back in order to move forward.

Christopher B. Knaus, Ph.D.,
Professor, University of Washington-Tacoma

Throughout his life, Dr. Lincoln I. Diuguid fostered respectable and uncompromising life-standards. I met Doc for the first time at a Science Center of St. Louis celebration for Doc in 2000. I was reluctant to approach such an esteemed gentleman. But he immediately put me at ease. He virtually exuded a caring, characteristic attitude, which enabled him to be so influential to neighborhood kids. That aura is what *Our Fathers: Making Black Men* is about. The depth of Doc's ability to communicate with others, and then insist that they learned life's values was a remarkable quality that needs to be replicated today.

Diane M. Kappen, Ph.D.,
Social Psychology, Johnson County Community College

Brother Lincoln Diuguid was a true Omega man in every sense of the word. He lived life firmly squared on the principles of manhood, scholarship, perseverance and uplift.

Glenn E. Rice,
30th Eighth District Representative,
Omega Psi Phi Fraternity, Inc. 2008–2010

Lewis Diuguid's latest book challenges America and provocatively sears the soul. But like life itself, the book demands a respect for unshadowed realities and untainted truths that exist beyond preconceived notions or prejudices. *Our Fathers: Making Black Men* is a must read!

Carol Charismas,
Kansas City Educator

Reading the story of Doc Diuguid is an opportunity to learn about what it really means to be a black man in America. The reality of having to be twice as good as whites and that failure is not an option held true for him as a black businessman. Those same truisms remain, despite our achievements. This story provides lessons for those wishing to link the long struggles of the past to those we face today.

Earnest L. Perry Jr., Ph.D.,
Associate Dean for Graduate Studies Missouri
School of Journalism, University of Missouri-Columbia

OUR FATHERS

OUR FATHERS

Making Black Men

Lewis W. Diuguid

Universal Publishers
Boca Raton

Our Fathers: Making Black Men

Universal Publishers
Boca Raton, Florida • USA
2017

www.universal-publishers.com

978-1-62734-099-1 (pbk.)
978-1-62734-100-4 (ebk.)

Typeset by Medlar Publishing Solutions Pvt Ltd, India

Publisher's Cataloging-in-Publication Data

Names: Diuguid, Lewis W.
Title: Our fathers : making black men / Lewis W. Diuguid.
Description: Boca Raton, FL : Universal Publishers, 2017.
Identifiers: LCCN 2017932463 | ISBN 978-1-62734-099-1 (pbk.) |
  ISBN 978-1-62734-100-4 (ebook)
Subjects: LCSH: African American men--Biography. | African American
  chemists--Biography. | African American business enterprises. | Saint Louis
  (Mo.)--Social conditions. | United States--Race relations. | Black lives matter
  movement. | BISAC: BIOGRAPHY & AUTOBIOGRAPHY / Cultural
  Heritage. | BIOGRAPHY & AUTOBIOGRAPHY / Science & Technology. |
  SOCIAL SCIENCE / Discrimination & Race Relations.
Classification: LCC E185.97.D58 A3 2017 (print) | LCC E185.97.D58 (ebook) |
  DDC 305.89/6--dc23.

TABLE OF CONTENTS

FOREWORD

As you crack open the cover of *Our Fathers: Making Black Men*—after reading the book jacket—you must be wondering: "How can the stories and experiences of an African American man born in the early 1900s be relevant for me, today?" Sadly, I can assure you that Doc Diuguid's stories are very relevant, even vital today. While much has changed in the last 100 years or so, one constant is *trauma*. Trauma impacts us now in many ways, as it always has.

We are globally traumatized by the terrorist attacks in Paris and ISIS threats around the globe. We are traumatized as a nation by the 9/11 terrorist attacks, the shootings at Sandy Hook Elementary School in Newtown, Conn., and a list of many more too painfully long to include here. We are traumatized by the killings of young black males around the country, including Oscar Grant in Oakland, Calif.; Trayvon Martin in Sanford, Fla.; Eric Gardner in Staten Island, N.Y.; Mike Brown in Ferguson, Mo.; LaQuan McDonald in Chicago; Tamir Rice in Cleveland, Ohio; Freddie Gray in Baltimore; Philando Castile in Minneapolis and again, too many to recount here, and the number keeps growing. The subsequent protests and unrest after the police killings of black men and boys also traumatized and polarized us to a point of action and the creation of activist groups like Black Lives Matter in St. Louis, which was also the birthplace of Du-Good Chemical 70 years ago. The Black Lives Matter organization and movement works to bring awareness to and address the issues of the black community. Seventy years ago, Doc Diuguid opened Du-Good Chemical and as a small businessman worked for more than 60 years to help address the issues of St. Louis' black community one young person at a time who came to his door looking for a job.

While all the killings I referenced took place in recent years, the trauma they create is not unlike the trauma that shook communities in the early 1900s. In 1917, the year of Doc's birth, one of the bloodiest race riots of the 20th century traumatized both the black and white communities of East St. Louis, Ill., while destroying the black community. Whites were angered by black workers being hired in factories to replace striking white workers. The whites rioted, killed many blacks, burned homes and businesses, devastating the black community. In 1921 a similar incident took place in Tulsa, Okla., completely destroying a very successful black community that had been known as Black Wall Street. Perhaps even better known is the 1923 trauma/riot called the Rosewood Massacre, that effective ripped the middle-class black town of Rosewood, Fla., off the map. After the massacre only nine citizens of the town, the general store and one home remained.

All of these incidents traumatized and polarized local communities as well as people across the country. Jim Crow and segregation were the law of the South in the 1900s, keeping tensions high and trauma a part of daily life for people of color. Doc was born into this trauma. He knew trauma well. It greeted him at birth and never left his side. Trauma was his constant companion, but not his friend. For Doc, trauma became a motivator. He always knew he had to fight for everything, thanks to the lessons taught by his constant companion—trauma. It pressed him to be driven, competitive, determined. Trauma was also what he faced in the final years of his life, cutting tragically short what should have been many years past 100.

During one of my many visits with Doc, late in his life, I mentioned that I was also the "baby" of my family. Upon hearing the word "baby" Doc launched into a passionate rant about being the youngest in his family meant he had to fight for everything—from fighting to get even a little bit of attention from his parents, grandparents or other family elders, to fighting to get a few scraps at the dinner table. Those early battles prepared him for the battlefield of higher education, the sciences and business as a black man.

Doc's battlefield was wide—like mine and many fair complexed blacks—the attacks came from all sides. Being a fair-skinned, highly educated black man, he had to take on the known and expected battles with whites. They were always challenged by the fact that he was usually the first African American in his field and in his professional encounters with whites. But he had challenges with other blacks as well. Because of his fair complexion, he felt he was always fighting for trust and acceptance by blacks. Unfortunately, he had to fight for acceptance on all fronts. This was something we discussed often because he knew that this was a dual battle that I fought, as well, made only more challenging because I am a woman. He always encouraged me to demand respect and recognition as an intelligent African American/Native American woman. He told me it was a battle I should become accustomed to because it would always be with me. My own life experiences—from childhood until today—support this and his many other important lessons.

I admired and appreciated Doc for his accomplishments, wisdom and the great lessons he shared with me. What I admired most was his self-confidence. Whether we were discussing science, golf, history or current events, he was confident in his knowledge, confident in his ability, confident in himself! You might even say he was cocky! (And you would be right!) Whenever we had the opportunity for these private lessons the thing that struck me the most was his absolute belief in himself!

Trauma experts today say that one of the most important keys to overcoming trauma is a long-standing, strong belief in one's self—no matter the circumstance. Experts in trauma also believe that trauma survivors having a realistic grasp on the world around them and the things that life can throw at them is also vital. According to the experts, another key to recovering from trauma is hard work. A strong work ethic is vital to trauma survival. All of these trauma survival keys describe Doc Diuguid to a "T." He knew that he was exceptionally brilliant and that he was usually the "brightest bulb" in the room. He also knew that life in 20th century America was not kind or friendly to a person of color—especially a black man. Yet, he never let that stop him from striving and achieving anything he set his mind on. It also pushed him to help others overcome trauma and succeed.

Doc Diuguid believed that helping others reach their dreams, their potential was required in this life. He never believed in giving anyone a handout. But he was always ready and willing to give someone a hand up. From his own life experiences he knew that the young black men in his community needed the greatest hand up, although many of the young people he guided and mentored were women of color, also.

After Mike Brown was killed in Ferguson, just miles from Doc's nursing home, I often wondered how the influence of someone like Doc and the other black business owners from his old St Louis neighborhood would affect communities like them all over America.

I know the answer for this generation's trauma is not that simple. In 21st century America we are dealing with trauma that is every bit as severe as the traumas of the early 1900s. Despite the efforts and sacrifices of the great civil rights leaders and movement of the mid-1900s, we are dealing with 21st century Jim Crow and the more devastating segregation twins—race and poverty. But unlike in Doc's time, the issues and causes today are more cloaked. It is not always clear who is waging the battle. What is clear is that the only way to win this war is to find a way to get beyond the issues of race, bigotry and discrimination.

No, the answers are not certain or simple! But as we face the complexities of 21st century biases we can certainly use the wisdom of brilliant, determined, successful black men. We would benefit from the examples of how such a person, along with a strong community of black businesses, was able to speak into the lives of so many black men and women.

Enjoy *Our Fathers: Making Black Men* and learn from Doc, as I have.

Bette Tate-Beaver
Executive Director
National Association for
Multicultural Education (NAME)

BLACK FAMILY IMPERATIVE

The last of four lines lit up on the old shared phone system at work. It was an afternoon of deadlines, and every one of the half-dozen newspaper people was working getting stories done or ads locked down for the weekend paper. How that call of all calls got through was a miracle. I answered the phone. My mother was on the other end. That was unusual, too. The first thought any of my siblings and me would have had about a midday call from Mom was, "Oh no! Who died? Did something happen to Dad?" He was 15 years older than Mom, and she always chastised him about taking too many risks.

It was 1988 on a warm, sunny afternoon. I calmed down a bit so I could hear what she really had to say instead of worrying about what might come through the receiver. Mom's rare phone calls are a Depression-era thing. "Every penny counts," and "The meter is always running on long-distance calls." Also, "If it can't be put in a letter, it isn't worth telling," Mom would say. Something serious must be amiss for her to want to talk with me at the newspaper. I looked out the narrow, floor-to-ceiling window in my office when I said hello. I could see the Truman Farm Home. It wouldn't take much to flip a rock from The Kansas City Star's Grandview, Mo., bureau and hit the two-story, green-and-white clapboard house with a shingled roof.

At the turn of the last century, Harry S. Truman, the 33rd president of the United States farmed the surrounding acreage as a young man, including the land that accommodated The Star and all of the existing commercial buildings. Mom always liked Truman. He was Missouri's only president, a straight-shooting, brutally honest person just like her. Wouldn't you know that both were born in May with all of the endearing qualities of Taurus the Bull. Truman took bold stands such as integrating the U.S. Armed Services in 1948 when doing so was deemed political suicide. Mom was just 16 years old then. She grew up as Nancy Ruth Greenlee in a traditional nuclear family of seven children—two boys and five girls. She went to college to become an educator. That's where she and Dad met and were later married. Each knew that Truman took courageous stands on behalf of all American, which no black person in Missouri or elsewhere back then would forget.

Looking out the window at Truman's home set off daydreams of being in St. Louis, sitting at Mom's kitchen table, listening to her homespun, common-sense wisdom crafted in the form of stories that only a journalist could tell or admire. Mom had wanted to be a journalist, but that avenue was mostly closed to black women when she came of age as an adult. So she helped make such a journey possible for me.

After exchanging hellos and other niceties, Mom jumped to the point of her call. Yes, the long-distance meter was running—and it mattered most when the charge was on her end.

"It really scares me what's happening to black men and boys," she said, nearly 30 years before the police shooting in Ferguson, Mo., of Michael Brown and the start of the Black Lives Matter movement, calling attention to unwarranted killings of African American males by white cops. "All you see on the news is how they're getting into trouble."

I couldn't argue. Crack cocaine had become *the* drug in many inner-city neighborhoods. It was highly addictive, cheap and once on it, people did the most profoundly foul and deadly things. It was a poor person's narcotic. Stories filled the press of crack-cocaine-fueled shootings in schools, gangster-style killings, drive-by shootings, car-jackings, and parents abandoning their children or living with them in dangerous dope houses with violent people. Authorities and the media responded with the war on drugs, adding more police on the streets, zero tolerance law enforcement policies, longer prison sentences, the construction of more prisons and ramping up the schools-to-prison pipeline disproportionately affecting black males. It was far different from the political, social and news media response to the opioid and heroin epidemic in 2016, in America's white and mostly suburban and rural communities. For it, authorities talked about treatment programs to prevent overdoses and fatalities and ways to help people overcome their addiction. U.S. Sen. Claire McCaskill of Missouri held hearings in the state. I know firsthand of the nationwide sentiment because I wrote sensitive, compelling editorials for The Kansas City Star, urging a compassionate response and help for those who suffered opioid or heroin addiction. In radical contrast, the news media stories and commentary on the crack cocaine crisis included black women working as prostitutes to get money to get high. This was how the radio, television, newspaper, magazine and other media called themselves "covering" the black community. The negative news only helped perpetuate the problem and cause many young blacks to live down to the negative stereotypes and self-fulfilling prophesy whites had of blacks. Black women also felt unfazed about raising children alone. Black boys and men didn't think anything about having multiple children with multiple women. That often made the news, too.

Because I worked for a newspaper, Mom wanted me to do something to change that. "You need to write more positive stories about black men and boys," she said. She worried about her grandsons—my sister's three kids—and all of the other black boys in America who didn't have positive role-models in their lives. She worried about her granddaughters—my two girls and my older brother's two daughters—and all of the other black girls who wouldn't know what real black men were like. She feared these girls would be taken in by thugs, perpetrating as strong, protective men when they were nothing more than very scared, very insecure, untrained, uneducated and undisciplined boys with no hope or future for themselves let alone anyone else.

Mom's call didn't last long. She had to go. But over the years I've thought a lot about what Mom said. Her words and wisdom identifying a massive societal problem—an American problem—has lived beyond Mom developing Alzheimer's Disease not long after that call and dying an untimely death at age 62 in July 1994.

For that reason, this book is dedicated to answering Mom's call to write about black men in a way that people can see what she saw and respond in a way that existed when her generation and mine were going through childhood and the rebellious teenage years. Real black men in black businesses helped to raise and shape us into adults. They are missing today. But it is not just in the black community. In doing the research for this book, friends of all colors recounted similar tales of mom-and-pop businesses helping to guide and ensure the development of young people. Across America, these businesses have vanished, as if scooped up in some spaceship and taken to another planet, never to be replaced. They have been gone for so long that they are mostly forgotten as the hidden element missing in the lives of today's youths. Somehow, that positive element has to be recaptured so the massive problems facing today's young people can be fixed. The media play a role, but so do the schools, businesses, churches, law enforcement, the courts, penal system and most importantly, the community.

My sister, Renee Tolson, and my life partner and inspiration, Bette Tate-Beaver, worked with me to help make this book possible. Elizabeth Garcia, a former co-worker at The Star helped with the editing. The goal of this very important book is that by describing what's missing in America in the upbringing of our children, we can help to regenerate that cornerstone of character development in our youths' lives and never lose it in the future.

CHAPTER 1

LEFT FOR DEAD

The guard at Barnes-Jewish Hospital escorted my sister, Renee, and me to the basement of the building. Our younger brother, Vincent, followed on Sunday, Aug. 6, 2006. Vincent had been through the security drill at the hospital. But it was our first time getting security clearance there. Hospitals must be very cautious when people go into the intensive care unit as victims of violent crimes. It is for the victims' protection and the hospital staff as well. Trauma units at hospitals nationwide learned the hard way what sometimes happens when they don't take the stringent security precautions. It inconveniences family members and loved ones, but the extra protection is worth every bit of the costs. Our world has turned malignantly violent, and security is the only cure for this cancer.

Our drivers' licenses were checked, we were photographed and issued special security identification cards that we had to wear at all times. A slow trek back down the basement corridors and to an even slower moving elevator followed to the intensive care unit. Innocuous paintings, historical medical sketches and other artwork lined the hallways. They were visual background noise. Nothing stood out. Getting to ICU—without running as we had wanted to—was all that mattered. It was what brought Renee and me 250 miles from Kansas City to our hometown.

After the elevators and more hallways, we only had to clear electronically locked double doors. The medical staff directed us to the right room. The noise of the surroundings dampened, and the hospital lights seemed to blur. That always happens when my blood pressure suddenly jumps from the fight-or-flight stress of the unexpected that lies ahead. I know Renee felt it, too. Vince had already experienced it. He was the one who called us Saturday afternoon, and we knew we had to come. It was a trip that none of us wanted to make. Other human beings, some in hospital garb and some hooked to machines, filled the other bays of ICU. The patients were men and women of different ages. All had suffered; many from the violent hand of others.

Behind a curtain substituting as a wall in a crowded multipartitioned space that hummed, beeped and flashed with expensive medical equipment was a helpless, still-breathing 89-year-old body curled in a fetal position. Two probes protruded from his skull. Tubes ran to bags that were filling up with a constant drip of fluid under his bed. It was hard to watch. But none of us flinched. None of us cried. That was how the man before us had raised us. The most powerful, most intelligent, most awe-inspiring person in our lives lay at the mercy of the modern medicine, which he often ridiculed and despised. Lincoln Isaiah Diuguid had made it out of brain surgery. Doctors had drained away fluid that had accumulated from his head wounds. But Dad was far from being out of the woods, far from being the picture of good health.

Nearly everyone called him "Doc" except his wife, Nancy, and children, David, Renee, Vincent and me, Lewis. In these pages, he will be immortalized as "Doc." The thing that Doc had always done at the chemical company he had built and run with his family since 1947, the thing that shaped each of us and hundreds of otherwise throwaway ghetto kids into the stellar adults we are today was what landed Doc on the cold, concrete floor of Du-Good Chemical Laboratories & Manufacturers. The violence he experienced was among the hidden costs of Hurricane Katrina.

The unprecedented storm blew into the Gulf Coast region of the United States on Aug. 25-29, 2005, hitting Florida, Louisiana, Mississippi and Alabama. It killed 1,833 people, did $125 billion damage and caused hundreds of thousands of people to flee their homes. Katrina was the costliest storm in U.S. history, and it permanently displaced many people in that region; a large percentage were black and poor. They became the evacuees that the administration of President George W. Bush handled badly. But the United States always has. That is the nation's history, and millions of people continue to suffer needlessly because of it. Flushed from the Gulf Coast area among them were scores of criminals who had seared the streets of New Orleans with violence and crime. They now were displaced, too. They were spread like a toxin throughout the country, wiping out everything that had grown naturally before the coming poison. The finest of New Orleans' worst resettled their underworld behavior everywhere that the Bush administration dropped them.

Nancy R. Diuguid, Doc's wife, used to admonish Doc repeatedly. "You're too trusting, taking in every stranger on the street. The minute you turn your back one of those bozos will knock you in the head."

Doc would always blow her off. "I'm a good judge of character, and you mind your own damn business."

But Nancy, died on July 19, 1994. She had Alzheimer's disease. On Sunday, July 17, 1994, she walked away from the family home in the 3600 block of Lafayette Avenue. Her body was found three days later in the Mississippi River near Jefferson Barracks, Mo. She was only 62 years old. When Alzheimer's disease took her followed by the unimaginable death, Doc, who was 15 years older than she was, lost his best friend, intellectual equal and favorite sparing partner. Afterward no one was around to provide the cautionary voice anymore. Just as Doc had always done, he took a young man who was a homeless Katrina evacuee into Du-Good Chemical. The fence out front of the lab needed a new coat of chocolate brown paint. Doc needed help, and the man needed a job.

The fit had worked so naturally over the 59 years Doc, his father and brothers had converted the turn-of-the-century large animal hospital into a laboratory and chemical company. Alfonso, one of Doc's older brothers, was a master tradesman. He knew plumbing, sheet metal work, roofing and carpentry. A lot of the trades he learned while in prison. Alfonso had done time during Prohibition, running bootleg whiskey in Virginia with Jerry Falwell's family. That was how the Falwells made their millions. But they used to hire a lot of black drivers to get the liquor from the stills to underworld distributors, saloons and finally the customers. Many drivers would start out on different roads. The moonshiners figured that several of them were bound to get through. The best drivers made it. Many others were shot or arrested. Doc's brother was one who got nabbed and had to do hard time even though Prohibition only lasted from 1920 until 1933 when it was lifted as a way of getting the country through the Great Depression.

Doc remembered that people would bring ailing horses, mules and cattle through the double doors of the large stone archway that fronted onto South Jefferson Avenue. It was the receiving entrance of Dr. William F. Heyde's large animal hospital. It was where one of two veterinarians in the flanking offices up front would examine the large animals, do the initial work and then escort the four-legged patients out the side door into the alley, which was paved with 19ᵗʰ century bricks. Upstairs in the red-brick building constructed in 1895, which later became the lab, were cages for smaller animals that the veterinarian tended to. After Doc finished his post-doctorate studies in organic chemistry at Cornell University, the Lynchburg, Va., family pooled their money and resources to make the new business possible. In 1947, that wonderful Diuguid bricks-and-mortar dream was just 52 years old. The building at 1215 S. Jefferson Ave. was constructed in 1895, the year that famous abolitionist, newspaper publisher and fiery oratory Frederick Douglass died. Doc, the grandson of slaves, was named after President Abraham Lincoln, the famous emancipator, credited with freeing the slaves following the brutal Civil War. Du-Good Chemical would embody Doc's dream of being his own boss in his own company, giving him the freedom that Maya Angelou later would write about in her famous poem, "Still I Rise," as "the dream and the hope of the slave."

The Diuguid family stood together through many adversities. One day, Doc was on a ladder painting the front of his building when a union painter walked up and started to hassle the young chemist about doing the work himself. Doc advised the man to mind his own business, but the man persisted, threatening to pull the heavy, double, wooden ladder from under Doc. Doc was prepared to jump from the ladder on top of the assailant's head when his father, Lewis Diuguid, stepped from the building with a pistol at his side in his large right hand. He asked the man, "Are you looking for trouble?" The man said no and quickly left, allowing Doc to finish painting the building. Doc shared that story with some of the boys who later worked at his company, showing that families stick together—no matter what.

The unforeseen, however, did happen back in the manufacturing area, where Doc for decades had made his own paint. Doc had his back to the Hurricane Katrina evacuee while adding ingredients to the paint. The mixer that Doc had crafted decades ago was turning. It hummed, rocked and whirred filling the old manufacturing plant with its own noise of activity. Such sounds breathe life back into the old cavernous surroundings. It is music in the symphony of the industrial development of the nation—only this was the rare diamond, which was black owned and African-American made. Many layers of colors from years of other paints coated the metal trash-can size container and the paddles that stirred within it. Only once had workers cleaned that thing. It required cutting through multiple layers of paint. They were like rings on a 300-year-old oak tree. The 15-gallon container stood on bricks between two of the many posts that supported the 20-foot high ceiling in the broad shouldered and long torsoed manufacturing area. The concrete floors stretched 60 feet by 30 feet. Forty-year-old electric motors were bolted to a rustic 8-inch-wide, 2-inch-thick board that was 8 feet long and nailed to the two painted posts. Different colors had been fingered-painted over the years on the board from Doc testing various hues for how they looked and for smoothness and consistency.

Doc often talked over the chugging noise and rhythmic rocking of the equipment as the motor hummed and the two paddles sloshed the paint. Stories of great scientists and other people doing noteworthy things flowed like the smoothest brush strokes coating old, never-before-covered surfaces. The true tales of human accomplishments were meant to wash over all rough-hewn young listeners coating them with the possibilities of what they now were capable of doing, too. One coat was never enough—just as with paint over an old, untreated fence board. Refinishing kids who were hard cut by life took many layers of trying work and many stories of greatness for the sealant of a new life to finally sink in. Doc's PhD may have been in organic chemistry, but for the street kids captivated by his tutelage, his doctorate was in reshaping them from raw—often dangerous to themselves and others toughs—into well-refined, caring and taxpaying citizens. It had worked effectively on hundreds of kids. Only a few exceptions walked away undeterred from their errant paths.

The Katrina evacuee was among them. Doc turned his back to add ingredients to the paint and talked as he always had, following his habit of lecturing as he had during almost 40 years of teaching chemistry and physical science at Harris-Stowe State University. That was when the man he had taken in, the man he was planning to pay for the job of painting the fence, picked up a heavy item from one of the long manufacturing tables and struck Doc on the head. One blow was not enough to drop old Doc, who was built like iron. Doc struggled to get up unaware that he had been assaulted. The man struck him again. Still not down, the man struck Doc a third time, leaving him unconscious and to die in a pool of his own blood. The Katrina evacuee took Doc's wallet and fled leaving the door of the chemical company ajar.

Fortunately a neighbor happened by. He saw that the door was open, which never fit Doc's nearly 60-year-old habits at the company. The man wandered in hollering: "Doc! Are you there? Is everything all right?" He heard the paint stirring, but no one was around. He found Doc, on the floor bleeding. He helped him up, called 9-1-1 and Vince. After a lot of convincing, paramedics, the police, firefighters and others got Doc to go to the hospital. He had lost a lot of blood, and his head was massively swollen.

Vincent alerted the family, including David, Doc's eldest son, a physician in New York and an associate professor of Columbia University Department of Medicine. Surgery followed, and although a thousand miles away, David kept close tabs on the progress. Renee and I raced from our Kansas City area homes on the other side of the state to St. Louis the following day, finding Doc in ICU.

A nurse opened up the curtain in the semidark room and started checking the equipment. She said some reassuring words. The fluid from the head trauma Doc had suffered was putting pressure on Doc's brain. But the surgery enabled the drainage to occur just as the doctors wanted. Only time would tell whether Doc would return to good health without seizures or lost function.

While the nurse was in the room, Doc suddenly came to. She offered him a little water, which he gingerly drank. Some food also remained from his last meal. Doc normally had a robust appetite, but the meal remained untouched. The medication was doing its job, keeping Doc pain-free. We said hello, but Doc was out of it and slid back into a semi-sleep. However, he seemed to awaken and start talking. It was as if he were reliving the moments before he was assaulted only instead of the Katrina evacuee who hit him, Doc was talking to me as if I were still working for Du-Good Chemical.

"Stir the paint, Lewie," Doc said. "I told you to stir the paint!" He was quite emphatic and agitated as if no time had lapsed in the decades since I had worked under his tutelage.

Doc must have repeated the paint-stirring directive a dozen times while thrashing about in the hospital bed and pulling off his covers. The nurse was afraid he would fall out of bed so she lashed his wrists to the side of the bed with restraints for his safety. His massively large hands stretched outward grabbing for the person in his mind or for the paint paddles. Vincent had gone by then. Renee and I tried to make Doc think we were stirring the paint. But he couldn't hear us and wouldn't believe it if he could. After about 10 minutes and the nurse upping the dose of intravenous sedatives, Doc settled back into a restful sleep.

His elevated heart rate caused more fluid to flow from the probes in his skull through the clear tubes and into the bags below. The little hospital gown was hardly enough to keep anyone warm in that cold room, on that cold floor and in the cold hospital on that warm summer day. The linoleum floors functioned like the plastic panels of a refrigerator, reflecting back the coolness onto the bodies within. The sheet that covered Doc was hardly enough. We asked the nurse for a blanket and to turn the heat up. She did both. Doc, Renee and I settled in for a long encampment. Dad was asleep; the rest of us were worried sick.

A doctor came by to visit. He was nice enough, but none of what he said made sense. I got him to talk with David. They communicated in the same physicians' parlance. David translated for us. The surgery went as well as expected. We just had to wait now.

Renee and I traded turns walking the halls to burn nervous energy and all of the coffee we consumed on the drive. I hate that long, Interstate 70 drive on the four-lane divided highway. I always have. The spreading development of urban sprawl with the replication of fast-food restaurants, budget motels and indifferent filling stations marking the end of one suburb and the beginning of another—seem to knit Missouri's two big cities closer together. Renee and I have often joked that one day the outward expansions of both major cities and their suburbs will meet in Columbia, where we went to college at the University of Missouri, totally squeezing out the farms and the wilderness along I-70. We're not there yet. We were just stuck in the hospital—a far cry from where we had been.

Du-Good Chemical Laboratories & Manufacturers is all that's left of once thriving black businesses in the 1200 block of South Jefferson Avenue. The stalwart, red-brick, horseshoe-shaped main building is visible in the six lanes of traffic flowing in either direction on the north-south St. Louis artery. Three arched windows adorn the second floor. The middle window is slightly larger and wider than the two that flank it. Beneath those two windows are the arched front doors. They sit astride a big display window with a white stone arch built atop decorative glass bricks, which admit light to the inside but do not permit people on the street to see the goings-on inside. Du-Good Chemical helped erase the building's past as a large animal hospital like acid rain on limestone grave markers.

The main laboratory is on the second floor. That was where Dr. Diuguid spent most of his time. The north door is the main entrance and office for Du-Good Chemical. The other door opened onto what had been a chiropractor's clinic and then a beauty shop that existed off-and-on in the building when tenants could be found. Just beyond the office door and inside the plant was a filing area, the kitchen, bathroom and the big manufacturing room. It seems to stretch forever inside. The two-story front part of the building drops down in the big room with its 15- to 20-foot-high ceilings. This manufacturing area contains long tables for production and vats varying from to five to 500 gallons to satisfy the once-thriving production needs. Huge, wooden, turn-of-the-century sliding doors with grated glass windows open onto the alley. Big trucks rumble through the narrow, brick paved alley, shaking the buildings. The trucks barely miss the frayed and drooping electric lines atop the 30-foot-tall creosote poles. The utility lines seem to swing through the alley like arcing circus acts traveling along endless trapezes. A sloped ramp from the brick alley into Du-Good Chemical enabled shipments of all sorts to enter the concrete floor of the building. Boxes of glass and plastic containers arrived by tractor-trailer trucks. So did chemicals in 55-gallon, steel drums, feeding the plant's production capacity. The material all had a place, either in the big room, or workers would haul the stuff on two wheel dollies through the furnace room just on the other side of the huge double doors and beneath the second laboratory to the warehouse space in the back. That part of the complex paralleled the street and connected to the other side of the horseshoe structure. In the open middle was the yard area, where the company truck was always parked.

Using an old wheelbarrow, Du-Good workers hauled clinkers they pulled from the turn-of-the-century coal furnace. The coal was delivered by truck from the alley, too. Workers put the clinkers from the furnace on the ground in the area the truck occupied and broke up the sharp-edged, rocklike residue with a sledgehammer in a years-long process of building a road from the six-foot-high fence that paralleled the street to the warehouse section of the building. Those were Doc's orders. Nothing got wasted or thrown out.

The vehicles of Du-Good Chemical were always well-aged, red and decorated with signs that told of the company and its products. But the trucks were always discards from other businesses. They were all-purpose, work autos given a second chance at life and purpose at Du-Good Chemical. The first truck was a 1938 Dodge Humpback Panel Delivery Truck with huge fenders and running boards. An ancient picture of it parked outside of the company stayed hidden for years inside an old roll-top oak desk, which the previous owner had left just outside of the main office and behind the front display window. The second vehicle was a 1952 Dodge panel truck, which looked a lot like many sport utility vehicles today except without any side windows and amenities. The floorboards were made of wood planks except for metal in the driver's and passenger seat area. The truck had no upholstery. It contained choke and throttle knobs on the hard metal dashboard, which had to be used just to get the old vehicle started. The windshield wipers were activated by a knob that sat atop the dash, and a starter pole above the accelerator had to be stomped simultaneously with the gas after the key was turned in the hopes that the old vehicle fired by its 6-volt battery would kick on. The steering wheel was so big in circumference that it felt more like the paddle wheel on a steamboat. But power steering back then was only what the driver was able to provide to muscle vehicles of that vintage in and out of tight spaces. The Dodge also had large, professionally done white lettering on its sides and back doors to advertise Du-Good Chemical and the products that the company manufactured. "Quality through Research" and the logo "DG" were emblazoned on the vehicle. A white, used 1968 Chevy van came after the Dodge and a 1987 Chevy van followed that as the last.

The last stretch of the horseshoe shaped building was where building materials were stored for repairs on Du-Good Chemical and other properties that Doc owned. Among them were boards retrieved for a couple of bucks from buildings that were constantly being torn down in the inner city. The long shed also held bricks from this red-brick town. They were nabbed and stored for construction and reconstruction purposes. In addition, the concrete floor contained sand retrieved from the dredged Mississippi River. Piles of it rested and always got used for many repair projects to keep the Du-Good enterprise going.

The dogs shared the company parking area with the company trucks. The dogs' job was to protect the property, allowing no one admittance. They barked constantly, adding to the neighborhood cacophony of dog noise. Doc always said, "I keep cats to keep the rats out and dogs to keep the thugs out." In this old river city, he needed both. Doc liked to joke, too. He would tell people that his dogs didn't eat meat. People would scratch their heads and say they'd never heard of a dog that didn't eat meat. Doc would laugh and say his didn't because he didn't give them any. People hearing that would laugh, too.

The repairs and construction were ongoing and constant on the old property. Doc, and mainly his highly skilled brother, Alfonso, and father made up the construction crew, converting the turn-of-the-century, large animal hospital into the first black-owned-and-run laboratory and manufacturing company west of the Mississippi River. The Diuguid men refashioned wood, which had constituted the animal stalls, into cabinets, lab tables and drawers of varying sizes. They put in electricity, gas and water plumbing for the labs and manufacturing areas where none had existed. A pipe vice bolted and welded to a pillar in the manufacturing area stayed in constant use gripping steel pipe that ranged from three-eighths inch to 4 inches in diameter.

The Diuguids took out wood-burning stoves upgraded the heating system. Doc made linseed oil-based paint. The Diuguid men applied coats of paint inside the building and outside, which they wanted to last 100 years.

Du-Good Chemical was the first building on the block to go black. Inflexible, restrictive deed covenants strictly enforced by city laws and area business people prevented any property from being sold to blacks. African Americans were called Negroes and colored people then. Those were the polite terms. Niggers, darkies, coons, burheads, spooks, spades and spear chuckers were more common refrains whites used to dehumanize blacks. Such terms made blacks seem less desirable and less human to the white majority. Keep in mind it was only 51 years after the Plessy vs. Ferguson Supreme Court case made segregation the law of the land and less than a century after the end of the Civil War and slavery, and the Supreme Court's Dred Scott ruling of 1857. Justice Roger Taney wrote: Blacks "had for more than a century been regarded as beings of an inferior order, and altogether unfit to associate with the white race, either in social or political revelations, and so far inferior, that they had no rights which the white man was bound to respect."

Doc's family felt that racism in St. Louis, where the Dred Scott case originated. Doc also remembered it being in Lynchburg, where his father a few years earlier had to testify in a court case. His father easily could pass for white. The prosecutor in the case assumed that Lewis Diuguid, born in 1880 the son of a slave, was white and addressed him as Mr. Diuguid, which was a no-no in Virginia. It wasn't until after the trial that other whites informed the prosecutor of his error. He was livid. Blacks in town, however, laughed about the incident for years.

The Diuguids always knew that white people had a way of overcoming their prejudices when they need the money that blacks possessed. In St. Louis, times were hard in 1947, and Dr. Heyde, the owner of the large animal hospital, wanted out of the business. He was getting old, and cars had taken over where horses, wagons and buggies used to dominate. Treating dogs and cats didn't pay or provide the satisfaction needed to sustain the once thriving business. Trends in business constantly change. What may have been a growing concern and a money-making dream one day evaporates the next like ether on a sweltering summer day in a laboratory Petri dish as some new innovation muscles forward becoming the money-making, trendy thing that everyone demands.

The whites-only, hard line phalanx also had seen its day. In 1948, one year after Du-Good Chemical got its footing and three years following the end of World War II—President Harry S. Truman, a Missouri native, signed an executive order integrating the U.S. Armed Forces. That would have been unthinkable less than 50 years earlier. But the sun was setting on that part of America's past.

Racism in the United States was having to yield ground yet again as it had with the end of slavery following the Civil War. As it had with Reconstruction and blacks allegedly receiving all of the freedoms of whites in the United States because of the 13th, 14th and 15th amendments to the Constitution. Under those amendments, blacks could start schools for their children, so their offspring could get the education that laws prevented them from receiving. They could found colleges, allowing their children to move into a higher tier, helping to contribute more to making this country great. They could hold elected office and help to endure the best function of our democracy. And they could move anywhere in the nation and be welcomed as Americans. But that changed with the end of Reconstruction in 1877 when Republican Rutherford B. Hayes was elected president and made a deal with the Solid South to withdraw U.S. troops. It was three years after Doc's mother, Bettie, was born and three years before his father birth—each the offspring of slaves. They felt the punishing effects of being black in a time when whites were turning their backs anew on Africans in America.

White supremacist groups such as the Ku Klux Klan enjoyed a resurgence at the same time that the Industrial Age in the North was beginning to blossom. The Civil War was fast becoming a distant memory. Blacks had to make it on their own or not at all. Towns also decided that it was fashionable in the late 1800s to withdraw the welcome mat that they had extended to blacks. Many Negroes found themselves unwanted and targeted for hatred and scorn. That quickly turned to violence with whites evicting, lynching and killing blacks and taking over their property. Towns that had been tolerant overnight become "sundown towns," where blacks were only welcomed during the day as laborers. Doc often recalled seeing signs well into the latter half of the 20th century going in and out of hamlets, saying "Don't let the sun set on you, nigger." Blacks had to be gone at night or face horrible retribution from angry white mobs.

The green of dollar bills always has been the color of choice, helping people overcome their worst prejudices. The Diuguids showed up in 1947 with $60,000 in cash for the property at 1215 South Jefferson Ave. In 2013 dollars, that would amount to $617,673.30. It was an absolutely unheard of feat in 1947, and certainly would be incomprehensible now. But that was the power of family, and Doc never forgot it always sending annual dividends of his company's earnings to his brothers and sisters who had invested so much in his dream. Dr. Heyde, the veterinarian who wanted out, relented and sold the property. William Sherwood Diuguid, a Howard University law school graduate and one of Doc's older brothers, made sure the deal was legal. Du-Good Chemical became the first stake in the ground, changing the south side of St. Louis from all white to eventually all black.

A steep hill flowed down from Park Avenue past the Du-Good complex and continued on to Chouteau Avenue. A masculine viaduct lifted Jefferson Avenue over the century-old railroad yard. On most days, especially during rush hour, traffic crawled over the bridge, frustrating drivers on their way to and from work. The red taillights seemed to blur into one long serpent snaking over the curving road. Coming in the opposite direction in the evening traffic headed toward the 1200 block of South Jefferson Avenue. The headlights of vehicles, flame like white-hot fires in the rush home. Trains would park in the acres of yards waiting to be pulled by locomotives to destinations all over the country. They are large, powerful, menacing, historic and unforgiving as they rumbled, clacked, screeched and bumped along parallel ribbons of shiny steel tracks. The trains carried people and cargo to places where smiles and joy waited for the bounty. Steam engines that once powered the transportation and commerce of the country were replaced by diesel locomotives. Times and technology constantly change. Keeping up is the rule when change is the only thing anyone can expect.

A century ago, tall, decorative, gravel-textured and tapered, concrete-and-steel pillars topped with huge globes were the gas streetlights lining South Jefferson Avenue and the rest of one of America's oldest cities. Eventually each was filled with wires and a electric bulbs as the technology changed. Cars made of steel and other metals sometimes veered into those unmovable streetlights, and came out the worse from the collisions. Dashboards with their sculpted decorative metal interiors were unforgiving to passengers who then had no seat belts or airbags for protection. The breakaway light poles and interior vehicle safety devices were decades away. People back then took their chances as they did with smoking. Nearly everybody puffed on tobacco products. Folks got by never knowing any better.

Darkness in the evenings wasn't helped much by the streetlights back then. The lamps rested near the curbs like the many fireboxes that sat atop cast iron pillars. People without telephones could use the fireboxes to summon help by breaking the little glass in the top of the rectangular box and pulling the lever inside. The lights with the fire alarm boxes rested near the curbs of the 12-foot wide South Jefferson Avenue sidewalks. The concrete walkways were cracked and well-worn in more than a few places. The sidewalk on Jefferson Avenue was three times the normal width of those in the surrounding residential neighborhoods. The sidewalks were like those that bordered the streets downtown, indicating that they for years had been heavily traveled by people shopping in the area and going to and from work. In the winter when it snowed, the foot traffic was so intense that if Doc didn't have his kids or some of the boys get out immediately and shovel the wide sidewalk, the snow in a matter of a couple of hours would be hopelessly packed down, making shoveling it up impossible. Yet, Doc always had the kids get out there and try. They never argued with Doc after struggling to shovel up the snow after pedestrian traffic had trampled it into lumpy, impossible to remove ice. The sidewalk was nearly impossible to walk on, too, when the snow was packed down. That always made Doc nervous because he worried that someone might fall and hurt himself.

Cars still parked on both sides of Jefferson Avenue as traffic patterns permitted. The fast flow of cars was heaviest in the mornings going north to jobs mostly downtown. So cars parked on the west side of the Jefferson. The evening rush hour mandated that cars park on the east side of Jefferson Avenue giving traffic three full lanes of unimpeded flow for cars, trucks and buses to reach their destinations. Doc liked to park his car in front of Du-Good Chemical on the west side of the street. It made a statement. First there was a rusted out, 1940s Ford that he drove to St. Louis from Cornell University. Then he bought a 1955 black Lincoln Mercury new with a loan. Afterward, Doc only paid cash for his cars, buying a powder blue 1962 Pontiac Catalina, a gold 1968 Pontiac Catalina, which got stolen when it was parked in front of Du-Good Chemical while Doc was working there. He replaced it with a green 1972 Dodge Coronet. It was Doc's first automatic. For months, he would stomp his left foot on the floorboard of the car thinking he had to shift gears. A used 1981 Ford LTD followed that and his last vehicle was a used 1986 Ford Crown Victoria/LTD. The cars and trucks changed over the years, but Doc proved he was at the company to stay, and everyone knew it when they saw his vehicles parked outside or behind the 6-foot high wooden fence, shielding the loading area.

A four-story apartment building abutted the wood-and-brick storage part of the south side of Du-Good Chemical. On the first floor of the apartment building on the corner of Rutger Street and South Jefferson Avenue was a dry cleaners and tailors' shop, Wide-A-Wake Cleaners at 1225 S. Jefferson Ave. On the north side of Du-Good Chemical was an alley. Across the brick alley, which was deeply rutted from heavy vehicles using it, sat several one-story structures. A shoe-shine parlor, Carter's Shoe Shine Parlor at 1213 S. Jefferson Ave., was in one part of the building. The other housed various businesses—mostly vacant and those that did try to make it didn't last long. Those low-rise units were connected to an apartment building. Kemp Egg & Poultry Store, 1209 S. Jefferson Ave., occupied the first floor of that structure.

All of the people in the red-brick houses, apartment buildings, schools, businesses and churches that filled the neighborhood were white. No blacks were ever to frequent Buder Park two blocks west of South Jefferson Avenue or Chouteau Elementary School across the street from the park, or the Catholic Church at California and Rutger avenues. Lafayette Park, historic and stately in its early origins of the city about a half-mile south and east of the lab, was off limits, too. Rich people from the city's early days lived there. Whites only was the way the area was established, and that was the way it was to stay. But Doc and his family changed that. The racial covenant in the deed restriction on the animal hospital crumbled when the Diuguids paid cash for the property. Doc often said, "Money talks. The realtor said, "Besides, no one will know what these fellas are because they don't look colored." But people have a way of finding out.

The neighborhood started to change slowly and then quickly as whites moved out and blacks moved in. St. Louis like many northern cities became a stopping point for many blacks leaving the South for factory jobs in the North. The Great Migration continued more than a half-century trend. When black people came north from Mississippi, Alabama and Louisiana, they needed housing. They needed schools, and they needed jobs. These folks stood out. They were darker than most blacks in the city, and their hair generally was shorter and kinkier. They had a hungry look of need about them, and many adults and children were ready to fight in a heart-beat.

Poverty breeds a kind of cancerous anger and aggression. But everyone seemed to know and get along with Doc, who was also from the South. In addition, they knew him from his longtime company. But they also knew Doc from advertisements that he placed in St. Louis' many black newspapers, including the Argus, the Sentinel and the American. Doc also had a following from the hundreds of students he had had as a chemistry and physical science teacher at Stowe, Harris, Harris-Stowe College and Washington University. For the homeless and alcoholics on the street he always had a buck or two—regardless of whether they did any work for him. To every passer-by, Doc offered a kind word.

But he was a curiosity, too. Doc looked white, but he talked decidedly black when he encountered black people. But he also used every ounce of his college education and Phi Beta Kappa status when greeted by whites. His multilingual talents were a wonder to behold, and every black who worked and rubbed shoulders with this self-described, hill-billy from Lynchburg, Va., learned to do that kind of code switching, too.

Often people who would see Doc with his four children—the first three born a year apart in the mid-1950s—would scratch their heads and wonder. His wife was a brown-skin black woman born and raised in St. Louis. She was an educator, too. She'd send the children to work with Doc. Their idea of when their kids should go to work at the company was when they could hold their bladders, their bowels and a broom. Each started work about age 3, and there was no shirking hard work from then on. They lived in the hard-scrabble, unforgiving, square frame of the Ds—discipline, duty, determination and diligence, which their parents created.

People who didn't know Doc that well would see this seemingly white man with three and later four light-skinned, definitely black children. They'd see him lead them to Du-Good Chemical. Some black and white people would stop Doc on the wide sidewalk, before he could key his way into the arched entryway of the company. They would rudely ask, "What are you?"— as if they were entitled to an answer. It was a question people might ask an alien from another planet. But people of all colors lacked the vocabulary to talk sensitively and appropriately about race.

The Civil Rights Movement was in its early years in the late 1950s and early '60s. Segregation prevented colored people from mingling with whites unless work mandated it. So people just bluntly asked Doc what he was. Doc remained consistent, having heard that question all of his life. He would stomp his foot on the concrete sidewalk and emphatically but nicely tell people, "I'm an American." It was a difficult concept for people to swallow. The rule in the United States was that anyone with one drop of black blood was considered black. Doc would proudly volunteer during the cover of hard work that he was part Cherokee; part Ibo, a tribe in Africa; and part Scottish. But that would come out only when people bothered to get to know him.

St. Louis was supposed to be that better place—a city where a black man or woman could shed the prejudice yoke of the South and feel accepted like anyone else. They could feel embraced for the merit of their work and prosper.

It was to have been that place where black people could have their piece of the American pie and realize their American dream. Doc's brother, William Sherwood Diuguid, who studied law under Charles Houston at Howard University, found St. Louis to be more open and inviting than other places. He established a law practice in town and went into a drugstore business with friends. His stories of the town being progressive attracted Doc after two years of post-doctorate studies at Cornell University. Frustration had been building in Doc. His breakthrough work in developing a plasticizing agent from aviation fuel was stolen from him resulting in multibillion-dollar gains for oil companies. Doc often lamented, "I didn't even get my name on the patent. All I barely got was a handshake and pat on the back." Other ground-breaking discoveries of his followed in which he saved major corporations from certain product-deficiency-forged doom. Companies that normally would compete to attract a person of his caliber were standoffish or offered him jobs provided that he either disown his family and any connection to being black or go to work and home having no contact with white workers in the factories. The price they were asking for a mere job was too high. Doc was unwilling to pay it. Doc always said, "If you're passing for white, you're failing as black." He declined the job offers, opting instead to go to St. Louis to establish a breakthrough microanalytical, independent, research chemical company with a manufacturing arm. The youngest of nine children had a dream of greatness. The world was changing for black people, and he felt that he had a better shot than most of making it big.

The 1200 block of South Jefferson Avenue changed rapidly after Du-Good Chemical became established. Word got around that the area was no longer all white. The sidewalks stone curbs and brick buildings were the same. The mortar hadn't shifted or crumbled. But something was decidedly different. The inflexible, whites-only, color-coding had been breeched, prompting white business owners and white families to worry whether their property values would fall and how long they had to hold out before the door closed completely on getting out. Real estate predators also hurriedly infiltrated the area, and the block busting began with a vengeance. People were encouraged to sell their businesses and homes at a loss feeling lucky that they got some money out of what they had owned. Black business people and families were then sold the same property marked back up at full or greater value. It was a big-money game that realtors played for profit.

People's unforgiving prejudices toward blacks ended up costing them a fortune. It cost St. Louis and other cities throughout the country dearly. Property was sold to black families and black businesses. But no loans or training were provided to enable the new business and homeowners to maintain the places. Disrepair was inevitable. With it came a self-fulfilling prophesy verifying the prejudices by the conditions that bigotry helped create. For several years black people and business owners forged a social infrastructure that helped create a sense of community and an incubator for the development of young people. The 1200 block of South Jefferson Avenue was one of those places. They existed in the thousands in every city and small town in America. They were part of the uncelebrated, unappreciated village that helped to raise boys to men, girls to women and each to taxpaying, civically engaged citizens. When these businesses disappeared from the face of America so did the guidance they provided as well as the back up and support for families reinforcing the values and virtues of everyday life.

Sam Fowler's Wide-A-Wake Cleaners, 1225 S. Jefferson Ave., occupied the first floor of the apartment building at Rutger and South Jefferson. Du-Good Chemical stretched from there to the alley. Carter's Shoe Shine Parlor at 1213 South Jefferson Ave. was on the other side of the alley. It was run by Henry Carter, but everybody called him Shorty. An attached four-story apartment building towered above with a gray-painted, wooden stairway connecting back porches to each unit. Jeff's grocery was tucked into the first floor fronting on Hickory and South Jefferson. Across from the lab was Rev. C.L. Nance's church, The Second Corinthian Baptist Church. It was a brick apartment building, too. But it was painted white and had the storefront look of a place of revival. Behind the church in the 1200 block of South Jefferson Avenue was Earl McDaniel's garage. It was a one-story brick building that had two sets of garage doors that opened onto the alley between Hickory and Caroline. If Rutger Street had continued eastward, it would have run into the alley. Many people in the neighborhood took their cars and trucks to Earl's garage for repairs. Doc did, too.

The people who owned the businesses also lived within walking distance of them. Driving to work didn't make sense except on the coldest, snowiest days. Even then walking was the way to be seen so that shoppers would know that the places they wanted to visit were open. Doc sometimes rode his bicycle when he needed the added speed. These black men in their leather-bottomed shoes slapping the uneven brick sidewalk of the old city would wave to their neighbors and talk with people on the street. When it rained, puddles of water would pool with mud in their path making navigating the walk and talking a challenge. Big trees by the curbs provided an abundance of shade. They were oaks, hickories and maples—made to last. They added a cool soft beauty to the hard, hot city of brick, stone, concrete and tar. Preschool-age children bundled mightily against the cold winters or wearing stripped pullover shirts, shorts and no shoes or socks often played on the sidewalk and in the street as the men walked to work. The kids skipped happily together and played sidewalk games, never giving a care about the world they'd have to someday face. The white world most days couldn't stand the blackness of them or their neighborhood's humanity.

The America in the blocks surrounding South Jefferson Avenue was not unlike white America. It's just that few in the mainstream bothered to look. It's where dogs barked and children skinned their knees. Sticks in playful little hands rattled fences like machine gun fire. Here is where mothers, grandmothers and aunts hung from windows and kept a watchful eye over all who walked and played before them. It's where mothers cried, people died and fathers went to work. Parishioners couldn't dupe themselves into skipping church if they saw the reverend hiking to the chapel, and those folks who were employed in the businesses knew not to take the day off.

Bunches of older men born in the 1800s also would gather at Samuel Fowler's Wide-A-Wake Cleaners and Carter's Shoe Shine Parlor. The black men of the neighborhood would hang out, talk, read the newspaper and drink a Coke or two. Shorty and Sam kept soda machines in their shops for that purpose. It was a way for enterprising black men to make a little change from the fellows who would otherwise sit around endlessly taking up space and a lot of air time talking. Smoking seemed like a pre-requisite. Everyone smoked, and cigarette machines and ash trays of all shapes, colors and sizes in Shorty's and Sam's easily accommodated those urges, too.

Neither place was much to look at. The walls looked as if they had not been painted in years. Smoke stains from wood burning stoves and coal-fired furnaces filled the interior. An elevated area in the front window of Sam's Cleaners was where most people sat. It had to have been where mannequins dressed with the latest fashions or other goods were once set up for display in the two big windows for passers-by on the street. Shorty had a few tables and chairs set up around an old pot-belly, wood-burning stove. Nothing matched. His place more than any of the others loudly and deeply hummed with the many stories of old men.

It was in Du-Good Chemical Laboratories & Manufacturers that something very different happened. Boys who walked the street aimlessly sometimes rang the doorbell. Others would see Doc painting on his building or working out front on his car. Doc would stop and talk with them. He'd instantly become the father that a lot of the kids never had. But it didn't end there. The boys who'd walk, bike or roller skate by the lab often would get drawn into whatever work Doc was doing. He'd ask them about school, their teachers, what they were learning and their grades. He wanted to know everything. He would question them intensely, carefully listen to their answers and then expose the illogic in whatever they'd reveal that sounded off-kilter.

Strangely instead of the kids getting fed up with the constant probing and picking into their lives and never returning, they would always come back, yearning to tell more, be questioned more and to work more for this strange man whose curiosity about them they couldn't satisfy and who inspired them to be curious, to ask questions and to think for the first time. Doc made them start to believe in themselves and what they had to offer beyond the unforgiving dead-end of the streets. He would take the urchins off of South Jefferson Avenue into his lab and build them into men. Many ended up going to college, which was a galaxy beyond the expectations where they were raised in homes where their parents never finished grade school. Many of these urchins of the street ended up in science careers because of Doc.

CHAPTER 2

BLACK FAMILY—ALPHA TO OMEGA

Butch was one of the kids from the street who helped Doc dig the cellar for his house using only a hand shovel, pick and wheelbarrow. They even mixed the concrete by hand and poured it in the finished area—one wheelbarrow at a time. Butch, sweating mightily, pointed to Doc's then two preschool-age sons and said: "I don't envy you. This is the kind of work and unforgiving direction you'll have to take for the rest of your lives!" Doc and his wife, Nancy, laughed. Nancy often told that story and told how Doc bragged mightily about Butch being one heck of a hard, dependable worker. Butch tuck-pointed the back wall of the company in the warehouse area when neither of Doc's nephews—one who became a nuclear physicist and the other a psychiatrist—had the staying power in St. Louis' summer heat to get the job done.

Doc also liked to tell about a young man named Ray Grant whom Doc encountered in an area liquor store. He talked Ray Grant into quitting that job to continue college. Ray Grant had left school figuring he could make more money working behind the counter in the liquor store. Doc saw that Ray Grant had something "on the ball," and the same assessment came from teachers who knew the young man's work. Ray Grant had to be convinced that school would be his long-term salvation compared to the liquor store, which paid well, but was dead-end work—possibly in more ways than one. Ray Grant knew Doc had a point, although the money from the liquor store was hard to give up.

The man explained his circumstances, his family and his obligations. Doc, however, would not relent. He told the man that the money might be good for now, but what if someone came in with a gun, held up the place and shot the student? The young man said he knew the risks and knew that the money in part was high to compensate him for that danger. Doc explained that the man would be on his feet all day dealing with nothing but drunks and people trying to forget their problems through self-medication. The man said he knew that, too, and actually had fun talking with the customers of the store. Doc said that would only last so long. When that's over, the job will be tedium, and those drunks will be a pain in the student's backside. Science and math offered so much more, Doc said. The man remained unconvinced. Doc also said that the money with the liquor store would not last. The job may not be as secure as the student thought. Doc kept at the young man. Finally the young man could see that Doc made valid points. He went back into college and stayed until he got his degree. The man eventually earned his PhD and then through Doc's help, he got a job with Monsanto. It is difficult for people to see the big picture. The money is easy, and people need it. But there are people in the world like the men in the 1200 block of South Jefferson Avenue who have seen the panoramic view, and they help explain it to others.

Doc also shared with the man the story of his father, a brakeman for the Norfolk & Western Railway Co. He had convinced Doc and his brothers that what looks like big money now will eventually disappear. Doc and his brothers hated their dad for not getting them jobs on the railroad as other men did for their sons. Doc's father, like the black Pullman porters, had been exposed on the trains to white, middle- and upper-class riders and their sensibilities.

Doc recalled that because of his father's job, he and his siblings were able to ride the trains anywhere in the country at no charge. They had to sit in the segregated cars, but it was a sacrifice they made for the ability to travel freely. Once, one of Doc's siblings encountered Mary McLeod Bethune, a famous black newspaper publisher and civil rights worker who used the pages of her newspaper to fight the lynchings of black people at that time in this country's history. She had been asked to visit with President Franklin D. Roosevelt in the White House. When she boarded the train, the porters tried to escort her to the colored section. She cursed them and refused, saying she was going to Washington, D.C., on the invitation of the president and would not settle for a second-class seat. The porters relented and escorted her to the white section of the train. Doc enjoyed telling that story to the boys who worked for his company to let them know they had to stand up for their rights.

Doc and his siblings took advantage of the free rides they could get on the trains. That made the idea of working for the railroad that much more desirable. But each realized at the insistence of their father that a college education was the way to higher wages and a white-collar job with dignity instead of the back-breaking work on the railroad, where being treated inhumanely went hand in hand with being black. Doc asked Ray Grant, "What do you want to do, work for drunks all of your life?" That question was the clincher. But Doc also told Ray Grant the story of his own family and college. Against the protests of his friends, Doc's dad insisted that all of his sons and daughters—nine in total—get a college education. In the early 20th century, sons were supposed to work feeding badly needed money into the family home especially during the Great Depression. They were Richard, born 1899; James, 1902; Alfonso, 1907; DeWitt, 1908; William Sherwood, 1910; Hubert, 1915; and Lincoln, 1917. Lewis Diuguid's daughters, Sherley, born 1905 and Elwyza, born 1912, were, according to people at that time, supposed to get married. College seemed an extravagance that many families—let alone those that were black—could not afford. But getting a college education was the only way for the Diuguids. Doc said Ray Grant as a liquor store clerk couldn't ignore his logic. Ray Grant eventually went back to college, earned his PhD, was hired by one of the area's biggest chemical companies and ended up retiring after a long, fulfilling career as a chemist.

Education was the only path in life, as far as Doc's father, Lewis Walter Diuguid, was concerned. He wanted it for himself and he wanted it for his children. He had gotten on a different road—one that most former slaves and the children of slaves like him couldn't help but trod. Lewis Diuguid often was mistaken for a white man, although he never hid his heritage, being part Ibo, Native American and Scottish. Diuguid, after all is a Scottish name, although following the pattern of slaves taking the name of their masters, the family name should have been Thornhill, but Lewis Diuguid's mother didn't care for that family at all so she took the name of the Diuguids in Virginia, who lived on the plantation across the road. Lewis Diuguid's sister was among about 14,000 blacks who each year before the Civil Rights Movement, dropped out of the black community and passed into white society. Doc recalled riding with his father and sister Elwyza to Atlanta to visit that aunt. Doc remembered that his Papa told him and Elwyza to stay in the car while he went inside to see his sister. Doc also said he had an Uncle William in Brooklyn who was passing. Uncle William had married a black woman. Then, without divorcing her, Uncle William married a white woman while passing. Neither wife knew of the other's existence. When Uncle William died, he was buried in the white folks' cemetery, until people found out that he had a black family in another part of town. Doc surmised that Uncle William wasn't looking to remaining in the white folks' graveyard.

Doc, like most black folks, couldn't blame others who passed. They were able to shed a lot of heartache, misery and pain and in return enjoy the privileges that went with being white in America. Doc also recalled professors' comments when he announced that he was studying to be a chemist: "It will only make you unhappy because you won't be able to find a job anywhere in America." Doc said they were right. He got turned down repeatedly by some of the biggest chemical companies in the country despite his credentials, post-doctorate work and discoveries. Doc's Papa still knew that education was the only path to a better, more successful, less prejudiced life. Initially Lewis Diuguid dropped out of school and landed a job as a brakeman on the Norfolk & Western Railway. He walked to work in the rail yards from his home in Lynchburg, Va. He always took long deep contemplative steps. His thin, muscled 6-foot 5-inch frame demanded it as did his powerful underappreciated intellect. The job paid decent money—especially for a black man. But in the late 1800s, it was dangerous work—the kind that whites left for colored men to do. It went beyond the heat or cold, the rain and the snow that railroad workers caught from working outdoors. It was dangerous because the brakemen were responsible for slowing down the cars of the train. They had to stand on top of the tall rolling wood-and-steel structures and turn a large wheel at just the right speed, applying just the right pressure to slow down the train cars. If they spun it too fast they would get thrown from the top of the cars to sudden death. If they turned the wheel too slowly, the car would crash into others, also pitching the brakeman off. If he was lucky, he only lost his job because of the damage done to the train. Diuguid did slip up once and got thrown from the top of a boxcar for it. He herniated himself as a result—an injury he carried with him the rest of his life. But eventually, air brakes were added to trains. That caused the job of brakeman to become fairly easy and far less dangerous. When that happened, those jobs shifted from blacks to whites almost instantly. Diuguid managed to hang on to his position until he retired in the 1940s, carrying a pistol with him every day that he went to work. He knew well people's hatred for blacks, and he'd tolerate none of it. Others knew that, and gave him a wide berth.

Diuguid was a tough man of unforgiving thrift. But he also enjoyed telling stories. One was of a cousin, Henderson Fields, who was thought to be the strongest man in Virginia. He easily could lift a set of boxcar wheels in his teeth. Diuguid also told of Henderson Fields, a black man, going to have a drink after work in a white bar. People in the tavern took great offense. One man insisted on throwing out Henderson Fields. The bartender warned him not to trouble that black man. The caution was not heeded. Henderson Fields picked up one of the men and used that man's body like a club to beat the others unconscious. He then finished his drink. Doc said Henderson Fields worked in the mines alone. He saw the other men as children who just got in his way. He was credited with easily doing the work of five men. An industrial accident, however, left Fields, the most powerful man in Virginia, on crutches. Even then he still amazed people by carrying a 200-pound load of coal for his stove in his teeth.

Doc also often repeated the story of Thomas Fuller. Doc grew up hearing the story and thought it was one of his Papa's tall tales. But books such as *The Black Presence in the Era of the American Revolution, 1770-1800*, the *Negro History Bulletin* and a 1959 issue of *Jet* magazine verified the story, which had been handed down by blacks like Diuguid since slavery. At age 14, Fuller was kidnapped from Africa and sold into slavery near Alexandria, Va. He couldn't read or write but became known as "the Virginia Calculator" for his ability to solve difficult math problems in his head. His owner, Elizabeth Cox, would lend Fuller to other white people, who would do such things as have him walk the boundaries of their land to compute the acreage for government records. Fuller performed the complex calculations for plantation owners' bookkeeping and construction needs. But his problem-solving often wasn't instantaneous. Whites would tell him their problems and give him the mathematical variables, and he would go about doing his normal chores. A day or so later he would give people the correct answer. William Hartshorne and Samuel Coates of Pennsylvania doubted Fuller's ability. They challenged him to calculate the seconds in 1½ years. Fuller correctly said 47,304,000 seconds. Then they asked for the number of seconds in the life of a man who had lived 70 years, 17 days and 12 hours. Fuller responded, 2,210,500,800. The men, who had done the problem on paper, yelled that the Virginia Calculator was wrong. Fuller, however, replied, "Massa, you forget de leap year."

The scene reminded Doc of a story his father used to tell about the black men who worked for the Barnum & Bailey Circus. They were among the last to get on the trains when the circus left town and the first to get off to begin unloading the tents, animals and equipment. Doc said his Grandmother McCoy, who lived with his family, would take him when he was a kid with other children to see the circus when it pulled up on the trains. Doc remembered seeing black men skipping off trains with sledgehammers. They'd pull out the tents and long metal stakes that had to go in the ground to anchor the heavy canvas structures securely against high winds, rain or other weather. Once the ground was clearly marked, the men then with their well-worn sledgehammers would begin the process of driving in the stakes. Doc explained to the boys who helped him that the black men would stand around in teams. One man would start a song. The others would sing the chorus. Often they sang Negro spirituals. The blues hadn't quite come of age yet. The sledgehammers swung mightily by as many as five black men would each hit the steel stake, driving it into the ground with a ringing rhythm to the song's beat. The men's muscles rippled, and perspiration on warm days drenched their bodies. The metal stakes seemed as if the Earth swallowed them even when the ground was hard. Doc's Dad also told how prejudice was the constant interloper even for black men working for the circus. One day, P.T. Barnum interrupted the men, asking them to grab hold of a 2-inch in diameter hemp rope. They did, wondering what the old huckster was up to. Mr. Barnum asked them to pull on the rope while he held the other end and pulled in the opposite direction. The black men were perplexed with one saying, "Why Mr. Barnum, you is no match for us mens." Barnum insisted that they do as he had asked. The men complied. Just as the men had said, Barnum was no match for their strength. Barnum finally said: "There! You, boys, have witnessed one of the greatest feats of all time—a team of blacks all pulling together to accomplish something!" He laughed and walked away firmly fixed on his stereotypes and prejudices against black men. The prejudices went against everything that the black circus workers constantly did to keep the circus afloat even as they were paid precious little for the vital work they did compared with white circus workers. As a matter of fact it fit another old slave story of Willie Lynch.

Willie Lynch was thought to be a British slave owner in the West Indies who in 1712 traveled to the Colonies, which later became the United States after the Revolutionary War. Now keep in mind that slavery had only existed in the Colonies since 1619, with the delivery of about 20 slaves to Jamestown, Va., by a Dutch slave ship. Slavery had existed in other parts of the New World since 1502 when the Spanish started the process of stealing people from Africa and taking them to the Caribbean, Central America and South America to work in the mines and fields. That enabled Europeans to grow fat and wealthy from the misery and suffering of black ancestors and mine in the so-called New World. As a matter of fact, the world in April 2002 should have recognized the 500th anniversary of one race of people enslaving another in the start of a global trade of rich black human cargo. Some estimates say that 50 million black people were captured for the slave trade. Millions died before reaching the New World. But only about a third of them survived the journey. Just think of what a great power Africa would have been if that theft and brain drain had not occurred. That holocaust marked the first globalization of trade and it was quite bloody. Sharks changed their migratory habits to take advantage of the dead and dying black cargo that was thrown overboard slave ships during the Middle Passage. Also during that period, the West Indies and the Caribbean islands south of the Colonies were where breaking plantations existed at which Africans were conditioned to their new role as slaves. It was there that Willie Lynch was said to have traveled from to talk with plantation owners in the American Colonies. You see, they had a problem with the threat of slave uprisings, and they sought Willie Lynch's help. Here is some of what he is thought to have told them:

"In my bag here, I have a fool—proof method for controlling your black slaves. I guarantee every one of you that if installed correctly it will control the slaves for at least 300 years. My method is simple. Any member of your family or your overseer can use it. I have outlined a number of differences among the slaves, and I take these differences and make them bigger. I use fear, distrust and envy for control purposes. These methods have worked on my modest plantation in the West Indies, and they will work throughout the South. Take this simple list of differences and think about them. On top of my list is `age,' but it's there only because it starts with an `A.' The second is `color' or shade. There is intelligence, size, sex, sizes of plantations, status on plantations, attitude of owners, whether the slaves live in the valley, on a hill, east, west, north, south, have fine hair, coarse hair or are tall or short. Now that you have a list of differences, I shall give you an outline of action, but before that, I shall assure you that distrust is stronger than trust, and envy stronger than adulation, respect or admiration. The black slaves after receiving this indoctrination shall carry on and will become self-refueling and self-generating for hundreds of years, maybe thousands. Don't forget you must pit the old black males vs. the young black males, and the young black females against the old black females. You must use the dark skin slaves vs. the light skin slaves and the light skin slaves vs. the dark skin slaves. You must use the females vs. the males. And the males vs. the females. You must also have your white servants and overseers distrust all blacks. But it is necessary that your slaves trust and depend only on us. They must love, respect and trust only us. Gentlemen, these kits are your keys to control. Use them. Have your wives and children use them, never miss an opportunity. If used intensely for one year, the slaves themselves will remain perpetually distrustful."

There are quite a few people now who challenge whether Willie Lynch really existed. But I think that what was said shows how the negativity and the sense of self-hate and self-destructiveness may have developed.

After decades as a brakeman, Diuguid retired, but decided to go back to school to get his high school diploma. That amazed his older grandchildren, and he challenged them to keep up with him comparing the grades he earned with theirs. Diuguid also went on to college at Virginia Seminary, astonishing even more people. Education was important to him, and he thought his actions would demonstrate it far more than mere words could describe.

Doc remembered growing up in Lynchburg, Va. He recalled his chores, which included milking the cows in the morning, feeding the chickens and gathering the eggs for breakfast. Doc also remembered the long walks to school, losing a childhood friend because the white boy said the word "nigger," and that boy being chased off by his mother, Bettie, who was six years older than Doc's dad. And Doc remembers watching the Ku Klux Klan parade down Main Street in Lynchburg. The Klan in the 1920s was a much revered, white, Christian, men's organization that looked out for the well-being of the mainstream way of life. It protected Americans like them from threats by blacks, immigrants, Catholics, Jews and other undesirables. The Klan maintained the established order and white supremacy. All of it was a hangover from slavery. The South may have lost the Civil War, but its traditions of whites feeling superior to blacks in every way never died. The resentment that oppression fostered eventually led Doc to form his own company, Du-Good Chemical, and make it into a well-established business. Doc often paraphrased Dante saying it was better to be king in a place he had of his own than to serve in a so-called heaven, where he could never be respected as a man.

Doc's strong independent streak grew from the red, overworked soil of Virginia. It's where the mountains tumble along the Earth and against the beautifully blue sky and the sweet smell of the open atmosphere compels its native sons to forever breathe free its wonderful air. People who grow up here love it. But the love also comes with an extreme contradictory feeling of loathing for African-Americans and anyone else who is not white. The rolling hills and open fields rich in history are stained with the sweat and blood of slavery and racism. Doc, his brothers, sisters and parents felt its salty sting every day. Because of strictly enforced segregation, Doc and his siblings went to a segregated grade school just for black children. Whites went to better schools across town. Doc went to Dunbar High School. He remembered disdainfully how white children living nearby traveled miles from the colored school to attend the better white schools. However, he also recalled how the teachers he had were second to none. They were strict disciplinarians and made sure that the students they instructed learned the material.

Doc was an excellent long-distance runner. He remembered running the mile in under five minutes measuring the distance along the railroad tracks. In addition to being an intense intellect, Doc also played football at Dunbar High School. But an ankle injury sidelined him early in that pursuit. He forever maintained a great interest in sports. Doc's brothers were also athletic. They managed to get into trouble, too. Doc's brother, Alfonso, was a crack shot with a pistol or rifle. One day he shot the porcelain knobs off the light poles in Lynchburg, Va., for sport. Naturally the police were called, and Alfonso was fingered as the culprit. The cops not being of the highest ethical standards wanted $10 in that pre-Great Depression era to make the charges that Alfonso faced go away. But that amount of cash was like $130 today. Doc's Papa told Alfonso that he shot out the knobs like a man, he had to face the consequences like a man. Doc often shared such object lessons with the boys at his company after they had broken tools or bottles or caused other problems. It was to teach them responsibility and to be accountable for their actions. He also told them stories about his dentist brother Hubert, who "hoboed" his way to Chicago with friends, riding railcars but who after getting there didn't feel like riding the rails back to Lynchburg. Hubert wired Papa seeking money to return on a passenger train. Doc remembered that their father told Hubert that he was man enough to find his way to Chicago, he had to be man enough to get back on his own. But Doc's sister Sherley who was older, sent Hubert the money to get back.

The hardscrabble conditions of the Depression caused people to sometimes forgo being honest. Jimmy, one of Doc's older brothers, worked for an automotive repair and tire sales company. When business became a little slow, the owner would have some of his workers take some tacks out and scatter them sparingly through some of the streets to drum up business. Sure enough, some drivers would limp into the shop needing either an inner-tube repair, a new inner tube or a new tire and tube if the nail was fortunate enough for the shop owner to have stuck in the sidewall of the tire.

Science captured Doc's imagination. Doc was good at science, too. In school he was told he did a perfect dissection of a pig and should pursue a career in medicine. So much was happening in the sciences in the early part of the 20th century. Albert Einstein had risen to rock-star fame with his theories in physics and for winning the Nobel Prize. Thomas Edison was taking the groundbreaking work he had pioneered in the late 1800s and turning it into popular applications with telephones popping up in homes and businesses, phonographs becoming the thing to have, motion pictures and the innovation of sound and electricity powering lights and many more households and industrial convenience items.

Doc is quick to share that he went through college the hard way. He went to West Virginia State College, starting in 1934 when the Great Depression was in full bloom. His goal was to get a chemistry degree. But professional careers during the Depression were rare, and for black men they were unthinkable. Doc's Papa provided only limited funds for Doc to get through school, saying that if Doc couldn't come up with the balance through his own ingenuity and grit then Doc didn't have any business being in college. Doc managed to stay in school through "creative financing" in which he and Hubert began several enterprises on campus to make the extra money they needed to get through college paying all of their bills on time.

Doc's dean put him on a two-degree program—chemistry and education. Teaching would have been the fallback, allowing Doc as a black man to be able to teach in one of America's many segregated black schools. It was one of the two mainstays of professional careers for black people—preach or teach. But Doc remembered the dean cautioned him that if his grades dropped in either degree program, which he pursued simultaneously, that Doc would have to drop one of them. The determination, discipline and confidence of this Lynchburg native, however, was unstoppable. Doc graduated magna cum laude in 1938. He also pledged Omega Psi Phi with one of his older brothers, Hubert, who went on to serve in the Army as a lieutenant during World War II in a colored regime and became a dentist getting his degree from Howard University.

Doc also was fond of telling many stories from his college days in West Virginia and often on vacations to Lynchburg, he would stop in Institute,

W.Va., to visit for hours with some of his black college professors. When he and Hubert pledged, Doc remembered the frat brothers kept them up late with the other pledges and then insisted that they do laundry for the big brothers in the fraternity. Neither Doc nor Hubert was fond of laundry and neither was good at it. Doc washed all of the clothes in hot water shrinking nearly everything. "Hubert fell asleep while ironing clothes and burned holes in several pairs of pants," Doc recalled laughing. "That was the last time they put us on laundry detail."

To also earn money to pay their college bills, Doc explained that he and Hubert pooled their cash and opened up a hockshop loaning money to students for goods the young adults put up for Doc and Hubert to hold. When the students repaid the loan with interest, they would get their possessions back. Doc remembered getting stung once when a guy brought in what looked like a nice suit. He got his money, $5. Doc and Hubert later found that the pants had holes in them. They ate the loss. The guy never returned for his clothes. Then college officials got wind of the enterprise and shut it down. Doc said he and Hubert simply rebranded the operation as "buying and selling."

Doc recalled that students had to wear shirts and ties to eat in the college dining room. But he and Hubert liked to sleep in getting up just in time to get to the cafeteria before it closed. "Hubert had cut out a shirt, which he could pull over his head. The tie was already tied, making the chore of getting dressed a snap. Hubert threw on a sweater a pair of pants and some shoes and took off for the dining hall getting there right before the door closed. Man, sometimes it was close," Doc said.

Football players then as now were accustomed to getting the best of the food that was served. "But often as the food zigzagged from the head of each long table to the end, the last person would find no meat was left," Doc said. "Arriving late had definite drawbacks. One football player knew the score. He got there late and saw as the plate of meat was making its way toward him that he was going to get shorted. He marched up with his fork in hand, stabbed a couple of pork chops and dropped gravy on the heads of everyone back to where he was sitting. Man, that sure was funny. He was not going to be left out," Doc said laughing each time he retold the story to workers at Du-Good Chemical to help them know not to settle for the way things are.

The dining hall also was a place of reckoning. It was during the Depression, and students had a hard time keeping up with the bills so they could stay in school. Doc and his brother, being industrious, also would cut men's hair to earn a few bucks. When students got behind in their tuition or room and board at the college, they were kept from entering the dining hall for meals. Once the dining hall tried to lock out a number of students for late or nonpayment. A crush of students rushed the door bursting inside so they could eat anyway. Times were hard like that. One of the greatest delights Doc had at West Virginia State College was hearing George Washington Carver speak on campus. Doc said Carver, who died in 1943, told students they no doubt stepped on a blade of grass on the walk to the lecture. "In that blade of grass lies the secret of life," Doc recalled Carver saying. "All you've got to do is tune in on the right idea to solve problems. It's like a radio. You've got to get on the right frequency." Doc shared another story about the clothing Carver wore to visit with the king and queen of England. Carver often wore a black suit coat that was a different shade from his pants. The reason: When the pants wore out, Carver replaced them. But he never replaced the coat. Carver's colleagues took up a collection to get him a new suit for his royal family visit. When a well-dressed man gave Carver the money for a new suit, Carver retorted, "Son, if they wanted to see a suit of clothes, they would have invited you."

Doc was a member of the pledge club or Lampados Club. That group consisted of men interested in joining the fraternity and participated in various activities. That included Doc being the editor of the Omega Psi Phi Oracle, a newsletter for the fraternity. He became a member of the Omegas after graduating from the pledge club. In a December 1935 issue, Doc wrote:

> Once again the pledgee club of Theta Psi Chapter sends its greetings to all Big Brothers and Pledgee brothers and all other chapters. Our officers for the year 1934-35 are as follows: James Pettris, President; Hubert Diuguid, Vice-President; Spencer Roberts, Secretary; Joseph Underwood, Treasurer; and Oliver Arnold, Chaplain.
>
> We have men starring in all activities and a variety of fields of education.
>
> On the football field, we have Knute Burroughs, the mighty tackle; Isaiah Israel, the shifty halfback; and Ennis Williams, an end player. Israel and Burroughs are members of the "W" club.
>
> On the tennis club we have the following enthusiasts: Spencer Roberts, "Spence"; Thomas Fawcette, "The Devil"; Edward Waugh, "Wow Wow"; and Lincoln Diuguid "Duke."

Kinkle Spencer, better known as "Papa Long Legs," is the great imitator of Cab Calloway and also he is the ladies' fancy.

Lincoln Diuguid, an assistant in the Chemistry department, was awarded a scholarship trophy by Coch Hamblin for the Lamp, having the highest average, (2.81) for the past semester.

Donald Smith "Smitty" is manager of the football team, and Oliver Arnold is the assistant manager.

Hubert Diuguid is vice-president of the Agricultural club and is a member of the Dramatic Society.

The "Lamps" gave a "Be On Time Program" in chapel on October 12, 1935, and Oliver Arnold made the main address. "Like all other "Lamp" affairs, it was a swell success."

The Lamps presented Miss West Virginia, (Miss Alma Wright), and her two attendants (Caroline Hill and Sarah Wright) at the Home Coming Game between Bluefield State Teacher's College and West Virginia State College on November 2. This, too, was a hit for the "Lamps."

We are planning for the annual dance to be given by the Pyramids and the "Lamps," which will be on November 23.

Now we are on the verge of the burning sands and until we have safely reached the Promised Land, we bid you farewell.

LINCOLN DIUGUID

Editor

Doc gave an earlier account in the Oracle newsletter of that same year for his fraternity:

Lampados Club, West Virginia State College, Institute, W.Va.:

Once again, the members of the Lampados Club send their greetings to all the big brothers and pledgee brothers of all other chapters. We have been carrying on the great work, exemplifying at all times the Omega spirit. During this year we have successfully accomplished many of our aims. On the first day of the year, we distributed printed copies of ten beneficial New Year's resolutions to each student of the West Virginia State College.

Our volleyball and basketball teams entered their respective intramural tournaments; although we did not win the tournament, we exemplified good sportsmanship, manhood and perseverance throughout.

We helped the big brothers with their ninth annual spring frolic held in Manhattan Hall on April 12, 1935. It was a gala affair, and it certainly gave us something to look forward to.

A check on our outgoing mail would have shown that our "Drop-A-Card Movement" for Easter and Mother's Day accomplished great results.

We are now planning projects for the ensuing year. Outside our regular program, we have thus far planned a "Welcome Program" for the incoming students of this college.

We are doing all that is within our power to exemplify the true Omega spirit and we are coming closer to our goals as the days go by. We are still traveling down that narrow and straight path, and until we have crossed the burning sands, we bid you goodbye.

LINCOLN DIUGUID

Editor

Doc was a sophomore at West Virginia State College in 1935, having entered in 1934 and graduated magna cum laude in 1938 with degrees in chemistry and education.

At West Virginia State College, Doc said he got to hear another national giant at that time speak. He was noted historian and lecturer Dr. Carter G. Woodson. It was an impressive talk. Woodson, one of Harvard University's first black PhD graduates, started Negro History Week in 1926 because he was troubled by black people and others accepting the media images back then picturing African-Americans as cowardly, booty-chasing, thieving, untrustworthy, underperforming and lazy buffoons. Woodson was the founder of the Association for the Study of African American Life and History. He was called the Father of Black History. Woodson picked a week in February for Black History Week because of two great Americans' birthdays: Frederick Douglass, a runaway slave who became a newspaperman, abolitionist, civil rights advocate and fiery orator, and President Abraham Lincoln, who is credited with freeing the slaves with the signing of the Emancipation Proclamation in 1863. Negro History Week became Black History Month in 1976 as part of the nation's bicentennial celebration. It was a time to celebrate black people's triumphs over tragedies. Doc recalled that Woodson instilled in the West Virginia State students a sense of pride, which countered everything they had heard about people like them.

The positive lessons about black people from Woodson, Carver and other scholars at West Virginia State College and the possibilities each individual offers to America got picked up by Doc, enlarged and transmitted like electricity, building enthusiasm and inspiration in every African American Doc met from then on.

When he wasn't in school, Doc tried to get on at the steel mill back home in Lynchburg. But he was always told he was too small for the big man's job of hauling billets in a wheelbarrow-like contraption and dumping them out. Doc remembered that one guy had to move about a thousand pounds each time and do it repeatedly during the work shift. Doc proved that he could do the work. He wanted the job desperately for the extra money. But the foreman wouldn't hire him because he was not the right size. Doc could see that the other black men with the high wages that the job paid wore the best clothes, drove the best cars and were able to attract the nicest-looking women. But that job wasn't to be for him.

Doc valued the education he got at that black college. It would carry him much further than anything he could have hoped to get from working in the steel mill. Doc picked up the basics—particularly in how to develop lesson plans for teaching. He remembered falling woefully behind in one class with an unforgiving teacher. Doc was to be the presenter that day before the entire class, but he also overslept. Doc hurriedly dressed. Using his imagination, he scooped up some dandelions as he sprinted to class, taking care to get yellow ones and those that were ready to go to seed. He arrived just before the bell rang to find the teacher there with the dean. Doc started lecturing about "the lowly dandelion." He asked the class how that dandelion spread all over campus. "All hands shot up with people wanting to give answers," Doc said. He showed the seeds of the dandelions and asked whether any of the students wanted one. "All hands shot up. I said, 'One at a time!'" He drew some images on the board. The bell rang saving him from stretching the lesson out more. "The professor and the dean came up and shook my hand saying that was the best science lesson they had seen. I was making it up as I went," Doc said laughing. But sometimes that is as much a part of teaching in a creative and innovative manner as planning is. Doc often went back to West Virginia State College years after finishing graduate school and starting his own company. He took his wife and children to visit his former professors who were still teaching on campus. Fond memories of how they helped launch him into a stellar science career and into being a mentor for others still provoke wonderful stories of the past.

Doc earned his master's degree at Cornell University in 1939. Getting into graduate school there was no cakewalk. He recalled applying for admission and being told in correspondence that the school would only admit one black person in any discipline over a four-year stretch. Once that person left or completed his degree, the one position would open again to another black student. It was an early version of affirmative action. Doc insisted on checking once more, refusing to accept that the school wouldn't let him in. He was told by the admissions department that it had not received his transcript. He sent money to West Virginia State College and had the transcript sent. An admissions letter followed. Doc recalled sitting with the head of the department who was disgusted that Doc had the audacity to show up. The guy knew they had corresponded. But when he went to a file drawer to retrieve his copy, he realized that the university had overruled his rejection of Doc. The school year started with Doc enrolled as a master's candidate, but it was not without hardships.

Doc was placed with a family who provided him with room and board for the work he did in their home. The food the couple provided "wasn't enough to feed a bird," Doc recalled. "I stayed hungry the entire first semester."

When Doc tried to study, the "man of the house" was constantly on him to add more fuel to the coal furnace. "Finally I fixed him," Doc said. "I stuffed the furnace with a bunch of coal so when he went to check on the fire, the flames in the furnace roared out of the hole when he opened the door spilling hot coal on the floor," Doc said laughing.

Another time, the couple was entertaining dinner guests, and Doc had to serve as a waiter. The cook knew the couple was underfeeding Doc so she let him have one of the entrées, which was supposed to provide seconds for the guests. When the people had finished their first round of food, the mistress asked Doc to bring in more for seconds. Doc let them know there would be no seconds because he polished it off and it was a delight. Again, the lesson for workers at Du-Good Chemical explained how blacks often supported and aided each other in many "backdoor" ways especially when they worked in white America.

Doc got a grant for $90 a semester the following term. It allowed him to eat better. His grades also went up.

The lean, hard era of the Great Depression helped shape Doc's generation. Nothing went to waste, and Doc often shared such stories with his employees. The lessons of thrift, renewable resources and recycling had a firm foundation at Du-Good Chemical. One of Doc's favorite sayings to the boys from the streets to whom he gave jobs was: "It's better to have and not need than to need and not have." Depression-era habits also fit with the ways of old black folks. They were handed down from generation to generation from slavery. Doing without for slaves and freed folks afterward was a way of life. People had to make a lot out of every little thing. With industrious efforts they could stretch food for what seemed like forever. It also is from people with great needs that the most innovation emerges. Sometimes the stories were sad, but they were always meant to help the boys at Du-Good Chemical understand that no matter how bad they had things, they were better off than others. There were humorous and sometimes sad exceptions. Doc told how his brother Jimmy had a grocery store in Brooklyn. "The hottest-selling item in the store during the Great Depression was Strongheart Dog Food," Doc said.

Strongheart was named after a German shepherd who became one of Hollywood's earliest film stars, living from 1917 to 1929. The dog food was named after him in 1931.

"People would troop into Jimmy's store and buy cases of Strongheart," Doc said. "The only problem was in the entire neighborhood there was only one dog. My brother knew something wasn't right, but as long as the customers wanted Strongheart, he kept selling it. But one week, Jimmy wasn't able to get a shipment of Strongheart to restock his shelves. He got Pointer instead. One fellow came in and asked for a case of Strongheart. My brother said he only had Pointer and explained the problem. The man took the case and grumbled about it. The next day he brought the case back. One can had been opened. The man shook his head and told my brother, 'My dog didn't like this kind of dog food at all. My brother asked, 'Why not?' The man said, 'It's too salty!' That's when my brother knew that those people were eating that dog food. How could the man know the dog thought the dog food was too salty unless he was eating that dog food himself?" Doc always asked that when inquisitive looks from the boys at the factory let him know they didn't get the point of the story. That happened a lot. But Doc wanted them to pick up problem-solving and deductive-reasoning skills.

Doc also would explain using Depression-era stories with the workers why they had to give their full attention to the job they were assigned to do. The environment of the Depression was crushing, prompting people to apply a different logic and survival skills in order to continue working. Complaining wasn't part of the landscape—just hard work and working harder to get the job done. "One guy decided he was going to speak up for all of the men about the difficult hours and bad working conditions," Doc said. "The supervisor listened politely, giving the man the impression that he cared about the worker's concerns. When the worker was done the boss man pointed out the factory window to a line of men waiting for a meal at a soup kitchen. 'See that line' the supervisor said. 'Any one of those men would be eager to be inside this warm building doing this work no matter how hard or bad the working conditions so they could get a paycheck and feed their families. I suggest you get back to work.' The man complied." That often was enough to quell any unrest at Du-Good Chemical over the long hours and difficulty of the jobs that the workers had to do. The boys were preteens and teenagers who were not employable elsewhere.

Sleeping on the job was a huge no-no. Again, Depression-era stories helped to instill a sense of discipline, duty and commitment. Doc said: "A guy at one plant had a habit of going into the bathroom and falling asleep on the toilet when he should have been working. The plant manager suspected that was happening. One day he followed the guy to the john and just as he suspected, found the man dead asleep with his pants around his ankles. The plant manager carefully wrote a note in the nicest cursive script and pinned it to the man's shirt. The note said: "I saw that you were sleeping here in the bathroom and didn't have the heart to wake you from such a peaceful slumber. However, when you wake up and read this, you're fired!"

Doc also stressed professionalism and a sense of decorum. Workers were admonished to be punctual and arrive on time every day for school and work or call ahead to let whomever know they would be late and why. They also had to have on clothes that fit the occasion. Work clothes were for work. School clothes were for the seriousness of studying. And play clothes were for playing. In addition, Doc taught the boys to address older men like him as "sir." It was a simple courtesy. Making eye contact with people was essential. That was hard for many black boys because eye contact was an immediate sign of defiance and signaled a brewing fight. They had to unlearn that and many traditions in the black world in order to pick up another way of communicating in the white world of good business. Firm handshakes spoke volumes as well about an individual's character. Doc punctuated the lessons on behavior with a story about a guy who was seeking a job and had a prospective employer call his previous boss for a reference. "The boss said so-and-so is a hard worker, he has excellent credentials and he gets along well with others. But if you want to hire a drunk, that's your business." The walk-off line was the killer. Doc wanted to make sure that the boys under his tutelage were aware that, when seeking a job, they were being watched and scrutinized constantly. Even after they had secured the work, they were being assessed and evaluated, and even more so as young black men. The rule was black men had to be at least twice as good as whites to be considered half as qualified. Again, those Depression-era stories helped to cement in sound behaviors for young men who otherwise would have little guidance or direction.

Doc saved every nut and every bolt, every board and every nail whether bent, straight, rusty or new. Again, it was a holdover of living through the Depression. The boys often laughed at him for being a packrat but never when they needed some item to complete a job.

Part of the hard times traces to academic and make-ends-meet struggles Doc faced after getting his master's degree at Cornell University. He was hired at Agricultural, Mechanical and Normal College (AM&N College)—Pine Bluff, Ark., in 1939, to head the chemistry department. Sight unseen, the president of the college promised Doc $100 a month minus room and board, which ended up being about $50 a month. When Doc arrived for the job he learned the cold truth. "But by then it was too late to back out," Doc said. The president of the college wasn't happy with what he saw in Doc either. The guy said, "If I had known you were this young I never would have hired you," the man barked in a fiery tone. Doc was only 21 years old at the time. Doc retorted, "If I had known you were only paying $50 a month I never would have come!" But they were stuck with each other as the Great Depression with its stupefying 25 percent unemployment, huge bank failures and crushing home foreclosure rate raged on.

But Doc was a hustler. He got a hold of an old truck and did some light hauling to make some extra money while he worked at the college through 1943. In addition, he worked as an analytical chemist at Pine Bluff Arsenal from 1939 through 1943. Part of it was during World War II. Doc was involved in the production and testing of chemical weapons. He and lab assistants had more than a few close calls handling such dangerous materials as nerve gases. Doc remembers that the Pine Bluff Arsenal plant used black laborers for some of the most dangerous jobs. This was standard in American industries from coast to coast. At Pine Bluff Arsenal, black men worked in the production of acetylene. The manufacturing process was highly explosive. The right mixture of water and chemical was required. One guy perched over a huge concrete bowl-shaped structure had to watch a gauge and turn a water valve to keep the production constant. It was a very tedious, boring job done during the graveyard shift. Often the black workers would fall asleep.

"That was always curtains," Doc remembered. A huge explosion would follow, destroying the wooden platform over the concrete bowl and the worker with it. "What would happen? The plant would rebuild the platform the next day and put another black worker up there until it would blow again. Black people were expendable—always have been in this country."

Teaching chemistry got Doc started on what became his passion—directing young black men and women into the sciences. He was good at it. Like his parents and his own black instructors throughout his academic career, Doc would hold his students to seemingly impossible high standards and then congratulate them when they were successful. Often it was a mild acknowledgement. "Now you're coming!" was his way of letting his students know they had done something that surpassed his expectations. Doc wanted his protégés to continue to strive for excellence long after his contact with them had ended. He wanted his voice compelling them to go further, to become their own. He wanted his hand on their backs pushing to become the force within them to go even faster and further. Saying, "Now you're coming," was his way of letting them know they were on the right path, getting close but not quite arriving. It's like life. People must always strive to climb higher, never relaxing, never resting because that is when sloth, apathy and failure overtake even the most talented people. African Americans can afford to relax even less than others. It is when the relentless prejudices, bigotry and discrimination overtake black students and black workers. Racism is always waiting, always hungry, always willing to verify people's worst impressions of African Americans. The ugly feeling dates back to slavery and serves to feed white privilege and a sense of white superiority. It weighs like a crushing boulder on the backs of blacks judged for generations in America as intellectually, emotionally and physically inferior. Overcoming that takes constant effort, and Doc knew that just as his parents did and his professors as well.

The climate in Arkansas was more like Doc's home state of Virginia. Arkansas was more temperate albeit it quite hot in the summer. The winters were moderate—not like the horrible cold that Doc faced at Cornell University in Ithaca, N.Y. Snow piled on top of snow there. "The cops would take a long stick to feel down several feet below the surface of the snow to see whether a car was illegally parked on the street, and then give the offender a ticket," Doc recalled. "It got bitterly cold there, too. It was not uncommon for the temperature to drop to 10 below zero Fahrenheit." Being a chemist, Doc always made that Fahrenheit/Celsius distinction.

Doc also remembered driving on iced-over roads in Ithaca. Often his tires were in bad shape. The Depression and the war made getting good tires nearly impossible. One night Doc was out late working in the lab on campus. A police officer was off to the side of the road. The weather was bad. The cop was there to warn motorists. Doc just thought it was curious that the officer was out that night in the middle of nowhere. The officer was positioned just before a two-lane bridge, which had iced over. Doc slowed down, but he hit that black ice on the bridge. "It felt like the steering wheel had come off," Doc said laughing. The car managed miraculously to get to the other side. It was one of those instances in which there was nothing Doc could do. His fate was in the hands of providence.

When World War II broke out, Doc was in Pine Bluff, Ark. He and his brothers did what many young men did at the time. They went to enlist. Doc and his brother Hubert had advanced college degrees and were supposed to be admitted in the Army as lieutenants. Hubert got in that way. Doc in Arkansas would only be accepted as a buck private, which he said was unacceptable. He was rejected anyway because of a severe sinus infection caused by working with poisonous gases at the arsenal and an ankle injury from playing football in high school. Doc afterward took the opportunity to go back to Cornell University to get his doctorate in chemistry. When he arrived in Ithaca, he found a draft notice from Uncle Sam waiting to admit him in the Army at the lowest rank. The military was segregated then, and black draftees were to go into all-black units doing mostly menial, support-oriented tasks. The prejudices for black people were strong in the 1940s. Following white American prejudices, black soldiers were viewed as not as brave, not as trustworthy and not as hardworking. Other soldiers of color were viewed the same way. But nothing could be further from the truth. Each time minority units were in combat, they distinguished themselves. They were fighting for their country, fighting for their families, fighting for people of color everywhere in the United States, fighting against the prejudices and fighting to prove they were just as good as any Americans. At the draft headquarters in Syracuse, N.Y., Doc went through the physical examination with the other young men. Working with the poisonous gases at Pine Bluff caused him to have a terrible sinus infection, making it difficult for him to breathe. He also had his ankle taped up. His high school football injury had flared up. Doc, however, made it through the inspection to the final station. He tried to explain to the men in military uniforms that he had been rejected in Arkansas, but they weren't hearing it and kept him moving through the admissions process. Doc got to the end of the tests. "They wanted the men to jump up and down and wave their arms," Doc said. "I knew if I did I was in the Army, and there'd be no getting out so I didn't move. Some fellow came up and started yelling at me saying, 'What's wrong with you, mister? Didn't you hear the instruction?' I said yes, I heard it, but I couldn't because of my bad ankle. He told me to get out of the line and to sit down. I sat there the entire day. Finally, an officer came over with my file. It was marked with big red letters that said C-O-L-O-R-E-D. Make no mistake about it. The man asked: 'What seems to be the problem, mister?' I explained to him what I told the other guy. I told him I was in the doctorate program at Cornell. He asked, 'What kind of work do you do?' I told him I worked with antimalarial compounds and was having some promising results. He yelled: 'What the heck are you doing in here then? We lose more men to malaria than to bullets. Go on back to that college and finish your work.' He marked my file in big red letters '4-F.' I said 'Yes sir,' and left."

◆   ◆   ◆   ◆   ◆

If Doc weren't unconscious and hooked to myriad beeping machines in Barnes hospital, he would be smiling. He always did when telling and retelling that story. His middle-age children sat in chairs around Doc's hospital bed in the ICU and waited. They hoped for the best, hoped for a miracle, hoped that the indomitable spirit within their father would will his way past the injury the Katrina victim inflicted on Doc, will his way past the broken body and stand again in the forceful form of his old self.

CHAPTER 3

FROM CORNELL TO JEFFERSON AVENUE

At Cornell University, Doc was hired as a research assistant in organic chemistry. He worked while he completed his studies in 1945 and 1946. He was a research associate from 1946 to 1947, doing post-doctorate studies. During this time he solved some of the thorniest problems, which led to breakthrough research in the use of aviation-based fuel. From that, Doc synthesized a plasticizing agent that is still in use today. Doc's ground-breaking work made plastics possible along with that part of the oil-based industry. But the professor he worked under got the credit and that man's name is on the patent. Intellectual property rights work that way. A major U.S. corporation made billions of dollars from the work. "All I got was a handshake," Doc lamented throughout his life. Doc found himself the victim of many other such intellectual property thefts, prompting him to decide to go into business for himself. He saw self-employment as his only chance to enjoy the fruits of his genius and hard work. Doc continually told the boys who worked at his lab that Thomas Alva Edison was fond of saying, "Genius is 1 percent inspiration and 99 percent perspiration." No one worked harder than Doc.

Doc was continually frustrated and angered by the racism, prejudice and discrimination he encountered. Even though he was quick-witted and a great problem-solver, he often did not get the credit for the innovations he devised. Doc's professors at West Virginia State College were very complimentary and encouraging unlike many of the white professors he encountered at Cornell University and in American society in general.

To survive, Doc became a student of American culture and society. Black people at that time were at the bottom of the economic, political and societal pile. It was a holdover from slavery. White supremacy had blacks and other people of color in what seemed like a constant concentration camp-like lockdown, which was brutally enforced. Doc and the few other blacks on Cornell's campus felt it every day. Some decided to say the heck with the struggle of getting a college education or an advanced degree and took jobs bussing tables or serving as bellhops at hotels. But Doc was possessed. He was driven to succeed and prove even the worst racists wrong. He and other young black men and women were driven to expose white privilege for the lie that it historically has been. They knew that knowledge and ability were never the sole provinces of white males—even though American society had convinced people worldwide that it was. The only way to break the cycle and the lie of white supremacy was to succeed, besting even the best of their white contemporaries. That was the greatest lesson Doc got from his parents and the black community that raised him. That is what black people everywhere were taught. They were raised to be revolutionaries fighting within the system against epic oppression. They didn't do it by marching in the streets or staging sit-ins at lunch counters. They did it through their everyday acts showing they were competent, capable and just as good and better than those whom white privilege favored. They were the quiet activists, but they were just as angry and demanding. They didn't get fire hoses turned on them during demonstrations, have the police dogs rip away their flesh or get their heads split open by the cops' billy clubs. They went against the mammoth white machines in college, businesses, politics, churches, communities, government and industries. They got bloodied psychologically, mentally and emotionally every day. They took the punishing blows. To succeed, they had to compete in white America. They had to constantly fight the system of bigotry that barred admission to blacks.

That was impossible to see from the 1200 block of Jefferson Avenue in the 1950s and 1960s. The street contained a well-established black commercial district, starting with Du-Good Chemical in 1947. Because of white flight, black children growing up in the surrounding neighborhoods rarely saw or rubbed shoulders with white people. The children lived in a sheltered environment—a cocoon away from the cold, arctic, racist and discriminatory tornadic winds. The gusts hit black America with the harshest conditions. They threatened the economic, social, family and community environments of African Americans. Together as businessmen and as members of the clergy, the black men created a safe haven away from the worst hurricanes that threatened the existence of themselves and others like them. Together they were the urban heat, the temperature inversion that kept the titanic atmospheric winds of racism from coalescing into a force that would destroy them. Strength in numbers has always drawn people of color together. It is what created many black business enclaves like the one in the block Du-Chemical has called home.

College is its own societal bubble, protecting young, impressionable students from the real world. Doc's Cornell University professors encouraged him to apply for jobs in businesses and industries needing talented scientists. Doc applied at Beech-Nut Chewing Gum, which was seeking a chief chemist. The person who interviewed him said Doc had excellent credentials and was amazed that Doc had done as much as he had in such a short period of time. The man offered Doc the job, but said that for Doc to take it, he would have to abandon all of his family. Doc, who had straight hair, fair skin, gray eyes and the features of a white man, was told he would have to pass as a white man. That is the only way he could be hired and that was the only way he would be accepted at the company. Doc declined the job. He remembered that his father's sister had moved to Florida and like 14,000 blacks each year she had vacated the world of black America to "pass" into the world of white America undetected. She would occasionally return to Virginia to visit her black relatives, but they were never, ever to visit her. There is a terrible trauma and terrible shame associated with surrendering the part of ones past that helped to make the person whom he or she is. Doc didn't have to think long before he told the man who wanted to hire him that he could not take the job. The personal cost was just too high.

Doc also interviewed with other major companies. One guy in authority wanted to hire him, but again there were restrictions. The man said: "There are some very prejudiced people who work at this plant. The only way we will hire you is if you promise to come in every day, and speak to no one. Just do your work and leave." Doc said the personal cost associated with that job also was too high.

But not everyone felt that way. There weren't too many black students at Cornell University, and Doc knew just about every one. A black football player on campus graduated and accepted a job at a corporation. Doc often shared the story about him with his workers at Du-Good Chemical as an object lesson. Doc's classmate was told by the white guy who hired him: "Some of the black workers will come to you with many grievances. I want you to listen to them, take notes and let me know what you hear." Doc's friend from Cornell did just that. He took notes and then presented the findings to his supervisor. To his amazement, the guy chewed him out for bringing him the complaints and for thinking that something would be done. "I hired you to listen to their complaints. You are to pat them on the back and make them think we are concerned. You are to do nothing. If that is too much to ask of you then I will have to hire somebody else for the job!" Doc recalled that his college friend thought about that and decided to follow the boss' orders. The college friend figured that the boss would get another black to do the job, and he would be black-balled for life. Doc's college friend decided to look out for his own self-interests. He rose through the ranks of the company, became president of an East Coast black college, headed a major nonprofit and was appointed an ambassador in Europe. Doc's Cornell University black colleague was highly successful by choosing the path of least resistance—not making waves against white America. But there is no courage, strength, integrity or character in going against the best interests of black people. Flowing with the white-American river of rage against African Americans is easy and self-serving. Going against white culture and white privilege was a killer then as it continues to be now. Doc set a different path for himself, following that of his father's. Doc put a high premium on his integrity, his sense of pride, morality, ethics and his dignity as a black man. Give those virtues away, and one has nothing, Doc would explain to Du-Good Chemical workers.

The alternative to sacrificing one's soul and indomitable spirit to white America to become a totally broken house-Negro was to go into business for oneself. That was the path Doc chose. He pulled a page from John Milton's mid-1600s epic poem, "Paradise Lost," in which Milton wrote, "Better to reign in Hell than serve in Heaven." Doc's defiant attitude toward American racism fit the theme of the book involving disobedience and therefore the following loss of the so-called paradise—for the black man—at least of the place where white America wanted to keep black people. Doc forever railed against religion in black America teaching obedience and patience and encouraging blacks to wait until after death when they would get their "milk and honey." Whites weren't God. They merit dominion over no one—especially blacks.

Doc is a believer of Dr. W.E.B. Du Bois theory of blacks possessing a double consciousness pulled from Du Bois' 1903 book, "The Souls of Black Folks." Du Bois described how blacks see the world both through the prism of Americans like everyone else but also through the lens of being Africans in America. It gives black people the gift of vision unlike what whites possess. It enables them to be infinitely more than the stereotypes people have of them. It gifts them with problem-identifying and problem-solving abilities beyond what most people in this country possess. Black people just have to realize their special talent, harness it and rocket to success, taking the rest of America with them.

Those thoughts were what propelled Doc to start his own chemical company. "I can do just fine on my own," Doc often defiantly shared with his workers. Like immigrants to this country, Doc and many black entrepreneurs felt the push and pull of self-employment. The pull was from that ever strong Horatio Alger spirit in America. People like Doc knew that with a little money, the support of family, a lot of elbow grease and a lot of luck they could make it big in whatever endeavor they immersed themselves in—body and spirit. That was the enthusiasm behind the launch of Du-Good Chemical, and that is what helped it endure. The push was from the crushing racism and discrimination that black people felt in the country that they loved and fought for. It was a push that said they would never be fully accepted into the privileged world that whites controlled and dominated. Yet, old black-and-white photographs of Du-Good Chemical and Doc exhibited a tremendous amount of pride for what the company meant to the 1200 block of South Jefferson Avenue and to blacks in that community. Doc possessed a determined defiance to living the hanging-head, stooped-shouldered life that most blacks suffered because of racism. Like his dad, Doc was determined to shed the yoke of oppression and never let white people's limitations for blacks deter his drive for success in business or science. Doc had a swashbuckling pride from creating Du-Good Chemical and its products—what no one ever could give to him. He didn't get any lucky breaks. He got what he was able to provide for himself with the help of his family. The old black-and-white pictures made that clear, but what was even more striking was to see the three-dimensional images in living color.

Generations of boys who have worked at Du-Good Chemical have had zero knowledge of the dynamics behind the company or behind the other black businesses in the 1200 block of Jefferson Avenue. What they saw was a string of struggling entrepreneurs who had a dream of being their own boss. They saw black men who didn't want to work for anyone else. It was so American and yet diminished often because the businesses were merely black and small. In the seclusion and protection of the black neighborhood, the boys couldn't know the truth, and no one in the 1200 block of Jefferson Avenue or in any other black enclave of businesses throughout America could articulate the rocky path well enough for them to know. Yet it was real. All the boys got were instructions on what to do and what not to do to stay on the straight and narrow path of staying in school, getting good grades, being good workers and getting ahead.

When the factory machinery was off at Du-Good Chemical and the boys were taking a break, they would look south along Jefferson Avenue at Harold's Tavern, 1405 S. Jefferson Ave., on the corner of Park Avenue. It was where black men and women congregated after work to relax, drink and crack jokes—it didn't matter who was the butt of the humor. The boys working at Du-Good Chemical longed for the day when they, too, could go inside to enjoy the gregarious banter with beers. The spirited, loud talk often elevated into riotous laughter. People who were daily subjected to great strife and sorrow also knew and openly expressed wondrous joy when the moment hit. Sometimes, though, it was at the expense of a fellow bar patron. Black men in the bar often played the "dozens," an exchange of insults, picking at each other over what someone else didn't have or boasting about their own possessions. The banter mainly focused on women, clothes and cars. Cadillacs were a mainstay. Many black people didn't have much. So many people coveted and flaunted any outward show of wealth so others would think they had made it. Having the latest style in clothes or the newest Cadillac meant a lot even though most of the bar patrons lived in the unbanked, less-than-poor-credit world of people whose only currency was cash. In one "dozens" session, a bar patron bragged about the new 1961 Cadillac Coup de Ville he had just bought from the dealership. Someone else immediately shouted that he had owned the car the week before, but it was repossessed because he got behind on his payments. People widely knew that the dealership kept certain cars for black customers. The car salesmen knew they could recycle those vehicles because of nonpayment. They made their money that way, and blacks driving the car around provided ready advertisement in the neighborhood. That caused others to want a chance to own that car. The man with the car shot back, "At least my Cadillac is brand new unlike that 1953 Cadillac you've got that you need to get jumped every time you try to start it." The bar roared with more laughter.

Not to be outdone, the man with the old Cadillac responded: "I know you have that new ride. But I'm not eating cat shit to keep it." People in the bar howled. The noise could easily be heard by passers-by going to the store or to work. On weekend nights, people even talked over the loud music. The smell of beer belched into the outdoor air from the window air-conditioning units. Every so often when the banter got too heated, someone would pull a gun.

Shots would ring out. From the 1200 block of Jefferson Avenue, the boys at Du-Good Chemical would see people flee the bar in a mad rush. Men and women would dash helter-skelter into the street regardless of traffic to get away from any stray bullets. Poverty and its kissing kin, violence, dominated the lives of black people, who mostly struggled just to keep their meager-salaried jobs, pay the rent and utilities, and feed and clothe their children. Those primary concerns superseded everything else. Having fun and partying followed to relieve the stress of just getting by. Doc tried to explain to the boys working at his company that such goings-on—though funny and exciting—were part of the silt of ever-changing time. Doc said that when he was a kid, Cadillacs were not the vehicle that blacks craved. Back then the in-cars were Packards. But that company went out of business years ago. After Cadillacs, Mercedes and BMWs were the vehicles that African Americans demanded as status symbols. Then Lexus and Infinitis took over.

The history of the times and people's changing tastes were like an unending play with new acts, scenes and actors. It often has only a whispering effect compared with the day-to-day struggles of the large audience. The drama on stage is everything to the actors. The hot lights they are under mostly keeps them from knowing the goings-on of the larger world. The theater outside of their own is muted.

Sometimes the dramas onstage and that of the audience collide. People mostly watched the drama of unfolding history on TV. The newscasts brought them details of the John F. Kennedy-Richard M. Nixon debate in 1960 during the presidential election. The Cuban missile crisis was a huge concern because of the possible destruction of the world. The atomic bombs that most people feared from the Cold War were an ongoing menace. Interviews of Malcolm X making history about black power excited some folks, and angered and scared others. Missouri's own Harry S. Truman signed an executive order in 1948 when he was president integrating the Armed Forces. The 1954 Supreme Court Brown vs. the Topeka Board of Education decision ending legal segregation brought more cheers. Emmett Till's brutal death in Money, Miss., in August 1955 and his open casket in Chicago chilled and enraged the nation. It also inspired Rosa Parks, that unassuming seamstress and started the Montgomery, Ala., bus boycott, which led to the Civil Rights Movement headed by the Rev. Martin Luther King Jr. The Vietnam War took and then claimed some of the boys from the neighborhood. Nationwide anti-war protests followed. Long lines at gasoline pumps and higher prices followed the 1973 Arab oil embargo. The black community had its champions, which included Ralph Bunch, track star Jesse Owens, Jackie Robinson and Joe Louis. Muhammad Ali's antics in the boxing ring captured black people's attention. He was a hero both because he boasted of what he could do at a time when blacks were taught to stay quiet and in their place, and then because he carried out his words with great authority, which riled the white establishment.

People followed these dramas on television while their own life struggles dominated their waking concerns. Domestic violence often rifled people's homes with one or the other spouse being beaten. Children often got caught in the crossfire. The massive amount of corporal punishment among blacks was a holdover from slavery, where fear and beatings forced compliance. One generation handed down to each new one that followed that manner of raising children and treating spouses. Regardless of the family, children went to school and into jobs having heard parents or relatives warn that they'd better behave, "or I'll beat you 'til you bleed."

The black businessmen in the 1200 block of Jefferson Avenue were very familiar with such childrearing techniques. They knew the history of black people, and they followed on black-and-white televisions in their shops the history of the times projected into their establishments by the dancing light and incredible sound. Radio didn't capture the times as well, although radios in the 1200 block of Jefferson Avenue were always playing. The radios generally stayed on KATZ-AM, 1600 on the dial. Rhythm and blues along with the latest Motown hits generally played amid the incessant stream of disc jockey chatter. The station also played more commercials than songs. Doc advertised some of his products on KATZ. He also placed ads in the St. Louis Argus, The St. Louis American and the St. Louis Sentinel. He stayed away from the St. Louis Evening Whirl. It was a scandal sheet. The Whirl was well-read, however, being in The Whirl was not considered a good thing. The paper and the oddities it chronicled were more than "man bites dog." It was more like gangster cuts police dog's throat and throws the bleeding animal's carcass out the window before police shoot and kill the dangerous, cornered criminal. The Whirl sometimes included the front-page picture of two "lovers" literally in bed caught in the act before being killed by a jealous spouse. Never mind that The Whirl got the staff of the morgue to stage the photograph so it appeared that the photo was shot before the couple was.

Those were the unfortunate things that happened in the underbelly of the black community. They went on in the underworld of the white community, too. It's just that the white police, the courts and social service system were less inclined to show the dirty laundry of white people. For blacks, everything was on the table. It was funny and entertaining. But it also fed the stereotypes of black people, keeping individuals' prejudices alive and well. The news, however, failed to record the good, everyday life of black people.

The black shops and businesses in the 1200 block of Jefferson Avenue helped to set a normal tone for African-American children and adults. The businesses were the rivets helping to hold the village together. They provided many wayward kids an opportunity to enter these stalwart few workplaces and do different, and in many cases, menial jobs such as sweeping the floor, random dusting, stacking boxes, pumping kerosene, doing inventory or shoveling coal to earn a nickel, dime or quarter. In the process, the kids were lectured about how best to sweep the floor and do the other tasks. From these black teachers on Jefferson Avenue and many other streets like it throughout America, the kids learned that quality work matters. They learned the virtues of strength, persistence, enterprise, integrity, determination, character, discipline and confidence.

The old wood floors at the shops and businesses didn't give up dirt easily. The planks had been nailed to the cross beams in the 1800s so that they rested side-by-side. The years and a lot of wear had caused the boards to bend and bow and pull away somewhat from each other, leaving large cracks between the once perfectly placed planks. The floor covering also had come up after years of mopping. In some places the linoleum still stubbornly adhered to the old wood.; in others, only the bare wood remained. The 3-inch-wide boards were far from the pristine color of fresh oak that they were when the boards were first nailed. They had picked up the color of time—gray and well-worn with the constant shuffling of hundreds of shoes over the surface. Sweeping cleaned away the dust and the dirt that accumulated, but it settled quite comfortably in the cracks and the grain of the old boards. The corners also picked up mounds of caked-on dirt, which would take a scraper to dislodge. If Shorty was feeling particularly ornery, he would have some hungry kid scrape out the dirt from the corners with an old screwdriver. Mopping the floor would follow. That happened rarely—maybe four times a year. Pine-Sol would be used in the scrubbing. When the work was done, the floor always looked the same—only wet. It made the place smell good, which was an oddity above the odors that the regular clientele brought in with them and the constant cigarette, cigar and pipe smoke smell that filled the one-story room. The sweeping, scraping and mopping were good for the boys and the occasional brave girl. Despite the ridicule, the kids got hammered with many noble characteristics such as enterprise, a good work ethic, determination, pride, thrift, perseverance and courage, which aren't taught in school. They also picked up Doc's confidence, which the rest of America still tries to beat out of black people. Doc insisted, however, that the boys who crossed his threshold know they were as good as anyone else—actually better—they had to be to survive in the United States as African American men. None of those good, solid character traits can be bought, and once in place, they can never be taken away. Those exemplary character traits have to be forged. The giants of the 1200 block of South Jefferson Avenue were the blacksmiths who put the kids in the intense, unforgiving flames of hard work and then pounded out the kinks in the children's unruly spirit, shaping them into the future African-American champions, which the community and the country so desperately needed. It wasn't about how much money the boys made. It was the fact that they were rubbing shoulders and learning from real black men.

Kids on the street were hungry. They would learn from each other that Shorty was giving away nickels at the shoe shine shop. They'd go in and have the brazen audacity to ask for the handout. The older black men sitting around a couple of deteriorating folding tables on rickety chairs or wooden crates would look up from checker boards and riotously laugh. White hair peaked from under hats and open coats in the often unevenly heated room in the winter. An unforgiving floor provided no padding. A dirty and cracked front display window offered the only light. Wood crackled in an improperly vented potbelly stove. Shorty, who stood just a little over 5 feet tall, wore suspenders, a checked shirt most days and trousers with laced-up boots. A railroad cap pulled tightly down on his head made him look as if he'd just stepped from a caboose waving a kerosene-fueled lantern. Shorty like most of the men in his shoe shine parlor wore several layers of clothes. Most of them were rumpled from being unironed and less than impeccably clean.

One day, Shorty stepped away from the potbellied stove where he was warming himself while waiting for a paying customer to enter his shop. He approached the unflappable boys. They exhibited plenty of brass and chutzpah. The streets and the tremendous needs in the black community do that to kids. They have to be boldly and shamelessly brazen. Often, it's the only thing they've got. Shorty walked slowly toward the pack of six boys. His knees didn't bend much beneath the well-worn, brown and dirty corduroy pants he had on. Too much kneeling and bending over shining shoes at the wooden stands he had built against the walls had limited Shorty's mobility. Years of hard work had caused his dark skin to look like the shoe leather he daily tried to make appear new. Shorty stared down at the boys, who were no more than 7 to 9 years old. "Which one of you boys is ready to do some work for that money you want me to *GIVE* you?" Shorty barked. The men in the place laughed again. "You tell 'em, Shorty," one man at the card table called back the way people do in black Baptist churches when ministers start to whoop. The men's noise drowned out the background hum of the old red Coke machine sitting against another wall. It looked like an old freezer that opened from the top. The soda bottles had to be worked along a track to a gate that could be forced open if 10 cents had been inserted to pay for the cool, soothing drink. Most people would have been run off by the humiliating laughter and the short, old man's bark. These incredulous boys held their ground.

It was remarkably different from the youths who the St. Louis chapter of the Urban League in the early 1970s sent to Doc's company to work. Those youths knew they would get paid with federal anti-poverty money whether they did any work or not. Their attitude was blasé compared with the boys of a generation earlier who wandered into all of the black businesses in the 1200 block of South Jefferson Avenue hungry.

The boys from the street drew on each other's courage to stand up to the old men. The leader of the group shouted back. "Nobody said nothing about no work. We came for the nickel them other kids said you gave them."

Shortly barked back: "This ain't no get-without-giving world, boy! You've got to work for everything. Is you boys ready to get dirty doing some work because I've got plenty of it. And if you do it right, maybe I will think about giving you a couple of pennies for your troubles."

The black men laughed again with more catcalls. "I'll bet them boys is going to leave for sure now," one old man at a folding table said. The kids knew him as "Mr. Peabody." That wasn't his real name. They just called him that because he carried the perpetually strong odor of urine on him. He always had on a red flannel cap with a bill and a gray overcoat. Who knew what color the coat really was. Dirt and years of not being washed had left it earth-toned.

Mr. Peabody was happy to be laughing with the other men at the occasional boys who'd wander in seeking a handout. Often Mr. Peabody caught the brunt of the biting humor. No one will ever let him forget how the fire department had to be called to rescue him from the toilet in one of the apartments above Sam's Cleaners. The floorboards in the old building were not used to having commodes. Bathrooms were a turn-of-the-20th century added convenience. Homes, hotels and apartments that predated the trend had closets and bedrooms converted into bathrooms complete with indoor plumbing and drainage pipes. But the work wasn't always done right. Oak floorboards weren't always reinforced as they should have been. Holes were drilled into floors for the drainage pipes without the proper beams underneath. Mr. Peabody fell victim to that—literally. Most people are right-handed, which means most people sitting on the toilet lean to the left to wipe themselves. The weight of the commode, water and toilet user is bad enough on old floorboards. The added stress of constantly rocking to the left eventually causes any toilet to list in that direction. In Mr. Peabody's case, one day the whole commode fell through the floor of his apartment with him riding it nearly all the way down. Mr. Peabody screamed loudly, but it did nothing to stop gravity's pull. He found himself with his feet in the air and his hips wedged tightly in the jaws of the jagged old wood that the toilet had broken through on its way to the apartment below. Mr. Peabody's neighbor with the new toilet, gushing water from broken pipes and all of Mr. Peabody's smelly business called the fire department. The woman below wasn't at all happy about the bleeding, screaming, black butt-crack ceiling ornament decorating her apartment either. Firefighters arrived within minutes. They held back their laughter and managed after a time to cut Mr. Peabody out of the hole he was in. They bandaged him up. He declined to go to the hospital. Too embarrassed. He'd just as soon act as if nothing had happened. But word traveled fast about the load that Mr. Peabody dropped on his neighbor below. The damage was so bad that Mr. Peabody had to move to another apartment. People laughed about the water and building damage that Mr. Peabody's big stink had caused. They laughed about the neighbor below not appreciating Mr. Peabody's pimply, old butt, which she had to look at until firefighters came and about Mr. Peabody's load nearly condemning Sam's building. People are still laughing—everyone that is except Mr. Peabody.

This is a community that needs to laugh. It knows great hardship in the difficulty of getting jobs, the difficulty kids face in schools that don't want to teach them because there's the assumption that they have no ability or will to learn. There's the difficulty with death. It happens too often to the newborn and very young children who succumb to disease or poisons and to people who've barely turned adults killed on jobs or in the violence that stalks every heartbeat of life. There's the difficulty to pay for funerals and burials and the debt that those who've died early incurred in life. People laugh to sooth the pain and to cheer themselves when there's nearly nothing to laugh about. They crack on each other and on the sun, the moon and the stars. Everything is funny, and at the same time nothing at all. In many cases a strong sense of humor is the only thing most black folks have.

On this day it's the derelict-looking boys wanting a handout. Shorty asks their names, and they boisterously shout them out. He asks where they live, and they tell. He asks whether they are prepared to work for his hard-earned change. Two say they are. The rest leave muttering and swearing as they step back into the cold. Shorty gives the one named Ben a broom to sweep the floor. The other, Ernie, has to neatly arrange the tools and polishes that Shorty uses. The boys get instruction from all of the men. "Don't forget to get in that corner and get out that dirt, boy!" one man said. "You know you going to get called boy the rest of your life, don't you, boy?" The men laughed barely moving so Ben could pull the dirt from under the table. Shorty wouldn't let the boy half-step. "You can get all of that under there," Shorty said. "You want this nickel, don't you, boy? Get that paper wrapper, too."

Ernie had stacked the polish the way Shorty had instructed. Both boys were dirtier and more tired than when they entered Shorty's shoe shine shop about an hour earlier. Sure they had been harassed and hooted. Yes, they were upset and angry, too. But each left with an Indian-head nickel, which is more than what their friends had. They went to Jeff's store on the corner of Jefferson Avenue and Hickory Street. Ben bought a bag of Sugar Babies. Ernie got some Milk Duds. Their friends had too much pride to take the humiliating laugher and do the work. They also didn't have the nickels that Ernie and Ben got for their efforts, the candy that the money bought or the invaluable lessons that the old black men provided—albeit harshly.

Big-box stores and fast-food restaurants today such as Wal-Mart, McDonald's, Lowe's, Home Depot, Sears, Macy's, Walgreen's, CVS and Target offer goods and services at much more competitive prices than the mom-and-pop stores did. Nationwide, the corporations helped eliminate tens of thousands of mom-and-pop, small businesses, jobs in communities with proprietors of all colors. The profit-motive behind the small profit margin in no way replicated the goodwill and the rich teachings that the intimate, storefront settings provided. The corporatization of life in communities throughout America has ripped out the community rivets that helped shape young people into adults. The village has been robbed, pillaged and plundered with kids now raising themselves and families being overwrought by deplorable poverty and segregated conditions.

Left on their own without the guiding hand of African-American men, children end up living down to ever-present, negative stereotypes about black people. They become lazy instead of industrious. They turn into beggars instead of people who will work to earn their keep. They surrender instead of being determined to do a good job. They will resort to theft instead of relying on truth, honor, honesty, hard work and integrity. They will lie instead of being trustworthy. They'll have bad attitudes instead of possessing character, strength, a sense of duty and an unstoppable work ethic. Humor figures into that, too, along with a quick wit with a biting edge that enables the kids to give back the banter as righteously as they receive it. But the young people had to show a reverence and respect for their teachers instead of the ugly arrogance of unruly defiance and total irreverence for the lessons that they need to learn in order to survive. Most of them knew this and they complied. Some didn't try.

The slaves knew this, and they tried to instill the virtues in their children. Each generation passed those concepts of work and self-worth on to their offspring. It traveled from the South to the North with the Great Migration of blacks for more freedoms and a better way of life. Businesses and the churches like those on Jefferson Avenue became the standard-bearers for the community. They were carrying on a tradition as old as agriculture and the changing seasons. The harvest in goodwill and in community-minded adults was meant to ensure their survival. Adherence to the ways of the harvest meant more for black children. Missteps and messing up without the guidance meant trouble at home with kids not complying with their parents. Beatings often followed—sometimes the whippings went too far. That's a tradition from slavery, too. Such trouble walked into the schools, creating disturbances for the teachers. Suspensions and expulsions followed with kids who couldn't make it and couldn't conform. They'd land on the street—cold, hungry and alone.

The underworld of crime would eagerly take them in. Prostitution, alcohol, drugs, gambling, theft and violence were eager armies constantly seeking new recruits. Businesses and the churches on 1200 block of South Jefferson Avenue were the first line of defense keeping kids from succumbing to the darkness. If the black businesses failed, the police were all too willing to step in. They'd constantly round up kids walking the street, taking names, addresses and phone numbers. Most kids knew to run. Most parents knew to question the police when the cops were seeking the names of the kids. Trust was a non-starter when the cop cars rolled up. Nothing but trouble followed.

Watching and doing everything but cheering the black men anchoring the 1200 block of Jefferson Avenue was what most folks preferred. They'd surrender their kids to the hard work offered within any day rather than visit their kids behind bars or in graveyards.

The boys always loved to hear Doc yell his standard exit sentence when it was time to head for home. That time for Doc usually was around midnight. Not much else was moving on the street. Normal people were long-since in bed. Doc usually went home and graded his students' class assignments and test papers until 2 a.m. to 4 a.m. and then got up in time to make a 7:30 a.m. class that he had to teach. He was never happy about those early classes, and his students knew it. Late at night Doc always used to yell from the second-floor lab to the manufacturing room floor, "Let's get the hell outta here!" That was the boys' signal to shut down any remaining machinery, put the tools away, cut off the lights and head for the front door. Doc usually ran down the winding wooden staircase that led to the lab, and everyone went home. For years Doc ran up and down that rickety old staircase. It was wide enough for only one person. The stairs climbed to the south toward a square window with four panes overlooking the loading area and the basketball goal that Doc had nailed to a big tree near the long shed. The stairs listed to the east about as much as the Leaning Tower of Pisa does and people who were unsure of their stability held tightly to the well-used railing that Doc had installed. On the opposite side was a wall made of tongue-and-groove boards that climbed 15 feet high overlooking the trough. Right at the window where the staircase curved back to the north before entering the lab, one could look overtop the tongue-and-groove wall out onto the production floor in the big room. The greatest sight to behold was from atop the stairs looking out as the tables were filled with bottles that had been labeled and were ready to be filled and as the room sang with a cacophony of machinery while the boys and Doc yelled back and forth while mixers whirred and Doc followed his formulas empty-ing one ingredient and then another into a big tank or a 55-gallon drum. All of that activity took place on the concrete floor, where no spillage created any damage. Doc had put down thick red linoleum in the late 1940s in the lab and used the same linoleum to cover each step to the second floor, where he did his research and his longtime secretary, Ida Phillips, typed his reports, letters, invoices and papers he delivered at American Chemical Society con-ventions, which Doc regularly attended. The stairs got a lot more traffic than the lab floor did. Doc put down metal strips to protect the linoleum and the wood. But even that wore down. He then laid down some heavier, white tiles cut in the 1960s to fit each stair. That stuff stayed put for more than 40 years.

Home was a long way off now. Home was the family home where Doc's middle-age kids camped waiting for word that he had pulled out of uncon-sciousness and was getting better. It was where Renee and Lewis took out the old, broken window air conditioner that their mom, Nancy, had installed because she hated the pressure-cooker humidity and heat of St. Louis' summer. Doc always moaned about sleeping with the air conditioner on when Nancy was alive, saying it aggravated his sinuses. Grousing about everything to each other was part of their relationship. They argued over food, things that needed mending at the house and even the cigarettes they smoked. Nancy often joked that cigarettes got Doc into trouble a couple of times. Once he bought a case of Viceroy cigarettes at an impossibly low price. The entire box, which had several cartons in it, cost less than one carton. It was not a spoof or a rip-off like the "hot" still-boxed TV sets that guys who happened into Greasy Earl's shop often tried to sell. Those who were foolish enough to take the too-good-to-be-true deal found that when they got the "set" home that it consisted of a box with just enough evenly distributed bricks to convince the purchaser of "stolen" merchandise to think he was getting a "steal." Indeed that person was. Doc standing around Greasy Earl's shop waiting on work to be done on his car was talked into buying the case of cigarettes. It wasn't until Doc took the cigarettes home and Nancy started to smoke one that she realized that it had a funny taste and odor. She quizzed Doc about where he got the Viceroys. Doc explained. Nancy peeled the cigarette apart and found dozens of tobacco bugs throughout the cigarette she had already smoked. She yelled at Doc for being so gullible and from then on joked about the out-of-date and long-gone-bad "bug-a-rettes" that Doc had brought home for her to "enjoy."

Another bad run in Doc had with smoking was when he was on a TV news program. He was in a studio being interviewed about being head of the Leukemia Guild in St. Louis and about the cancer research he had been doing since his father died of cancer in 1955. TV interviews are stressful because words that are said on camera can never be taken back. So interview subjects have to be careful constantly. Doc was. However, he slipped up when the interviewer did his wrap-up ending the show. But the cameras continued to roll. Doc, thinking the show was over, pulled out his cigarettes and fired one up. That was captured by the cameras and broadcast throughout the city. Cigarettes at that time in the 1960s were suspected of causing cancer. It should have been enough of a warning for any scientist—particularly one doing cancer research—to stay far, far away from cigarettes of any kind.

Doc and Nancy knew better. Each was intensely smart. Nancy was Doc's intellectual equal and certainly her spirit was just as unstoppable. After Nancy got sick in her late 50s with the early onset of Alzheimer's Disease and died

in 1994, Doc lost any desire to smoke and he lost his best sparring partner. He began to sleep under the air conditioner in the summer and by all
accounts, enjoyed it. There was no one to complain to anymore.

◆   ◆   ◆   ◆   ◆

While Doc was in the hospital recovering from the assault, Renee and Lewis
bought a new window unit at Sears and installed it, using the skills they had
learned from Doc. It was therapeutic. Putting in the air conditioner was more
a wishful hope that Doc would return home his former self, needing the cool
comfort that the unit provided. It was a gift and a prayer that things would
return to normal, even though all signs indicated otherwise.

CHAPTER 4

DU-GOOD CHEMICAL, THE DREAM

A manufacturing company that was black-owned was unimaginable especially in the mid-20th century. Yet, Doc had the steel in his soul, the skills and the family support to make it happen. St. Louis had its own tradition of black entrepreneurs. Madame C.J. Walker got her start there at the turn of the century with hair-straightening products for black women. She grew that germ of an idea into a major business, becoming the first black millionaire in the country.

Doc figured that lightning could strike twice in the same city. He and his family turned the second floor of the old animal hospital into Du-Good Chemical's main lab with three aisles, long rows of lab benches, stools, water, electricity and gas connections and the latest analytical laboratory equipment. Doc set up a desk with a typewriter and hired a secretary. Above that desk on the wall beside the south window on the front of the second-floor lab was a picture of Louis Pasteur holding a rabbit. Pasteur was a French chemist and microbiologist who made unprecedented contributions in vaccinations, microbial fermentation and of course pasteurization. He developed vaccines against anthrax and rabies. Doc kept that photograph above his desk to inspire people who worked at his company. Doc often would tell the boys working at Du-Good Chemical that if it were not for Pasteur, humanity wouldn't know about germs, microscopic organism and the infectious diseases they cause such as the flu, chicken pox and pneumonia. Among Doc's secretaries were Alice Ridley, and then Ida Phillips. Miss Phillips worked for Du-Good Chemical for decades. Doc and his brothers constructed book shelves against the south wall, and even more shelves were set up for the chemicals Doc needed to do his work. Sunlight streamed in from the three east windows and depending on the time of day, the sun cast an orange glow through each window on the north over the alley and the south over the yard-like loading area. Doc built a hood by that south window to contain and vent hazardous chemicals, which he often worked with.

One of Doc's strengths was that he could dismantle just about any commercial product, determine what was in it and then reconstruct a similar product—only better. He also could give any client the engineering method that could be used to make the product. It was amazing to watch. Doc would work day and night until he came up with the answer. From the street, people would see him holding up test tubes to the fluorescent lights in the second-floor lab as he examined compounds. Doc would stir others in beakers over hot plates. A lot of the work required samples being put in titanium boats and then heated in special equipment to determine the number of carbon, hydrogen or nitrogen atoms. An ancient black vacuum pump elevated on a shelf above the middle countertop in the lab would rhythmically chug as it drew the air and water from whatever sealed container in the lab Doc connected it to. It was an additional part of Doc's analysis. He would take the samples to super-sensitive scales in the northwest corner of the second-floor lab. Those scales could weigh the compound down to one-one thousandth of a gram. Doc would admonish anyone coming up the winding staircase from the manufacturing area to the lab to stand still until he got an accurate reading. When everything was working, the large second-floor lab was alive with activity. Blue flames from Bunsen burners danced beneath the beakers, flasks and other equipment as Doc jockeyed back and forth from one to another. Motors whirred and pumps hummed. All of it generated a lot of heat, which made the lab the most comfortable part of the drafty old building in the winter and like a lower floor of hell in the summer.

Miss Phillips, Doc's longtime secretary, kept up with the paperwork, completing invoices, deciphering his notes for letters to clients and doing lab work herself. Her desk was in the southeast corner of the third aisle. It was a straight shot to the hood and the staircase. Two sinks were at the west ends of the long lab benches. Doc often worked in the middle aisle. The telephone and his large, old-fashioned calculator were in the first aisle. The calculator was the size of a typewriter, and it made a lot of buzzing and bumping noises when it was operating. But it really worked. Opposite the calculator was a large oxygen tank. Glass tubes ran from it to the middle aisle to aid in the analytical lab work. But Doc also used the oxygen when he needed to blow glass. He would make some of the glassware that he used in the lab and repair a lot of the expensive glassware that became damaged.

Over the sinks were many brushes of different sizes. The brushes were attached to long wires with a loop at the top so they could hang from pegs. An off-white soap powder that Doc made at Du-Good Chemical was used with the brushes to clean an endless number of beakers, flasks, test tubes and other glassware. Some of the glassware went in cabinets beneath the counters. Others went in large drawers, which the Diuguid brothers had built using the wood from the animal pins. They had then painted the unfinished wood with a gray linseed oil paint that Doc had made. The more expensive laboratory glassware rested on pegs above the counters rising to the high ceilings. They jutted above the laboratory equipment like the muscular smokestack industries across the countryside that powered America. When freshly cleaned the flasks and other impressive glassware sparkled. They were the poetry of the place—the sweet verse of the magnificent and impressive power of science. It is in our lives. But because it is everywhere, we just don't know it, and almost always we take science for granted.

Doc often pulled boys from the street wanting jobs and had them do the menial work along with his own four children. Doc started them off sweeping floors, and many lectures went with every push of the brooms. The jobs would advance to emptying the trash and burning it in the coal-fired furnace. Those who stayed on eventually got to wax the floors and wash the glassware. These boys had to prove they were trustworthy, capable and competent before they could handle the delicate equipment. Everything had to be done carefully; everything was expensive. Any breakage earned the culprit a lecture and cost the person whatever pay he had coming for that week and sometimes for weeks to follow. Stern lessons of thrift were doled out liberally with lectures about hard work and the need to do a good job the first time. Anything that wasn't right or spotlessly clean had to be done over. Repeatedly Doc would lecture the boys and his children, "Anything worth doing is worth doing right the first time! Otherwise why bother?" The floors—whether in the lab or the concrete in the manufacturing area—smelled of Pine-Sol. It offered a smell of clean that Doc liked. Although it took a lot of mopping and scrubbing to get the floors clean, and it never seemed to last more than a day, the Pine-Sol provided an invitingly fresh odor for anyone entering the company after the boys had spent a hard day of endless cleaning. The floors in the office and front and back labs also had to be waxed. Doc made the wax himself.

The shine would last about half of the week. Water and the daily wear of work usually did it in. Doc wanted the young people to know—particularly the black boys and his children—that they had to learn to enjoy hard work and to do it right. They did not have the luxury of making mistakes. Each mistake would be counted against them and any other African American who had the audacity to think he or she was doing enough to work in an all-white or predominantly white company. He repeatedly peppered the boys with lessons of thrift. Doc often told them: "It's not what you make that matters or even what you save. It's what you spend." A companion Doc-ism was: "It's easier to go from beer to champagne than the reverse." He wanted the boys to understand that living the high life and spending big money makes going back to living frugally and counting their pennies difficult.

Doc also wanted the boys to think as they had never done in the past. Doc often would admonish the boys and his own children when he thought they could have done better. "Boy," Doc would yell, "use your head for something besides a hat rack!" In this particular case, he was away from his company and depended on one of the kids to stay inside and answer the company telephone and the door if anyone came to purchase one of Doc's many products. Doc was emphatic with the boys on how they should answer the company phone, and he had no tolerance for deviation. It was always, "Hello, Du-Good Chemical." The boys learned telephone business etiquette at the company.

A woman came to the office door and knocked. But she didn't ring the doorbell, which was on the upper left side panel of the arched doorway to the main entrance. Because the woman didn't ring the bell, the boy inside didn't hear the knock and didn't answer the door. She put a note in the mail slot just beneath the window in the door saying she wanted to see some of Doc's hair-straightening and cleaning products. Doc was furious. That was a sale and a potential repeat customer who walked away. Doc could only hope that she might return. He told the boy a story about his childhood hoping it would help the kid realize that he had to think about everything and every possibility in order to succeed in life, and then outwit the next person to keep from being taken advantage of. Doc explained that when he was a boy, he liked to ride horses. Cars were just becoming the main form of transportation. Horses and wagons were on their way out. But a lot of people in Lynchburg, Va., still had several horses. Doc was out in a field one summer and spied a nice-looking horse and decided he would climb on the beast despite having no blanket, saddle or bridle. Once Doc had hopped on the horse's back, the horse got the idea of how he was going to get Doc off and pronto. The horse ran across a field directly at a low-hanging tree branch. He meant to teach Doc a lesson to never attempt to ride him again. Doc, who was enjoying the ride, realized what the horse was up to and slid off the horse's back just before he would have gotten clotheelined in the abdomen by the fairly substantial branch. The horse was out to teach Doc a lesson, but Doc saw what was coming and outfoxed the horse. He told the story to the boy so he would understand that he had to think ahead to keep from missing opportunities that might never return.

As soon as Doc advertised that he was open for business, he started to attract clients who shared his entrepreneurial spirit. They wanted to go into business, too, and they came in all colors. Doc's lab work helped others with their product concerns, improving and altering their products, and enabling companies to keep up with their competition. Doc also developed products, which he started to produce under the Du-Good Chemical Laboratories & Manufacturers label. In the arched, first-floor display window of Du-Good Chemical, Doc decoratively placed several of his products on top of silver-colored paper. He also added large lettering, photos and posters that advertised what his products could do to improve the lives of passers-by. In the winter, the display window, which once had been the horse-and buggy entrance to the large-animal hospital, would be adorned with holiday decorations. A "Seasons Greetings" banner was always draped against the glass for all of the traffic on Jefferson Avenue to see. It wasn't easy, however, to keep that big display window glass intact. Vandals would break it or someone would shoot bullet or BB holes in the plate glass. After it had been knocked out twice in one year, Doc replaced it with Plexiglas, which protected it from vandals, however, over the years, the plastic became so cloudy that it was impossible to see what products were inside. Also over the arched display window was the brick-framed rectangular company sign professionally printed on a thick glass background. Vandals in the 1960s broke that out. Doc rebuilt it using concrete as a base. He painted it with a yellow background and then black lettering. It lasted unmolested for decades, a testament to Doc's tenacity and a lesson for the boys who watched it happen.

Business picked up in the 1960s with a growing number of orders for Du-Good Chemical products. Doc was excited. But the growth brought new problems such as having the ability to meet the demand without the accompanying expense and swelled inventory. Doc secured a 150-gallon tank, which had the added capacity of heating its contents. He got motors with paddles for stirring. Doc picked up a large, old black compressor like the ones at gasoline stations, which enable people to pump gas in their cars. Doc used the air pressure to empty the 55-gallon drums into the large tank. A mixer affixed to the bottom of the tank turned while another whirred atop the tank. Doc would stand on the long manufacturing table and pour in ingredients. It was here and in a smaller tank by the furnace room door that Doc made his waterless, industrial-strength hand cleaner—the first in the nation that wasn't ammonia-based. It had a paste-like consistency that would liquefy when it picked up the heat of the user's hands. A pink color thanks to a red dye kept it from looking like lard. It attacked tar, paint, mechanic's grease, oil-based products and even printer's ink. People who used it could either wash the hand cleaner and the dirt away with water or towel their hands clean. Doc developed that product in the early 1950s, and it sold like hotcakes. Doc pulled eager boys from the street to work with his children. They manufactured, bottled, labeled, boxed, stored, inventoried and shipped the products. It was the only one of its kind on the market until corporate espionage enabled a couple of other companies to copy what Doc had produced. Because those companies had more marketing dollars, their sales quickly eclipsed Doc's. But Doc stayed in business selling Du-Good Hand Cleaner with the design of a chubby little man in a clean white painter's overalls and cap on the label primarily to black businesses, auto mechanics and distributors.

When Du-Good Chemical's production equipment was all turned on, the high ceiled large manufacturing room seemed to be filled with a whizbang kind of magic. Doc would be hanging on to the side of the 150-gallon tank filled with the pink-colored Hand Cleaner. Doc's children and boys from the street would have the gallon bottles all labeled and placed on the 4-foot wide, 40-foot long production tables. As soon as those 50 gallons were filled, the boys and Doc's kids would box them while Doc barked orders. They'd take the new product to the warehouse area along the western wall of the horseshoe-shaped building. Usually a Cardinals baseball game played during the summer on KMOX-AM radio over the din of noise that the machinery made. Cardinals football took over in the fall and winter and basketball with the St. Louis Hawks followed in the late winter and spring. The season of sports would repeat all over again, but the production stayed the same, with Doc in the center mixing the ingredients, hiring the boys from the street, giving them and his own kids manufacturing and life lessons. When things quieted down, lunch intervened with a sandwich and Coke or two.

The sounds of production were their own symphony. The large compressor chugged in the background vibrating the air like the big drums of a marching band in an industrial age parade. The two motors stirring the Hand Cleaner in the 150-gallon tank chugged, creating their own syncopated sound. They played off of each other like jump ropes in a fire-hot, double-dutch contest. When the stirring motors were turned off, a pump that looked like it was from a gas station was hoisted to the top of the tank by Doc, his kids and some of the boys. Two pipes connected it in place to a couple of two-by-four boards that were nailed to supporting posts that stood astride the 150-gallon, aluminum-painted tank, which had a dark-blue porcelain interior. That pump was connected to the big compressor. Then the rhythm in the big room really jumped with the top part of the pump hammering up and down. It drew the Hand Cleaner out of the tank, sent it through the black rubber hose and brass nozzle attached to the pump and into the gallon jugs. The upbeat sounded like hammering on a hollow piece of wood. The downbeat thumped like a muffled drum. That tempo would repeat itself several times a minute over a couple of hours until the tank of Hand Cleaner was empty and the product was all boxed and stacked neatly for the next shipment. One boy from the street, Jesse Talley, even remarked to Doc: "Hey, Mr. Diuguid, that sounds like music. Here's a new dance I just invented."

Doc replied: "Jesse, that ain't new. Black people been dancing like that for years. Now get back to work."

As usual, Doc was right. Having the benefit of living through the most exciting times of the century with progress for black people had exposed Doc to nearly everything possible under the sun.

In the summer Du-Good Chemical picked up the heat of the outdoors. The brick walls held the temperature like merciless ovens. Opening the 2-foot-square windows in the bathroom and over the trough helped a little. A fan in an additional square window in the manufacturing area blew the hot air from inside the building, but it never seemed to be enough to vent that big room especially when the lights were on and all of the equipment was running. Even the dogs at the company panted breathlessly as they lay on the cooler concrete floor. It was hot down there, too. Doc would shed his shirt and tie and strip down to a skinny T-shirt that revealed the rippling muscles in his arms. That impressed the boys, who often took off their shirts entirely and perspired profusely throughout the manufacturing work. Sometimes the boys would open the sliding door to the alley to pick up more cross-ventilation. It never seemed to cool the place. Storms offered some relief—but never enough.

Winter was worse. Ventilation pipes from the massive, octopus-like furnace in the back room fanned out through the big manufacturing room. The pipes were a foot in diameter. Each was wrapped with reams of asbestos paper—a no-no by today's anti-carcinogen standards. The asbestos helped reduce the energy loss as the heated air coursed its way to the main lab, the office, the kitchen, bathroom or the other front room, which was rarely occupied after a beautician, to whom Doc once rented the space to, had vacated the place. A pipe from the furnace also pumped heated air into the big room. It was an unadorned venting—just an open pipe a foot in diameter. Sometimes the boys at the plant would stand under it just to pick up a little heat. When it was 20 degrees Fahrenheit outside, it was about 45 degrees inside. Keep moving; stay busy was the rule to stay warm, Doc said. He would have one of his children make a pot of lima beans for the workers. The beans were a Depression-era food. It was cheap to prepare, and the boys could have as much as they wanted. When done right, the 3-gallon pot went quickly. When done poorly—either burned from inattention or made with too much salt—those beans would last for a week. People often joked about those lunches and the gas that followed. But the hot bowls of bean soup kept the workers warm. Stop working and they knew they'd get cold. The plant and Doc's philosophy had an old-world, other-century cast to it. But the motivation was clear. People stayed on their toes. They were actively working, and that kept them warm and out of mischief. The upstairs laboratory, however, was always a lot warmer. It was at least 60 degrees when none of the equipment was running and even comfortably warm with many Bunsen burners or hot plates going when Doc was busy doing lab work. When idle time did strike—usually late into the night—some of the boys would creep upstairs with Doc's children to get warm.

None of the youths got special privileges. Doc's children worked side-by-side with him and got just as dirty and blistered as the boys who came to earn a little change. Doc's kids also got paid a lot less for the hard work that they had to do. Doc would admonish all of them when they came to the main lab upstairs. He would give them more chores to complete, sending them back into the big room or the warehouse where it was even colder. The boys caught on quickly when the primary tasks were finished—don't go upstairs. Doc would become so engrossed in his work that he wouldn't think of the gold-bricking, as he called it, that the boys and his own children might be engaged in unsupervised downstairs. They often would open the main door to the old furnace and let the heat out in the closed furnace room. Despite the high ceilings with exposed rafters, drafty windows and doors and brick walls, the furnace room area would heat up nicely. A light bulb hanging from a solitary wire illuminated the big room. Flames from inside the furnace danced in the fire chamber. The fire heated the faces and bodies of the boys. The light the fire created reflected differently in their skin, shining like a mirror in those who were darker and in reflective tones in the boys who were of lighter complexions. They sat around and talked of the work; talked of what they would do when Doc paid them; and talked of coming back the following week for more. No one ever said they loved the work or loved Du-Good Chemical. They worked harder there than they had in their lives, and they cursed about it around the open fire of the furnace. Yet they learned a lot. They valued the boundaries Doc set for them. They valued the lessons they picked up and valued that someone in that hard-knocks community truly cared about them and made them think.

The boys, who came back to work day after day at Du-Good Chemical, picked up so many lessons. They learned about manufacturing. They saw what a chemist was and the work that he did. But they also picked up character lessons such as an unbeatable work ethic, perseverance, duty, responsibility, discipline, diligence and trustworthiness they learned about getting a job done even when it seemed impossible. Doc knew he had no contract with the kids. He knew they might never return. But he always hoped they would. And they each expected Doc to raise the middle window of the lab—the one without the screen—and either say, "I'll be right down." Or they expected him to toss them his heavy set of many keys so they could pick out the one to Du-Good Chemical and then unlock the door, letting themselves in. That was trust. But Doc also taught the boys that if they were going to be late or if they didn't think they would make it the next day, that he expected them to call him ahead of time so that he would know and could plan on getting workers from elsewhere. Those are lessons that few parents and schools teach. But they are essential to individuals' succeeding in life. Doc's lessons were vital to building the character of the boys who knocked on the door of Du-Good Chemical.

The boys learned to think their way through problems. They learned to use math to determine the number of jugs to put on the table to prepare for the production process when the bottles came in 8, 16 or 32 ounces and the size of the mixing container was 55 gallons. The boys also had to estimate the number of feet of a plumber's snake they needed to put in a drain to unstop a plugged up sink. They needed to figure out the cost of materials if Doc sent them to a store to make a purchase. He expected his exact change. Nothing less would do. They also would have to do the math when lab work was involved in calculating nitrogen and hydrogen atoms in a compound. Those measures were set aside for only the elite of the boys who entered Du-Good

Chemical. In the process, the boys also learned what real men were. Hard work made men—nothing less was acceptable.

Many of the boys would land at the door of Du-Good Chemical after school. During the summer months they would come from youth programs that were offered in the surrounding neighborhoods. There were basketball camps and arts and crafts programs. Some community and church-based efforts even took the youths on field trips and overnight camping outings. They were designed to give the kids something constructive to do and to keep them off the street. They served a purpose during the morning and afternoon hours. But the evenings generally landed the kids back on the street with little to do except hang out. The black businesses took over then. Kids would wander into those establishments—again, looking for a way to make some money. They also had a curiosity about those black men whom they watched go to work every day. They wondered what those men did and how they did it. They wondered what made those guys tick and what set them apart from everyone else. Why weren't these guys hanging out on the street corners with other black men they encountered? Why weren't they drinking out on the street? Why weren't they chasing women? Why weren't they shooting dice against the curb having just gotten paid? Why weren't they home with their spouses and kids spending endless hours in front of the television? The boys had so many questions, and the only way to learn was to rub shoulders with the black men. It was how the boys learned to be men.

Boys who had a knack for working on cars would frequent Earl McDaniel's garage. They would camp with him in that dank, dark and greasy hole that opened onto the alley, which seemed like an eastbound extension of Rutger Street. The kids would ask Earl a lot of questions. He would have them fetch wrenches and other tools as he'd work on cars from throughout the South Side community. Many of the vehicles were old and barely ran. But Earl found a way to keep them going. He had no formal automotive school training. He just had a gift for tinkering. Earl kept dogs at his place, too. They guarded the cars or trucks that he kept overnight for work or that he had to keep because someone didn't have the money right then to pay him for his work. Earl had learned the hard way not to let the repaired car go until he had all of his cash up front. To do otherwise was asking for trouble. The whole community was on a cash-and-carry basis. The black men also imparted that lesson on the kids. Earl taught the boys how to change tires, replace batteries, do the timing on engines and even pull the engines and transmissions apart for repairs. Such tutelage was important for kids who wanted to someday open their own garages. But the kids nicknamed McDaniel, "Greasy Earl." He was a dark-complexioned black man. He always seemed to wear the same greasy overalls. He sometimes would visit Doc at Du-Good Chemical the same as Doc would go over there to share a Coke or beer. When Earl would rise up from the blue vinyl chair in the lab he'd leave behind a noticeable grease stain on both the seat and the back of the chair. It was an occupational thing, but it made the boys at the lab laugh because there always was the need to clean up the oil spill after Earl's departure and follow his footprints out the door, too. Cleanliness was not one of Earl's strong suits. Kids who frequented his shop left plenty dirty. But they learned, they always learned that life was neither about cleanliness nor about money or material things. They learned from the black business and civically engaged people on Jefferson Avenue that life was all about relationships. The relationships were the ones the kids returned to and nurtured as the black men took the time to nurture them. The give-and-take enabled the kids to harvest the riches. But life also is about letting go of trying to be cool to fit in with the fast crowd and easy money of the street. The kids learned the language of money only too well. It was piped out of the television and radio constantly, urging all who watched and listened to buy whatever the commercials offered. That same sentiment was reinforced by the kids' peers. Certainly the hard steady work of a job and saving pennies didn't cut the mustard against what looked fast, free and easy. But chasing that phantom world always leads to dead ends—often literally.

The collection of buildings housing black businesses look to outsiders as if the structures are on their last legs. Run your fingers along the brick and in the small spaces where there was mortar and an abrasion will likely occur. The wood holding the windows and the decorative trim showed the half- or full-moon marks of hammers that had pounded in nails securing the boards into place. They were held together by the will of the owners and the black men's desire to build the companies into mega-million-dollar dreams. Each place was infinitely more than the sum of the old building materials yielding the marginal—at best—appearance. They embodied the personalities and the hopes of the proprietors. They held the past, present and future dreams. They were as real as Moses' staff, as sweet as the wine Jesus made from water and as filling as the fish that He used to feed the multitude. The dreams like these in the 1200 block of South Jefferson Avenue were what a people prayed for, and after getting them, they prayed for more, and they needed to keep praying. These dreams were not only of the men who ran the places. They were the dreams of their parents, their parents' parents and back to the millions of

African slaves in the Americas. The men wanted those businesses to provide for their children and their children's children a future unlike black folks had ever thought possible. Each embodied a legacy more than words could convey. But the volumes of tales behind the companies came out in the lessons the men provided for the kids on the street.

Sam Fowler ran Wide-A-Wake Cleaners, which did dry cleaning as well as tailoring of men's and women's clothing. His shop at 1225 S. Jefferson Ave. was on the northwest corner of South Jefferson Avenue and Rutger Street. Sam attracted a different set of kids. They were the ones who had an interest in fashion and design. They would enter his corner shop with the big display windows and ask for a job. Sam would put them to work sweeping the floor initially. Some would have to sweep the sidewalk out front and pull the grass from the cracks in the concrete. Doc would explain to boys that the roots from the grass and weeds in the cracks would exert thousands of pounds of pressure on the concrete and eventually would result in cracks that would destroy the sidewalk. The boys who worked for Sam knew he would put them to work arranging the thread, which he or his wife sometimes would get out of order in their haste to finish a job. Sam had a son, too. But the boy seemed contrary about the work his dad did for a living. He always was displeased about having to work with his father. The streets had a great attraction to him. One day the boy was out with some of his unsavory friends. They had stolen into the always busy rail yard about a half-mile from Sam's shop. The boys thought it would be fun to hop the trains and ride them down the track. But something went horribly wrong for Sam's son. He slipped trying to get into a boxcar. The wheels of the train stop for nothing. They rolled over the soft tissue of his arm crushing the flesh. The boy was rushed to the hospital. Doctors were able to save the arm, but the muscle and tissue had to nearly all be removed. The boy was never the same afterward and not much use as a worker, either.

Sam was devastated by the accident. But he continued to run his shop. It was all he had. Doc would take his suits to Sam in the morning for them to be dry cleaned. When Doc bought new suits, he always took them to Sam to have them altered. Sam knew Doc's measurements and always got the clothes to fit just right. Sam mostly worked in the window of his shop, using the available light to save on electricity. Besides, it was good advertising. Like the other men on South Jefferson Avenue, Sam was thrifty. These guys were all young men during the Great Depression. They grew up without electricity, television sets and even radios. Those were all luxury items that came into their lives later. They treasured them, but they were not dependent on them. Each man tried to instill the same work ethic in the boys who came into their shops.

On the southwest corner of Hickory Street and South Jefferson Avenue at 1205 S. Jefferson Ave. was Jeff Johnson's Gold Star Market grocery store. It carried basic staples—meat, bread, canned goods, milk, baking supplies, frozen goods and some fruits, vegetables, beer, wine and snacks. Jeff had bought the place from a guy who was an immigrant and had run the store for decades on the corner. It had an established clientele, and Jeff planned to keep those folks coming to the store under his new ownership and management. The streetlight on the curb illuminated the place at night for passers-by. The sidewalk on Jefferson Avenue seemed to make a quick left turn at Hickory Street and go right into Jeff's store. Folks always seemed happy to be there. A bank of old cash registers at the checkout counters were the first things people saw in the place. Windows at the top along the east wall provided the most illumination for the inside. Old light fixtures with bulbs in them hung from the ceilings. Four aisles in the store fingered their way toward the back. At the end were the refrigerated sections with perishables and frozen goods. The selection wasn't as good as in the bigger supermarkets, but everyone going to Jeff's found what they needed or something that would do.

Jeff loved greeting people. Many parents would send their kids to Jeff's store for goods they needed to complete a meal. Onions were a favorite. Green peppers, too. Next to that were butter and milk. Wonder Bread was a big item. One could always trust that it would not go bad. Folks always seemed a little dubious of the prices and the quality. People in the South Side neighborhood lived on tight budgets and couldn't afford extravagances. Paying more for the same goods they could get elsewhere was out of the question. That was partly why the European immigrant who had the store before Jeff sold and moved. He could see the change coming, and got out while he thought it was still prudent. Jeff—like the other black businessmen in the 1200 block of South Jefferson Avenue—was hoping for his piece of the American dream. He wanted to be his own boss and have people enjoy what he provided and give him the respect for his services that he richly deserved. Timing was everything. But unfortunately it didn't always work in the black businessman's favor. Segregation had held black people captive so they were forced to shop at certain stores that accommodated them and accepted their businesses. But money is green. That was the only color that those businesses—black and white—cared about. Others wanted white patrons and money coming from white hands. It was as if it were cleaner and better that way. Racism is stupid. But it worked in black businesses' favor initially, maintaining a stable clientele for them.

When integration occurred, the chain on the gate that held blacks in the segregated community came off. Black customers flooded into white stores and shops. Doc's father used to tell the story about a black ice man in Lynchburg, Va., having customers who were black, and he depended on their business. One day, a competing white ice man decided to muscle into the black man's territory and persuade the black man's customers that they need to get their ice from him. The black ice man went to his customers and pleaded for them to come back, saying they had been with him for years and shouldn't change. One black woman responding to his plea said, "Don't you know, the white man's ice is colder!" It was the most ridiculous thing anyone could have said because the science of ice is that it is the same temperature regardless of who sells it. The racially tinged conditioning people have gone through in this country has them believing without any doubt that products from black businesses are inherently inferior to the exact same products sold by white merchants.

In sharing that story, Doc also added other history lessons for the boys. Doc was constantly amazed by how little history the kids knew and how unaware they were of their surroundings and the economics of daily production. He would ask the boys where bread, eggs and milk came from. They would always respond: "From the store, Doc. Everyone knows that." Doc in his usual forceful manner would say, "Wrong!" He would explain that such products were raised on farms, and that the agrarian economy kept the urban economy afloat with products that city dwellers took for granted. Doc also would tell the boys that huge blocks of ice used to be cut from the rivers, lakes and ponds in the winter and stored in limestone caves underground in the spring, summer and fall for use in what were called iceboxes, which had been major convenience items in people's homes until refrigerators were invented and widely used in the 20th century. Every home had iceboxes and bought ice from the iceman to keep their food cold and from spoiling in the warmer months. The rivers then were less polluted by industrial and household waste so the freezing point was not as low as it is today. The ice, once cut in huge blocks, would be taken by wagon to the caves and stored. Doc explained that straw was used as insulating material and layers of straw separated the blocks of ice, slowing the melting process and keeping the caves even cooler than the constant underground temperature in the 50s.

The ice once removed was cut into blocks to fit people's iceboxes and was delivered by horse-drawn wagons to homes and businesses. Nothing about people's impression of the ice, who delivered it or anything else was equal in the minds of the consuming public.

Jeff fought that racial conundrum at the location on South Jefferson Avenue and later when he moved to 1301 Rutger St., calling his store Country Style Market. But at Ohio and Rutger Street in the bigger location, Jeff also did what the white merchants wouldn't do. He let black kids wanting to make some money come into his store to sweep the floor, stock the shelves, bag groceries and do inventory. They also had to dust the products in the place constantly. Old stores attracted dust. People entering and leaving didn't help. What Jeff had that the other black businesses didn't have was a lot of temptation. All of the candy, potato chips and other knick-knacks would make the kids' mouths water. Sometimes resisting was impossible. Jeff was a good man, a kind man. But he insisted on kids working as hard as he did and as he insisted from his other employees who lived in the community. They benefited together or they suffered together. Theft was inexcusable. That was one of the many other lessons that the men in the 1200 block of South Jefferson Avenue taught the kids. The young people learned that they were not just hurting the proprietors of the businesses, but they also were hurting their individual reputations and their families'. Once they were caught stealing, the boys were told to never return to the store. They had broken a bond of trust, and that was a powerful thing. Trust and faith were hard-won virtues in the community of need. People were terribly used to taking advantage of any opening. Heck, they had seen the same thing inflicted on them at the companies where they worked and by the white people who abused and exploited them. Doing the same thing to others seemed as natural as breathing. Everyone did it, which was why Jeff and the other black men in the 1200 block of South Jefferson Avenue took it upon themselves to teach the black kids that honesty provided them with a better way of living. Kids who got caught weren't hurt by Jeff or anyone else at the store. They were made to understand in the harshest of words that they had done wrong and told never to return to the place. The store was small enough and the number of workers was few enough that once one person was banned, everyone knew it, and no one went back on the edict.

Across the street from Du-Good Chemical was the Second Corinthian Baptist Church, a storefront chapel that the Rev. C.L. Nance pastored at 2352 Hickory St. The reverend had a thunderously deep voice. He always wore a dark suit complete with a vest that seemed incredibly out of date—or maybe it was so stylish that it just looked odd compared with what others wore. The suit matched his dark-brown skin. His hair was dark and well-oiled. The Rev. Nance's hair was thin and nearly all gone from the top of his head. Suspenders hiked his pants above the waistline. The reverend always had on a white shirt and a dark tie. Often Rev. Nance would stand outside of his church and smoke a big brown cigar. It was his trademark. That man had an incredible voice. He could speak a person's name from his side of the street and made his voice thunder over the roar of even rush-hour traffic. No one talked as loudly as Rev. Nance in the entire neighborhood, and no one wanted to provoke his wrath for any reason. He had the gift of being able to make kids who misbehaved feel that they had sinned against God as well as against their parents and people in the community. Kids went cautiously into his house of worship, seeking extra change. They knew there would be a sermon with attached Bible verses, and if they were really misbehaving, they would provoke Rev. Nance to sweat and whoop. But mostly the kids went to the Baptist church because they were curious. They wanted to know more about Rev. Nance and have him explain the intricacies of faith and even life to them. Rev. Nance tried while getting the kids to stoke the furnace, scrub the floors, polish the pews and keep the light bulbs changed. Church had to be immaculate. Nothing less would do.

What the kids didn't pick up about honesty, faith, trust, honor and hard work at the other black businesses in the 1200 block of Jefferson Avenue, they certainly got it in mega-Jesus-doses at the Rev. Nance's church. They were Boy Scouts ready for heaven when he got done with them.

On hot St. Louis summer days whether saints or sinners, entire families would often step outside hoping for a cool breeze from the still moist air. The brick homes felt like ovens in the summer. The heat and humidity were unbearable. People became accustomed to sitting outside into the late evening hours watching the kids play on the sidewalk and in the street. They would talk about the goings-on that day. They'd talk about their families and what they had read in the St. Louis Post-Dispatch. It was one of the two mainstream newspapers. The other was the St. Louis Globe-Democrat. *The Post* was progressive. *The Globe* was a conservative rag. The Globe wrote several scathing articles about Doc's brother, William Sherwood Diuguid, and played them on the front page. Diuguid was the first black magistrate elected in the city, and that rankled the established order in town. They couldn't for the life of them understand how a black man got elected in the city and were set on seeing to it that he was discredited. They tried, but they never succeeded in bringing down Doc's brother.

There were also four black newspapers—The St. Louis Argus, The St. Louis American, The St. Louis Sentinel and the St. Louis Evening Whirl. The Whirl was a scandal sheet. The others were legitimate. People would pass by Doc and Nancy's house where their then-three children were playing out front and comment that they had seen the ad in one of the black papers that Doc's business had placed. Advertising was Doc's way of getting customers to buy his products. He manufactured mostly cleaners, cosmetics and hair-care products. They were sold mostly to black full-service gasoline stations and to black drugstores. Not to advertise in one of the black newspapers was suicide for any black business, and everyone knew it.

The black businessmen in the 1200 block of South Jefferson Avenue believed in capitalism. They banked on it in their businesses. They also believed in the community. It is why they took kids in from the street. Those young boys had been taught well to know the value of money and how they could never get enough. The kids were hustlers, which is something the men in the 1200 block of South Jefferson Avenue admired. They could look into the faces of the boys and see the same yearning and hunger for more that still radiated in them. The men also knew they had to take the desire the boys had for money and dampen it with a stronger passion for the boys to pick up the men's virtues to do good deeds for the community. They had to instill in the boys a need to care about the black community, its people and for each other. Relationships matter more than money. Relationships and connections to others will endure after the cash has vanished, after the adults have grown old and passed away and after the boys have become old men themselves. It's on the black men's shoulders then to teach each new generation the value of the things they were taught. Money is OK, but it is never enough, and everyone—no matter how rich—is always seeking more.

◆ ◆ ◆ ◆ ◆

A gunshot victim was added to one of the open rooms in the ICU at Barnes-Jewish Hospital. He was out of surgery and stable. Like Doc, he was there to recover before going to a regular hospital room. He had many more monitors on him than Doc did and even a breathing tube. Doc remained mostly still under the sheet and in his hospital gown. A nurse came in and pointed out to his adult children where she had put his dentures. He would need them to eat when he recovered. Doc's kids laughed, knowing that when Doc awakened his appetite would return in full force having been knocked down as Doc was at Du-Good Chemical. Seeing the dentures on the tray by the fluorescent-lit sink was another marker of hope that things would get better, would return to normal—whatever normal would be like when and if Doc came to and whether he could return to his company as the last holdout from an era that once flourished in the 1200 block of South Jefferson Avenue.

CHAPTER 5

THE SCIENCE OF SHARING THE DREAM

Doc strongly encouraged the boys who entered the doors of Du-Good Chemical to regularly visit the Barr branch of the St. Louis Public Library. Doc often said to the boys: "You can't take a jackass and make a racehorse out of him. But maybe you can help the jackass realize he actually is a race horse." The library was about a mile from Doc's front door. The walk there was not easy. It was up hill all the way. Temptations lay along the way especially after crossing Park Avenue. For those over 21, the taverns always beckoned. For the boys, there were many stores such as the Forum Five & 10 Variety Store, 1621 S. Jefferson Ave.; the F.W. Woolworth Department Store, 1627 S. Jefferson Ave.; and Zoller Bakery, 1613 S. Jefferson Ave. Any one of them could divert the boys. Sometimes they returned to Du-Good Chemical to proudly exhibit what they had. They called them "goodies." Doc called their acquisitions "useless crap."

A Kroger grocery store that opened on Lafayette and Jefferson across from the Barr Branch Library was a favorite place for the boys to hit. Yes, these kids did steal—quite bodaciously, too. The boys also stopped at the bakery to load up their bellies with doughnuts, jelly rolls, cheesecakes and gingerbread. Doc thought that was a mostly useless pursuit, to "fill your belly with junk instead of your mind with good knowledge." Doc also would have the boys urinate on a piece of litmus paper to show how the sugar content in their blood had become elevated because of what the boys had eaten. Doc would caution them that diabetes was in their future unless they changed their eating habits. The boys would always argue, but Doc was merciless in pointing out the flaws in the boys' logic. They came from communities of poverty and great need. Doc wanted them to start to think differently in order to rise above even their worst moments and circumstances. They all yearned for something different and better. That desire coupled with curiosity was what drove many boys to Doc's door in the first place. Telling the kids what they were seeking was too easy. Doc wanted the boys he let into Du-Good Chemical to deduce things for themselves.

At one time, Doc explained that big-band leader Duke Ellington could play every instrument in his orchestra and he could play it just as well as any of the members of his band. However, Duke Ellington knew that to have a first-class orchestra, he had to develop and manage the talent in each musician so that he could get the best from them and his band would sound outstanding. It wasn't about micromanaging but creatively getting the diversity of skills from each band member in a way that showed their true exceptional talent.

Doc had some of the boys help him make up a drum of Du-Good Dry Shampoo. It was a product beauticians used to clean women's hair without using water. He poured the ingredients into a tall flask first and then emptied the flask into a 55-gallon drum containing the base oil for the Dry Shampoo. Using a large pipe wrench, Doc screwed a long metal pipe into the larger opening of the drum that reached to near the bottom of the 4- to 5-foot-tall container. The insertion always displaced the fluid in the drum causing it to rise higher in the welded cylindrical container. Doc always asked the boys about that displacement of the liquid. He'd let them guess, and eventually Doc would tell them how Archimedes, when he understood the science of water displacement, went running through the streets of ancient Greece buck naked. Archimedes had just risen from a bathtub, yelling "Eureka! Eureka!" as he proclaimed what he had discovered—matter added to a liquid in a closed environment always displaces the fluid by the volume of the added matter. Doc wanted the boys to know the science, physics and engineering behind the work he was doing as well as each lesson's earliest origins. Doc screwed a short air-flow metal tube into the smaller hole of the drum. It did not go into the liquid in the drum. A hose from a smaller compressor was then attached to the larger pipe. Doc switched on the compressor, which forced air through the fluid. The small compressor sounded like a machine gun. The air bubbles the machinery forced into the liquid violently churned the ingredients through the oil creating a uniform mixture. Doc encouraged the boys to put their ears to the drum to listen. None of the kids could resist.

The boys received heavy doses of hard, relentless discipline and lessons on honesty and integrity from Doc in every work assignment and in every lesson meted out. They had to stay on the task to which they were assigned until the job was completed and then it had to be done correctly. Boys who responded, "Yeah," to Doc's questions were admonished by him to say "Yes sir" with enthusiasm. Eye contact was mandatory. Doc knew these were the "softer assets" by which white society heavily judged black Americans. Without the right responses or the right intonation in their voices, the boys' futures were sunk. Doc knew that unless he helped them to understand the vital lessons he provided, the boys would walk the streets of America hapless and hopeless like many of the younger and older men whom people often ridiculed. It wasn't as if the men on the streets had not tried to better themselves. Many just didn't have influential people in their lives to help build them into productive men. As a treat on the Fourth of July, Doc would take some of the boys with his own children to the fireworks display on the Mississippi riverfront. As the charges would go up from barges and explode over the water, Doc would explain how the fireworks originated from China and then tell the boys about the chemistry that went into getting the various colors. "Copper oxide produces the pretty blue that you like to see. The red comes from an iron oxide compound," Doc would say.

It seemed that in addition to helping the boys, the black men in the 1200 block of South Jefferson Avenue were constantly battling the city, its inspectors and its code enforcers. Doc owned two apartment buildings. Alongside one of the buildings, which sat on a corner of McPherson Avenue and Whittier Street, some large trees had raised the concrete sidewalks leaving the path grossly uneven. City inspectors who were poking around noticed it and slapped Doc with a notice to have the sidewalk torn up and replaced with new concrete. Doc was outraged. In all likelihood, it had something to do with being told what to do with his property by the government, but he also bristled at the white-dominated-and-controlled power structure of the city mandating unreasonable requirements of hard-working, though struggling, black businessmen. Doc knew that a $500 bill, which was a lot of money back then, for concrete work could put him underwater for the quarter in his efforts to either break even or make a profit with Du-Good Chemical and his rental units. For Doc, such situations always brought to mind an old saying that he shared with the boys: "A fool and his money soon part company." Instead of paying one of the city's "recommended contractors" Doc decided to raise the one-ton, 4-foot-square concrete slab, cut out the offending tree roots that were causing the problem and then lower the sidewalk back into place. However, Doc didn't have a backhoe or forklift. He only had four, 2-inch-in-diameter iron pipes he had picked up somewhere (because he thought they might someday come in handy) and some oak planks. What Doc thought to do was to use the boards as levers to raise the sidewalk up in the air enough to put the metal pipes under first one end and then the other. Doc and the boys he hired then would push the heavy concrete slab forward moving it with the boards out of the place where it was seated and onto the adjacent concrete slab. It would only work if the boys would move the heavy pipes to the front as the slab rolled forward, freeing the pipes in the back. Doc then planned to cut out the roots of the tree and roll the slab back into place. Doc explained to the boys that Hannibal, one of the greatest black generals of all times, accomplished similar feats when he took elephants over mountains in Italy to sneak up on the Romans and attack them from a direction they least expected. That venture required that Hannibal's troops lift the elephants and other tonnage in Hannibal's war machine over previously unimaginable great heights. Doc also explained that the Egyptians used similar methods, employing simple tools to build the great pyramids. The stones weighing megatons were hoisted into place using sheer ingenuity, which Doc had in great quantities. One of Doc's favorite stories whenever he had to use boards as a lever was to explain what the great mathematician Archimedes said about levers to show their incredible ability. Doc would say to every boy who entered Du-Good Chemical: "Give me a long enough board and a place to stand, and I will move the world!"

Doc's free method of fixing two panels in the sidewalk bordering the corner apartment building he owned worked like a charm. The city inspectors OK'd the work. It brought to mind what an old family friend in Lynchburg, Va., used to repeatedly say: "There is a right way to do something. A wrong way to tackle a problem, and then there's the Diuguid way." Success over costly and impossible odds usually inspired Doc to tell the boys at his company, "I'll keep my money in my own damn pocket!" Seeing such independent-minded behavior helped the boys know they were not helpless either. They learned from Doc's ingenuity that there were always other ways around problems—especially those that seemed impossible, insurmountable and expensive.

At the same two-story apartment building were two trees in the backyard that threatened to uproot the wooden fence that surrounded the property. Doc called them paradise trees. They were hollow on the inside and grew faster than weeds. They were tall and had deceptively large trunks. Doc knew those trees were trouble. Each sat near the brick, two-car garage, which Doc used for storage. But he didn't like the leaves that constantly fell on the garage because the decaying matter would cause the roof to go bad more quickly. Doc was also concerned about the trees because they were a danger in high winds. Any storm could send them toppling onto the garage, cause damage to the fence or fall into the street on someone's car. That was a liability that Doc could do without. So one Saturday morning, Doc, his children and John McSwine, one of the other boys who was working for him at the time, went to the apartment building in Doc's red 1952 Dodge panel truck. Doc had a hand saw, an electric saw, his ax, a lot of brown, hemp rope, his double ladders hanging out the back of the truck and a long extension chord. Doc showed his kids and John how to bring down those two big trees. Doc put the ladder as high as it would go in the first tree and then climbed to the top with the power saw and began cutting away the top branches. It was the job of Doc's kids and John to cut up what Doc let fall and then load the cut wood into the truck. Bit by bit, Doc reduced the first tree and then the second to just the trunk. What they couldn't cut with the power circular saw, Doc then used the hand saw and ax to finish. To prevent cut branches from falling and damaging the fence, Doc tied a rope onto the limbs and then had John and the kids pull on the rope so that the branch would fall away from the fence. That kept the fence from being damaged. Doc explained that they would do the same thing with the trunk of the tree. Everyone would pull on the ropes as Doc cut into the trunk so that the tree would not fall into the fence. Both thick trees were brought down methodically, and then cut up and loaded into the truck. The kids even saw for themselves that the paradise tree was hollow through and through, as Doc previously explained. John and the other kids learned invaluable lessons that day—lessons that would help them years into the future.

Doc wanted the boys at his company to take some time and think things through. Solutions often presented themselves. Doing nothing was never a good option. But it seemed that was what the city often wanted blacks to do—just surrender. Doc never pushed the boys to do what was humanly impossible. He had a saying for that, too: "If a bullfrog had wings, maybe it wouldn't bump its ass so much." That always made Doc laugh with all of the boys except those who were the object of his lessons at the company.

When property owners took no corrective action after a city-issued order for work to be done, then city inspectors would follow up and impose great penalties on black business owners. Often it would be a death knell for those companies. In these communities, there was very little margin for slip-ups and unexpected expenses. When city orders went unheeded, then the city imposed liens on homes or businesses. It often meant that the occupants would be forced to move, and the city would claim the property. But then the city would let the building fall into disrepair. Vandalism would follow with the plumbing being stolen, water damage occurring, the basement being flooded and finally the house or business being torn down. The pattern was repeated all over the black community with billions of dollars in worthwhile property and revenue being lost.

Racism and discrimination worked like a fungus consuming black neighborhoods throughout St. Louis and many cities throughout the United States. It was amazing to see conditions elsewhere in black neighborhoods that were replicated despite the hundreds of miles that separated major metropolitan areas. Those communities also had black businesses, churches and community outlets that worked quietly, diligently, persistently, consistently and tirelessly to counter the human effects of oppressive conditions. People's unfortunate tendency is to turn on each other instead of to each other in times of great strife. Bigotry in America is like a heat wave with accompanying high humidity that won't relent. There is a stillness in the air and a stifling feeling of being unable to breathe. It causes black people who are choking for oxygen to also wrap their hands around their own and others' necks. But the surviving black businessmen and other enduring anchors in the community counter that self-destructive, self-defeating behavior by introducing children who dare to enter their stores to "the softer assets." Harder assets were the telephone, mimeograph machines, cars and trucks. They were among the tools of many businesses. The softer assets are such things as a warm, friendly smile; a firm handshake; eye contact that is open and kind and not like the piercing stares of boiling angry people, spoiling for a fight. Softer assets also are proper attire, a clear voice and good diction. Doc regularly told the boys: "Use your tongue, your teeth, your mouth and your lips to properly enunciate each word so people can understand you."

These essentials were also character traits that the boys entering Du-Good Chemical picked up. They were the things that black businesspeople learned if they wanted to be successful—particularly when doing business with white America. The businessmen passed on the virtues to the children. It was a positive way of communicating without a word ever being spoken. Without these things, no business would ever transpire. People exhibiting such character traits would convey that they were trustworthy, dependable, honest, strong, sincere and that they were team players. Companies don't want and will not tolerate anything less. Without the early exposure to black adults who could teach these ideals, black kids who become adults struggle to be successful because the world they have occupied and the form of communication that is valued in that world keeps black children and the adults handcuffed to a poor education in unsafe communities with pathetic job opportunities, no health care and no future for the children. The black businessmen in the 1200 block of South Jefferson Avenue taught the softer assets and virtues through menial jobs they offered kids, such as sweeping and mopping the floors. The jobs and the lectures that went with the work lifted the kids to new ways of thinking and a different way of communicating and the virtues of the work opened up a future of new vistas to the kids who were desperately seeking a better way of life.

Doc smoked like a lot of men at the time. But he knew it was a bad, costly habit. He shared with the boys a story about a man who was more than 100 years old who smoked regularly. The man was approached by a cigarette company to do a television interview. More than ever, cigarette manufacturers were under the gun from doctors, health care advocates and the government officials who charged that tobacco products were the chief cause of many cancers, lung disease, heart disease and myriad other health problems. The cigarette advertisers wanted the old man on the television to show that cigarettes had no harmful effects on him despite more than 90 years of smoking. Doc explained that the cigarette company agent asked the man if he could be in the TV studios at 8 a.m. for an interview. The man said no. The agent said, "Well, OK, how about 10 a.m.?" The man again said no. The agent said he would then like to get the man on the noon television program. Television stations back then benefited greatly from cigarette advertising and were eager for the interview so they were trying to be accommodating. But the man again replied no. The agent asked, "Well why not?" The old man looked at him and said, "I don't stop coughing until noon." The boys at the lab laughed out loud. They understood that smoking had many harmful, costly effects.

Doc was trying mightily to unscrew a rusty 2-inch elbow from a piece of pipe that he needed in order to finish some plumbing work at Du-Good Chemical. It didn't take long before he commanded one of the boys, "Go get me the hammer." One of the kids who wandered in from the brick alley through the open sliding door went into Doc's tool room to get Doc's favorite hammer. Doc kept many hammers of different sizes and shapes. But like most men, he had one that he liked more than the others. Sam, who was dressed in frayed shorts and a T-shirt that he had worn on a few days, took the hammer to Doc. When something would not give way using the right tools, Doc always resorted to beating whatever he was working on into submission with the hammer. The boys who hung out at Du-Good Chemical always knew then that sparks literally were going to fly. But it was more than just sparks that they saw Doc make. The boys learned that black men could force the impossible to be very possible. They just had to have the will, the determination and the discipline to not give up. Doc's "Get me the hammer" mantra taught the boys that they, too, could wield control over their lives and their destiny. They, too, possessed the power and force to make the impossible, possible. They just needed the will, determination and discipline to make it so.

In the summer, Du-Good Chemical would get incredibly hot. Doc always took off his dress shirt and tie and stripped down to a thin T-shirt—the kind that had no sleeves. The boys who came to work at the company strangely enjoyed the sight. Even though Doc did white-collar work, he had the rippling muscles of a blue-collar iron worker. Doc swung his hammer with the ferocity and passion of a man who was trying to change the world—not just loosen a pipe from decades-old rust. The boys who hung out at the company laughed with glee partly because they saw each challenge as an epic struggle between Doc's irresistible force and some seemingly immovable object. But the boys' enthusiasm also was partly because they had never witnessed anyone who worked so incredibly hard and was so relentless in not giving up. Each time the kids witnessed it, they took some of that same dogged determination with them. But sometimes the beatings that Doc inflicted on pipes, boards or other stubborn things went too far. That's what happened in this case. The already thin, rusty threads on the pipe gave way, splitting the metal open. Doc said a few choice words and then instructed Sam to get the cold chisel from the tool room. Doc used the hammer to knock the elbow that he wanted lose from the thread of metal that it was attached to. Doc undid the pipe from the vice, which was welded and bolted to a wooden pole holding up the 15- 20-foot-high ceiling. Then he picked up the elbow from the floor and slipped the chain from the pipe vice around it and then tightened the vice.

Every job was an opportunity for a lesson. Doc told Sam: "Now you saw how that elbow fell to the ground, didn't you?" Sam and some of the other boys nodded. "What force caused that pipe to fall?" Doc asked.

"You're just asking that because you was just beating on that pipe," Sam said.

Doc retorted: "You mean 'You *were* beating on that pipe.'"

"Yes, you was," Sam said while he and the other boys laughed outrageously.

"No, knothead! "The correct grammar is to say, 'You *were* beating on that pipe!" Doc said with the same emphatic voice that he used when his college students were a little slow to get their chemistry or physical science lessons. "Beating on the pipe was not the force that caused it to fall to the ground.

Doc turned to Butch and asked, "What was the force that caused the elbow to fall to the ground?"

"I don't know, Doc. I was going to say the same thing that Sam said," Butch replied.

"What do they teach you about science in school?" Doc asked rhetorically. "Gravity was the force that caused that elbow to fall to the ground. Gravity applies to everything. Sir Isaac Newton discovered gravity. An apple fell from a tree and hit him on his head while he was sleeping under the tree. Newton realized that the gravitational pull of the Earth was what nearly knocked him unconscious. Gravity causes things to fall at a speed of 32 feet per second, per second. So things fall at an accelerating rate. Sam, which falls faster, a feather or an anvil?"

Sam said, "The anvil falls faster because it is heavier." The other kids nodded their heads in agreement.

Doc picked up the chisel and began to cut the pipe from the rusty elbow. "Wrong!" Doc said to Sam's answer. Doc would always set up the kids so they would reveal their flawed thinking and logic. Then Doc would hammer them with the right answer and the reasoning behind the correct response. It helped to cement in the boys' deeper understanding of science and life. Doc explained that gravity acts on all objects equally. If air were removed from the environment, the feather and the anvil without the resistance would fall at the same rate. The boys would scratch their heads and smile. They knew they had just been treated to another of many science lessons amid the sweaty work. The conversations with Doc were always rich, and there was never a idle minute.

Every hour working with Doc was an opportunity for him to teach. When Jesse talked Doc always tried to correct his punctuation and his grammar. "I'll git that for you, Doc."

Doc replied emphatically: "I don't want you to *git* that for me, Jesse. But you can *get* that for me.

Jesse said, "That's what I said."

Doc responded: "No you didn't. You said git, which is spelled g-i-t, and there is no such word. What you meant was g-e-t. Now that's get, and yes you can get that tool for me out of the tool room."

Jesse was also fond of saying: "Let me 'ax' you something, Doc."

Doc always responded: "How are you going to 'ax' me? I would think that would hurt."

Jesse said, "I don't know what you mean."

Doc replied: "What you mean to say is, 'Let me *ask* you something,' Ask is spelled a-s-k. It must never be confused with ax. An ax is something you use to chop wood, and you manage to do quite a lot of that with the English language without any help. I am trying to help you. The better you are able to communicate in this country, the more successful you will be."

Doc added: "Old Maude the mule kicks hard, but eventually she gets the message through—one end or the other. Using your head is the best way rather than have the hard knocks of life beat into you the right way to say and do things."

Jesse knew the other part of the lecture was coming. He was right. Jesse also was fond of asking, "Where's it at?" when he had questions about where to find something at Du-Good Chemical. That always triggered an automatic response from Doc, who was forever vigilant about going after bad language.

"It's between the 'A' and the 'T,'" Doc always responded. "No sentence needs to end with a preposition like that.

Jesse looked at Doc quizzically.

"You only need to ask, 'Where is it?'" Doc said. "It is totally unnecessary to add that 'at' at the end of the sentence. Boy, you can't chop up the English language and expect people to think you know what you are doing. Heck, no one will ever hire you if you continue to talk like that."

"But everyone I know talks like this, Doc," said Jesse who frequently challenged Doc.

Doc said: "I'd be willing to bet that everyone you know doesn't amount to much, either. I want to make sure that you end up better off. I am not picking on you, Jesse. I am just trying to make sure you get right what you mean to say so there is never any doubt whatsoever."

Part of the constant instruction for others was how Doc was raised with lectures of duty and discipline from his father and mother. Part of it came from having great black teachers in grade school, high school and at West Virginia State College who used every chance encounter with youths as teachable moments. Doc knew there were a few African-American kids who had an interest in science even though the second-class education they received wouldn't enable their talent to surface. So he took it as part of his personal mission to open the door of wonder and awe in scientific discovery to young people so they would naturally choose that career path. When working with boys who wandered into Du-Good Chemical, Doc would talk about his research as if everyone at the company were a PhD chemist like him. But he also would let the boys know how much they didn't know about the life around them and the science that made it possible.

"John!" Doc implored while making paint that the boys would use to apply double coats to the fences at one of his apartment buildings. "Did you have bread with your breakfast today?"

"Yes sir," John replied. John was inordinately tall and muscular for his age. He was a sophomore in high school and took boxing lessons at the nearby Buder Community Center. Like Doc, John had massive hands. He often pretended to box the head of Doc's big dog, Blackie. That always got the dog to bark loudly and ferociously and bite the air just as John would snap back each punch. The noise and the excitement with the dog always made John laugh. Blackie would get even more aggressive when John pretended to box at Blackie while Blackie was eating. Blackie and Mutt, the other dog, would eat from the upside-down lid of a big metal trash can placed on a 5-gallon ceramic tub. A 10-pound yellow brick held the lid down. The dogs were fed near the pipe vice, which was positioned by the tool room and an old icebox, where Doc kept the dog's food stored so rats and other critters couldn't get it. On top of the old ice box was a stack of metal and plastic funnels, which Doc insisted that the boys keep clean at all times for their use in the manufacturing of products. That icebox top also held oil cans, washers, nuts, bolts and anything else that might come in handy to keep the machinery humming at the company.

Whenever Doc would see the boys horsing around or goofing off or playing with the dogs instead of working, he would pull them back on task first by asking them questions to get them to think about their physical environment.

"Where does that bread come from, John?" Doc asked, pouring iron oxide into the linseed oil-based paint he was making in order to turn the white color red.

"The bread came from the store, Doc. You know that," John replied.

"Wrong!" Doc said.

"Well, where did it come from then?" John asked.

"The bread came from wheat that was grown on farms," Doc said "The wheat was harvested and then sent to the mills where it was separated and ground into flour. The flour was mixed with other ingredients such as yeast and then cooked in factories into the bread that was wrapped and shipped to the store where you bought it. People today don't have a clue as to how that bread gets to their dinner tables. You need to know these things. I remember when my momma used to make bread. But everything started with the farmer who saved the seeds from each harvest so he could plant his next crop of wheat so you can have more bread."

Doc often had his kids make a lunch of lima bean soup for the boys at Du-Good Chemical. Doc watched as the kids measured the salt before dumping it into the pot for seasoning. Doc asked the boys on the assembly line, "Where did that salt come from, and what's the chemical formula for it?"

"Why Doc, you know that the salt came from the store, too, just like John said that the bread we eat comes from there," Jesse replied.

"Wrong!" Doc shot back. "That salt is mined in such states as Utah. You need to get out of this city some day and drive west to Utah. There you will see salt covering the ground across the horizon. Everything is white with salt, and almost nothing grows in many places there because of the salt. The Great Salt Lake is by Salt Lake City. It has one of the highest contents of salt in the world. People who jump in that lake can't drown because the salt content keeps them buoyant. What does 'buoyant' mean, Tommy?"

"I don't know, Doc." Tommy shot back over the noise of the machinery that was running in the production of one of the products of Du-Good Chemical.

"Buoyant means that things stay afloat," Doc shot back. "Jesse! What is the formula for table salt?"

"Doc, I don't know that, either." Jesse said, filling the bottles on the table.

"Don't they teach you anything in school?" Doc asked, knowing that he taught many of the teachers at Harris Teachers College, whom the boys had in their schools.

"No sir," Jesse and Tommy said together. "All we do is music and art," Jesse said.

Teachers used such subjects to pacify unruly classes in schools that were overcrowded because of the baby boom and the continued migration of blacks from the South for over-promised jobs and over-promised better schools in the North.

"Those teachers are guaranteeing that you will be ignorant and second-class citizens for the rest of your life," Doc said. "The formula for salt is NaCl. That stands for sodium chloride. That means there is one sodium atom and one chloride atom in every molecule of salt. You use salt every day and don't have a clue of what that white stuff is that you are putting on your food."

"No sir, but it sure tastes good," Jesse said. The other boys exploded with laughter as they usually did when Jesse clowned, which always goaded Doc into stretching the lessons out more.

"That's what most ignoramuses say," Doc retorted. "In this region of the United States you have to be sure to buy the iodized salt because the ground in which your food is grown does not naturally contain iodine, which your thyroid gland needs in order to function properly. The thyroid gland regulates your metabolism. That determines whether you are fat or thin. If you don't have enough iodine in your system, then chances are you will be heavy all of your life."

"Jesse!" Doc said over the noise of the machinery. "What's the formula for lye? A lot of blacks use lye to straighten their hair. It damages the roots, and eventually the hair falls out. But few people can tell you why their hair falls out—although it seems obvious to me. My products don't damage the hair. My products leave women's hair straight and good-looking."

"Doc that sounded like a commercial," Jesse said, to more laugher from the other boys.

"Maybe so," Doc said. "But you didn't answer the question."

"I don't know, Doc," Jesse said. "What is the formula for lye?"

"They don't teach you anything in those schools," Doc reiterated again. "The formula for lye is $NaOH$. That's sodium hydroxide. A sodium atom is combined with an oxygen atom and a hydrogen atom. I have a whole drum of sodium hydroxide over in that southwest corner. If you got just a drop of that stuff on you, it would burn a hole clean through you before you could get to the water in the sink 50 feet away. Now imagine what it would do to your hair?

"Tommy!" Doc shouted. "Where does sugar come from?"

"I don't know, Doc." Tommy said. "Probably not the store because that was the wrong answer for the other questions."

"Well, at least you're starting to think," Doc said adding more ingredients to the paint. "Sugar is refined in factories, but it comes from sugar canes that are grown in such states as Hawaii and Louisiana. That granular sub-stance is a chemical. The formula is $C_{12}H_{22}O_{11}$. There are 12 carbon atoms, 22 hydrogen atoms and 11 oxygen atoms. You know there are a lot of carbon atoms in sugar. When sugar burns a black residue is what's left. The hydro-gen and oxygen burn off to form water vapor. You fellows learned something today despite your teachers' best efforts to keep you ignorant. When you let people keep knowledge from you, you enable them to exploit you because you don't know any better. What's the difference between today's exploitation and being a slave? In both ways you stay ignorant, and you aren't thinking for yourself."

None of the boys had a good response. Doc used the same teaching methods on his own children except he sometimes withheld such things as dessert from them until he got a satisfactory answer on the many science lessons he provided. Kids who hung around Doc eventually ended up thinking like a scientist, questioning everything challenging the status quo and experimenting every chance they got in order to learn more about the goings-on in life and its many interconnections.

Jobs that were not done right had to be done over at Du-Good Chemical. Doc would go behind the boys after bottles on the long tables were labeled, filled and capped. He would pull out a couple of the containers to quality check them. Sometimes the boys thought Doc was picking on them and making fun of their work. But instead, Doc just wanted to make sure the products his company was producing were up to his standards and make sure the boys knew that half-stepping was never going to be permitted from them anywhere. "The top of this bottle was not on tight!" Doc said emphatically. "I want you to go back over all of these bottles and make sure that every cap is screwed on good. There can be no spillage. This bottle has a label that is on crooked. Take it off and do it over. And don't let that happen again. That always looks bad on store shelves."

The boys would never get such instruction elsewhere. On other jobs they'd just get fired. They got instruction in mega-doses at Du-Good Chemical. Doc launched into another story with the young workers:

"An old man wanted to test his sons to see whether each was ready to go out into the world on his own," Doc said. He told each young man one at a time to come with him into the back yard of his house. Each boy followed obediently. The man had bundled together some sticks. He asked each boy to try to break the bundle in two. If the boy was able to do it, then the man knew his son was ready to go into the world. Each boy saw the bundle as a test of his strength. Each boy tried mightily to break the bundle in two with his bare hands, and each boy failed to accomplish the task. The father told each son he was not ready for the task of being on his own. The boys gathered together and confronted the old man in the yard, saying the task was impossible. No one was strong enough to break the bundle of sticks in two. They charged that the old man had meant for them to fail. The old man replied that the boys couldn't be further from the truth. The old man said he could break the bundle in half. The boys laughed out loud, knowing that each was stronger than his father was. But then the old man untied the sticks and broke each twig in two individually. The old man replied that the test of manhood for them was not in how strong each was but in how wise his sons were in understanding the problem and then solving it on his own."

The boys at Du-Good Chemical were not altogether impressed. But they understood the meaning of the story. Doc said: "Let me tell you another one that will get you to think. It is similar to the first but different. In this story, a man also wants to see whether his sons were ready to go out in the world to be on their own. He calls each into the back yard of his home. In the back yard is a rock garden. The man asks each son to move a rather large rock and tells each young man separately that he can use anything in the yard to help him with the task. Each young man squats down and tries mightily to move the large rock. Although each makes a lot of noise grunting and straining, none of the boys is able to move the rock. The old man shakes his head at each son's failure." Doc asks the boys at Du-Good Chemical what the sons did wrong. One boy yelled that they needed to pick up a plank of wood and use it as a lever. Doc said there was no wood in the yard. Another boy said they needed a two-wheel dolly like the ones at Du-Good Chemical. Doc said there wasn't one of those in the back yard, either. Finally the boys gave up in frustration, thinking that Doc was just yanking their chain with another one of his stories. But Doc said: "There is an answer to the problem, and it was as plain as the noses on the old man's sons' faces. The old man told his sons the answer when they confronted him saying that the task was impossible because it required great strength or machinery. The old man said that the one thing the boys neglected to use in the yard to help them move the rock was him, the old man. Again, this was not a test of the young men's strength but of their intellect and their ability to solve the problem by thinking of different solutions." It also fit what Doc's wife, Nancy, used to tell children—"Always remember, you're never alone."

The boys sometimes talked as Doc talked; sometimes laughed with each other over the stories. But all in all, they paid attention. The lessons mostly stuck. When the boys took the stories to heart, the street parables ended up enhancing the boys' lives. They added to the experiences the boys carried with them from then on.

The boys also were good at studying the black men in the 1200 block of South Jefferson Avenue. They knew who the most industrious men were. They knew which ones would work them the hardest for a few coins or a dollar or two. They knew whom to trust among the businessmen, which ones paid them the least and which ones poked the most fun at them while they worked. The boys knew Doc often had a half-dozen things going at once. He would monitor ongoing lab work with ovens and Bunsen burners going constantly while working the floor of the manufacturing area with the boys filling and labeling products. He'd have a repair project or two in full swing while supervising inventory. And in the midst of all that, someone would telephone or come to the front door wanting to buy Du-Good Chemical goods or seeking Doc's consultation on a new product they wanted him to develop. That was when he wasn't teaching at Harris Teachers College, or Washington University, or doing repair work on his rental property or working as a consultant for the government at Jefferson Barracks. The boys learned from Doc that they did not have to limit themselves to doing just one thing at a time. Working under Doc taught them that they could manage their time and maximize their productivity.

Generally when the boys could work one-on-one with the men, they would be all right. But when the men had other adults in their businesses or at the church, the boys were in for a ribbing and even more hard work. It was as if the men acted like they seriously had to get their money's worth out of the young workers or act as if they were competing to provide the best instruction with the work. Sam the tailor, Greasy Earl, Reverend Nance, Jeff the grocer, Shorty the shoeshine man and Doc at Du-Good Chemical often compared notes on the kids, too. They knew who would do the work, who would goof off, whom to trust and whom to never let into their shops again. Knowing which kids were the best caused them to depend on those boys the most as leaders for the others.

The boys also learned from the men in the 1200 block of South Jefferson Avenue that the black men also performed a lot of civic duties that helped push the Civil Rights Movement forward. The Urban League of Metropolitan St. Louis called Doc at Du-Good Chemical. Some of the major chemical companies in St. Louis—and there were many—had no black professionals on staff. The Urban League wanted to recruit Doc to test the companies to see whether they would process his application for employment. Doc has always been a staunch supporter of the Urban League, the National Association for the Advancement of Colored People and other civil rights groups. He agreed to go to some of the companies and put in job applications. Doc had a stellar work record and resume. Who wouldn't want to hire someone with his credentials? But a few weeks later, the Urban League called

Du-Good Chemical again. The woman said she thought Doc had planned to go apply for jobs at those companies as a test of whether they would hire blacks. Doc said he did put in applications at all of the places the Urban League requested. The woman replied that when she checked at the companies, they said no blacks had ever applied there. She was grateful for Doc's efforts because she knew she had caught the companies in outrageous lies. Doc's civil rights efforts led to those discriminating companies opening their doors to hire their first black chemists, engineers and other professionals. The door-opening that Doc helped provide was more than just a job and career for those workers. It gave blacks in St. Louis opportunities to live the American dream with middle-class earnings and the ability to own homes and put their children through college. Some of the boys who worked at Du-Good Chemical caught the germ of wanting to be scientists. Doc's mentoring helped those boys get a college education. Some corporations where Doc helped open doors for blacks later provided scholarships for minorities and then jobs for the best young black graduates.

The efforts went well beyond affirmative action. The boys from the hardscrabble streets of the inner-city brought with them tenacity, work ethics and problem-solving skills that they needed to make it. There was nothing cool or comfortable about the way they had to live growing up. Doc knew that, and so did the black men in the 1200 block of South Jefferson Avenue. They also knew that the black kids they helped train and mentor would give other businesses and industries in the city a new competitive edge that those companies needed. Kids who'd grown up in comfortable suburban settings just don't have the drive, the fire and the hunger in their bellies like the kids of color from the inner city. The black kids who had been made aware in places like Du-Good Chemical knew that they possessed what Dr. W.E.B. Du Bois called a double consciousness. They saw the world both as Americans and as Africans in America. That unique prism gave them a greater insight into many aspects of life and drove them to achieve when others were relaxing.

Unfortunately the rest of America didn't see it that way. Racism was then and still remains a powerful force, predating the Revolutionary War. Racism and discrimination ensure that people believe the prejudices about blacks over the truth.

Doc never forgot that because he was black, St. Louis University refused to hire him to set up an analytical laboratory. The university preferred to go with someone white even though he was less qualified and only had a master's degree in chemistry. That guy failed miserably in the project. University officials offered Doc a lesser position teaching chemistry to nurses. Doc saw both slights as insults and refused to take the teaching position at St. Louis University. Doc told the story repeatedly over the years to the boys who worked at Du-Good Chemical stressing that blacks often have to be twice as good in America to be considered half as qualified.

Doc landed a full-time position at Stowe Teachers College. It was the black college. Harris Teachers College was where white students went with all white educators. They were both part of the separate and unequal St. Louis Public School District. Segregation as the law of the land mandated the separate facilities. Classrooms, textbooks and other materials at Harris were superior to those at Stowe. However, the educators at Stowe were outstanding. Doc sadly noted the sometimes lackadaisical attitude of the black students. He was distressed that too many were trying to live down to the stereotypes that whites had of them. Doc insisted on excellence from the students in his chemistry and physical science classes. Those who did not get their work done during class had to follow him to Du-Good Chemical, where they made up what was needed to get a passing grade.

After the 1954 Brown vs. Topeka Board of Education Supreme Court decision ending legal segregation, Stowe closed and all of the students—regardless of color—went to Harris. Doc noted with great interest that the lackadaisical attitude of the black students ended with the merger. African American students suddenly had to compete with the white students, and came prepared every day for the challenge. Each pushed the other to be better than otherwise would have been possible. Integration had a positive, competitive effect on white and black students.

◆　◆　◆　◆　◆

Vincent, Doc's youngest son, made it back to the hospital ICU room. He had gone to feed the dogs and cat and make sure everything was OK at Du-Good Chemical. That was what Doc did daily, driving his car from the family home to his company. Each trip was an act of love for the company he and his family had built from nothing through hard work and an unrelenting grit. Doc never gave up keeping his American dream going even after fighting with a development company that wanted to take his property to build a McDonald's restaurant. Even after a fire mysteriously swept through the manufacturing area of Du-Good Chemical in November 1977, Doc rebuilt.

He always rebuilt. Doc's friends and family refused to give up hope that somehow he would rise from the hospital bed free of all the tubes and wires demanding to know how his company was, how his animals were, whether there were new orders that needed to be filled and asking who was ready to help get the work done. Doc was fond of saying there was never any shortage of work to do at Du-Good Chemical.

OUR FATHERS: MAKING BLACK MEN

In the section cover photo is Dr. Lincoln I. Diuguid with son and author Lewis W. Diuguid, attending one of Doc's grandson's high school graduation, in Kansas City, Mo., in the early 2000s. Doc always stressed the importance of education.

Du-Good Chemical Laboratories & Manufacturers in 1947 became the first black-owned business in the 1200 block of South Jefferson Avenue in St. Louis. Several others followed. The horseshoe shaped property that Doc and his family purchased had been a large animal hospital. Through hard work, the Diuguid family converted the property into the first black chemical company west of the Mississippi River. Du-Good Chemical pictured below in 2011 was the last of the black businesses on the block.

The manufacturing area of Du-Good Chemical (above) included 55-gallon drums and a 150-gallon tank for mixing products. An oak roll-top desk (below) was in the production area. Doc's father, Lewis W. Diuguid, (right) traveled from Lynchburg, Va., to help Doc convert the large animal hospital into the chemical company. Lewis Diuguid had a garden on the property and was fond of Doc's dogs.

Doc married Nancy R. Greenlee (left), and they had four children—David in 1954, Lewis in 1955, Renee in 1956 and Vincent in 1961. Doc is pictured below at the University of Missouri-Columbia, where he delivered a paper on his research. Below he is pictured with his brother and St. Louis lawyer, William (Shingy) Diuguid, mother Bettie Diuguid and brother and Lynchburg, Va., dentist Hubert Diuguid.

Doc (upper right) appeared in a photo at the front door of Du-Good Chemical in the 1990s. A large glass bottle (upper left) was used for mixing ingredients for products. It is backlit by sunlight streaming through one of many windows in the manufacturing area. Du-Good Chemical had two labs. Lewis Diuguid (below) is pictured in the 1970s washing flasks in the back lab for Doc Diuguid, his father, to use. Doc did most of his work in the front lab, which overlooked Jefferson Avenue.

Doc Diuguid is pictured (left) with his children, (left to right) Vincent, David, Lewis and Renee. Next, Doc is with his nephew, Ross Newsome Jr., Ph.D. Doc shares a moment with his friend and mentee, King L. Taylor. In the bottom photo are Doc's grandchildren, (back row) Danielle and Jillian Diuguid, (second row) Leslie and Adrianne Diuguid (front) Xavier, Skyler and Zachary Tolson. The photos of the family were taken in the late 1990s in front of Doc's home on Lafayette Avenue just west of Grand Avenue. Doc bought the house in 1969, paying cash for it.

Doc Diuguid (right) graduated in 1934 from Dunbar High School in Lynchburg, Va., where he also played football. He pledged Omega Psi Phi fraternity at West Virginia State College, graduating magna cum laude in 1938 with a bachelor's in chemistry. Doc received his master's at Cornell University in 1939, and then headed the chemistry department at AM&N College in Pine Bluff, Ark. During World War II, Doc also worked at the U.S. Army's Pine Bluff Arsenal, doing research on poisonous gases. Doc returned to Cornell, receiving his doctorate in chemistry in 1945 and post-doctorate in organic chemistry in 1947. Doc (below) was an avid golfer, competing in many St. Louis area tournaments, often winning trophies. He frequently took the black kids who worked at Du-Good Chemical to golf courses and driving ranges with him, where he would teach them the sport. People in the neighborhood would see Doc (bottom right) outside of the company he operated for more than 60 years as founder and president doing needed repairs and maintaining the grounds. Doc would offer black kids jobs to do the same work with him.

In the 1970s (upper left), one experiment Doc did for a scientific paper at Du-Good Chemical showed the toxic effects of forced-air heating units on laboratory rats. Working as a consultant for a base-board heating company, Doc determined that its products were safer for consumers to use in their homes compared to traditional gas-, electric-, coal- or oil-fired furnaces. The black air compressor (upper right) was a key piece of machinery at Du-Good Chemical. It and a second gray compressor provided air pressure to pump chemicals from 55-gallon drums into tanks and to fill bottles and jars with Du-Good Chemical products. Doc hired black kids in the neighborhood to work at the company. They labeled the bottles and jars, boxed, and then stacked the products in the adjoining warehouses. A cement bucket and trowel (right) were often used for repairs. Doc did all of the repairs at the company with help from kids he hired. In the process they picked up invaluable skills.

Doc (left) did cancer research in his lab in the 1970s. Above Doc is dressed for work at Harris-Stowe State College, where he taught chemistry and was chairman of the physical science department. Below Doc instructs his chemistry students in their experiments at AM&N College in Pine Bluff, Ark.

When Du-Good Chemical was a large animal hospital it was heated in the winter with large wood- and coal-burning pot-bellied stoves. In the late 1940s, Doc Diuguid, some of his brothers and his father, Lewis W. Diuguid, removed those stoves and replaced them with a large, forced-air, coal-burning furnace (upper left) to heat the rambling, horse-shoe-shaped, two-story building. Each day, Doc or one of the black kids he had working at the company would stoke the furnace with fresh coal in the morning and at night, open the door to the furnace (upper right) and remove hot clinkers. After they cooled, workers at the company had to take the clinkers in a wheelbarrow into the loading area and break them up with a sledgehammer to make the pavement for trucks. Nothing was wasted at Du-Good Chemical. Above the furnace door was a water reservoir that also had to be filled each day to add moisture to the dry winter air in the company. Regardless of how cold it got outside, Doc kept the temperature in the company low to conserve energy. Conservation was important to Doc long before it became the thing to do for many people in the rest of the country. The furnace was converted to natural gas in the late 1960s. A two-ounce sample bottle (left) contains Du-Good Rainbow Delight. The amber-colored dish detergent was among the many products that Doc developed, manufactured and sold to stores in St. Louis and nationwide.

Doc (top left) in his 90s continued to work at Du-Good Chemical. The St. Louis Science Center has standing exhibits praising Doc's work. Below is a picture of Doc in 2004.

Doc (left) at age 90 is honored by the St. Louis Science Center. Above he is pictured with his children and grandchildren. Below at the awards program Doc is joined by his longtime Du-Good Chemical secretary, Ida Phillips.

Above are a few of the awards Doc received for his work as an educator and for his many innovations at Du-Good Chemical. Below he is pictured with a plaque he was given in 2009 from
the St. Louis Gateway Classic Sports Foundation, which included having his name and bio in
the sidewalk (right) near downtown with those of other famous St. Louisians.

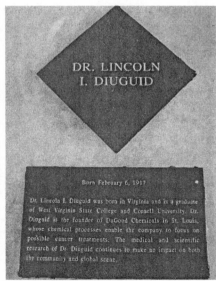

CHAPTER 6

OUR FATHERS, BLACK MEN

The boys kept chasing after 50 cents at Shorty's shoe shine shop, a buck or more at Jeff's grocery or a couple of bucks at Du-Good Chemical. But greater than the money earned were the lessons learned from listening to the different teachers in each of the businesses. Each black businessman had different stories to tell and different things to teach. The boys needed to hear all of the deep resonant voices and all of the stories. Often the boys didn't feel like paying attention or they laughed about what they heard. Nonetheless, the stories from the black businessmen sunk in, and they left deep lasting impressions.

Arranging the polish at Shorty's taught the boys the importance of orderliness and efficiency. Shorty would have a hard time pleasing his customers if he could not find the right polish for the shoes he had to shine. It would make him look disorganized and ill-prepared. To his customers Shorty would have looked as if he didn't know what he was doing. They would start to distrust his work and worry about whether he had done a good, lasting job on their shoes. So Shorty insisted on organization, and then delivered exceptional service.

Sam taught the boys patience and the importance of the right stitch, starch and not too much heat under the pressing machine. If it wasn't right, Sam would explain, the clothes, which make black men, wouldn't last. People would have their clothes come apart at the most embarrassing times, and that would be the end of business for Sam. His reputation as a tailor was on the line with each suit he altered, each button he added or each garment he mended, starched and pressed. At his store, Jeff implored the boys to always stock fresh, good-looking merchandise. Customers have other choices. Jeff wanted people to come to his store, and the only way for them to feel good about doing that was if he could ensure that they would get quality service and materials. Du-Good Chemical embodied all of those traits and more. Doc's customers were in states throughout the Midwest and South. The boys learned the importance of math, telephone manners when speaking with customers, how to use the telephone books—white pages and yellow pages—to look up names and companies, quality assurance in product production and shipping, and the importance of doing a job right the first time because often there wasn't a second chance. But the boys also learned the value of science and African-Americans' role in it. The boys saw that people who looked like them were inventors and famous people. They realized that they could have careers in science, too.

Those black business people were pillars in the community, and they definitely helped to raise the children. They were esteemed elders who also embodied and understood elements of America that most people didn't get. They knew that capitalism was the essence of the country. The men were mindful and embraced the hard and the soft elements of capitalism, and they prospered. They stood the best chance of living the American dream of owning a home, living in a safe community, being surrounded by good, like-minded, civically engaged people, enjoying good health, having a voice in everyday goings-on, feeling connected and well-regarded, sending their children to college, and eventually retiring comfortably watching their children pick up where they left off.

Achieving that level of success was the dream of the black businessmen in the 1200 block of South Jefferson Avenue. However, each man knew that building a fortress around his operation and not tending to the needs and desires of others in the community—particularly the children—would put his business and the community in jeopardy. Rev. C.L. Nance knew his church, the Second Corinthian Baptist Church, 2352 Hickory St., would only do as well as Jeff's grocery on the southwest corner of Jefferson and Hickory because people needed good food to survive, get to their jobs and function well. He knew he needed Shorty's shoeshine shop and Sam's cleaners because they enabled people in the community to look good so they could feel good at work and at church and stay employed. Rev. Nance knew he needed Earl because people with cars had to keep them running so they could get to work, to church and around town to shop. People needed Du-Good Chemical for the cleaning products, cosmetics and analytical services it provided.

Doc and the other businessmen gave the children something to which they could aspire. The kids knew they could make money and make their dreams flourish, too, if they just had the gumption to take a chance and do it as the men in the 1200 block of South Jefferson Avenue did. No one in the neighborhood could imagine how they would survive or how their kids would stay out of trouble without the guidance of the black businessmen. Everyone stayed out of harm's way because of the investment in America's capitalist business structure.

The St. Louis Metropolitan Police Department patrolled, looking out for the vested interests of the shop owners. Keeping the peace centered on commerce taking place unimpeded. As long as the shops were in place and the church was doing OK, the police were happy as was the community. But slowly things started to change. The police officers, who used to walk the streets occasionally in the 1200 block of South Jefferson Avenue, checking doors and saying hello to folks began to ride more in their patrol cars until riding eventually was all they did, getting out only on specific calls. The letter carriers, who used to deliver mail twice a day cut back to just once a day, and then no one was ever certain of the time the postman would arrive. Slippage occurred in these and many other areas, and the community and its children were sadly gut-punched by the effects of the withdrawal of adults as authority figures so closely connected with the kids.

The black businessmen in the 1200 block of South Jefferson Avenue always patronized each other's businesses. Doc sent the boys who worked for him next door to Shorty's with a dollar in change to buy 10-cent Coca-Colas for all of the workers even though it was a lot cheaper to get the soft drinks from the supermarket a few blocks away. The sodas were not as large as the ones that came from the grocery store. They came in the shapely 10-ounce bottles. Going into Shorty's for Cokes was always an adventure. The old floors creaked even with the light weight of skinny kids. It always felt as if the place was sitting over a cavern, and the floor was ready to give way and fall into a dusty abyss at any time. But that didn't bother the men who hung out inside Shorty's during the winter time and who occupied homemade benches that lined the front of the store in the spring, summer and warm parts of fall. The men were always playing some games—whether cards, dominoes or checkers. The card table always had a lively crowd around it with players seated doing battle. Getting sodas was not easy. Shorty's soda machine was ancient even by the standards of the black community and the 1200 block of South Jefferson Avenue. Black folks tended to get the cast-offs from white folks. As whites got the latest and the best, they either sold or gave to blacks what machinery they no longer wanted. Blacks always took it and got at least as many years of service from it as whites previously did. Shorty's soda machine had to date to the 1930s. The machine looked like a freezer except it was painted with the colors and lettering that said "Coca-Cola" on both sides. The top opened up, and inside were the bottles of Coke and other drinks. All people could see where the metal caps of the glass bottles poking above the metal racks that firmly held the drinks. People wanting the soft drink had to use their hands to advance the bottles of pop through a zig-zagging horizontal track until the full bottles finally came to a drawbridge-like gate that rose up if the right coins were placed in the machine when the person pulled the bottle up to release the drink. The purchaser pulled the drink upward and the cold, frosty Coke was his. Sometimes the machine refused to work. The boys would tell Shorty because they did not want to go back to Du-Good Chemical and tell Doc they had been shorted. Doc always blew a gasket and would send the boys back to either get the money back or the drink. It always took the fun out of the treat of having sodas. Shorty knew how Doc was so he would either get the machine to work or just unlock the machine so the boys could get the pops they paid for. The boys would cross the alley, swaggering and smiling broadly, ring the bell and get Doc to throw them his keys from the middle, second-story window so they could enter Du-Good Chemical like returning heroes from battle with their prize Cokes.

Many of the men in the 1200 block of Jefferson Avenue had pets. Doc always had at least two dogs and one cat. One of the first dogs he had at Du-Good Chemical was a blonde, short-haired German shepherd, whom Doc named Chloe. Doc usually picked scientific names for his dogs or something that described how they looked or their personalities. Chloe means "verdant" or "blooming." It fit the photosynthesis work that Doc sometimes had to do in his labs. But Chloe also proved to be an exceptional dog. Butch, one of the boys who frequented Du-Good Chemical, brought Chloe to the company when the dog was just a puppy. Doc didn't know it at the time, but Chloe was a female dog. Chloe also was exceptionally smart. Doc taught Chloe tricks such as how to hold a flashlight in her mouth and then walk throughout the company to police the property. Doc also taught the dog how to climb a double ladder. So Chloe would carry the flashlight and patrol the roof of Du-Good Chemical. Sometimes the not-to-nice kids and people in the neighborhood would jump the 6-foot-tall wooden fence, get onto the roof and try to gain access to the buildings. People often thought that a chemical company might have drugs they could steal. But there were none. Chloe knew that her job was to stop the unwanted visitors. The boys who worked at Du-Good Chemical reported to others that Chloe was an incredible watchdog. She became a legend in the neighborhood. People from throughout the community came by Du-Good Chemical just to see Chloe climb ladders. The real trick was watching the dog come down. But she always managed to place her paws in the right spots on the narrow rungs, balance acutely and not trip or fall. Doc's father became fond of Chloe. He often had Chloe at his side when he worked in the garden that he grew in part of the loading area at Du-Good Chemical. Doc's dad grew greens, beets, tomatoes, corn and a few other crops that Doc and others would enjoy. The boys got to see that black men as farmers could cultivate their own crops, which tasted good, too, rather than depend solely on grocery stores for food. When Chloe had a puppy of her own, Doc named it Pluto after the ninth planet in the solar system. Pluto was not smart. As a matter of fact, he was stupid. Pluto saw Doc's cat crawl into tight places such as under tables and under an old refrigerator that sat on stocky, short legs in the company kitchen. Pluto decided that he could crawl under that 8-inch-high space, too. Strangely enough, that big dog managed to do it and get out—although getting out was always a struggle. Pluto hated everyone and barked at everything. The deep, loud noise from that dog was more out of his own fear and insecurity than anything else.

Greasy Earl kept dogs in his garage, too. The dogs kept thugs from going into Earl's place and stealing batteries, radios, tires or rims from the cars or trucks that Earl stored there overnight while waiting on parts or payment for repair work. People needed their vehicles. But they were horribly slow at paying for the work. The dogs Greasy Earl kept helped to keep folks honest. Earl's dogs were mean. They sometimes even turned on him. One dog bit Earl on the right hand when Earl tried to take some food away from the beast. Earl went after that dog in a life-ending way. But he decided against killing the animal. Earl gave that dog, Blackie, to Doc instead. The dog ended up biting Doc, too, and through a near miss, that dog managed to avoid death yet again. When Blackie bit Doc, Doc swiftly reached for two brooms and broke one and then the other over Blackie's massive head before the dog could extract its tusks from Doc's left hand. Doc had incredible reflexes. The dog realized that it was on the losing end of the aggression it started. The dog bolted through the building to the loading area. Doc was hot on the dog's heals swearing and bleeding as he ran after the biting animal. Doc grabbed a piece of plumbing pipe as he ran like the track star that he was in high school. Blackie cut corners quickly as he bolted out of the furnace room, flew through the dog hole and ran outside into the loading area. Doc was hot in pursuit unlocking the outside door faster than most humans could think. Blackie dived under one of the company trucks just as Doc lowered the pipe in what could have been a death blow. The dog stayed under the truck until Doc calmed down—aided by the boys at the company wondering what the commotion was all about. Neither the dog nor Doc challenged each other like that again. The boys saw that the men in the 1200 block of South Jefferson Avenue could be highly emotional, sensitive, angry and reactionary. That has its place. But it does not need to frequently show itself to be effective. If it did, it would lose its currency and persuasive power.

On the weekends, people streamed into Jeffs's grocery store down the street. Traffic was especially heavy after what the boys called Mother's Day. That was around the first of every month when many single black mothers in the neighborhood got their government assistance from either food stamps or Aid to Families with Dependent Children. The government never gave the women enough to carry them through the end of the month—or that is how it seemed to a lot of the people. It always seemed to be feast and then famine. Sometimes the women picked up commodity peanut butter or cheese from the government. The peanut butter came in big cans. It wasn't the best. The stuff was so hard that it would bend knives that the kids used trying to extract it. Then if they did get a knifeful out, spreading the commodity peanut butter on any bread was impossible. That peanut butter would shred the bread. The commodity cheese wasn't much better. It came in long loafs similar to the look of Velveeta cheese and like bread except it was unsliced. The boys told stories of having melted cheese on sandwiches, cheese in potato dishes, cheese in rice, cheese in pasta dishes and ladled over vegetables of all types. It was extra calories and a little bit of protein. It was a filler. Jeff picked up the Mother's Day traffic, and he was happy to have it. He would greet the women who entered his store with kindness and respect, and Jeff insisted that all of his employees treat the women the same way that he did. How could they not? Many of Jeff's workers also relied on food stamps and received Aid to Families with Dependent Children checks. Like the other black businessmen in the 1200 block of South Jefferson Avenue, Jeff couldn't afford to pay his employees a lot. He gave them what he could so that he could meet his other fiduciary obligations. Jeff had more workers than most of the other black businesses combined. But that goes with owning a grocery store.

Either Doc would send his kids to Jeff's store or some of the boys in the neighborhood would happen by there. For Doc, they'd pick up bread, bologna, eggs or even a can of mackerel for sandwiches or they would get beans and other fixings for bean soup. Occasionally Doc would restock his supply of tea bags. In the evenings, especially on cold days, Doc would have the boys make tea in an old pot. He insisted on using one tea bag for four cups of water. That was sufficient, Doc said, for everyone to enjoy the warm beverage. In the summer, Doc would have the boys boil a couple of tea bags in a gallon of water, add some green mint leaves he had them pick from his garden in the loading area of the company with just a dash of citric acid he kept in the lab, and then refrigerate the concoction for refreshing ice tea. Even less often, Doc would have the boys pick up some cookies from Jeff's grocery store. That was when Doc's sweet tooth overruled his need to be frugal. Jeff always knew when one of the boys was shopping for Doc. The limited items that the kids picked up always told the story. But even though the boys were not supposed to linger, they would always wander up and down the aisles of the store, looking at all of the products on the shelves. Poor people in the neighborhood—and there were a lot of them—did that plenty. It's in communities of need that people often dream of riches and abundance. Wandering the aisles of Jeff's store was the best way to satiate that hunger. Jeff didn't mind. He understood how the people were. He just didn't want his inventory walking out the door without compensation with the many people who came to his store to shop a little and dream a lot. But some theft was inevitable. How was Jeff to police about seven workers and the eight to 15 customers who seemed to be in his store at any given time? It was impossible. He had to trust that the people wanted him around more to serve the needs of the community for the long term rather than for the short-term gain of them stealing his goods so they could fill their bellies or their households. Honesty was always Jeff's wish, and he drummed it into the heads of the boys who worked for him.

People who lived in the community surrounding the 1200 block of South Jefferson Avenue really didn't know the gold mine of riches that the black businessmen and civic leaders provided for the neighborhood and the area's children. Often folks didn't appreciate the value of these hard and soft assets until they were gone. But occasionally someone black from a small town wandered in, looked around and expressed absolute awe over the synergy that the community possessed because of the black businesses. Walter Tolson was one of those persons. He lived in Brunswick, Mo., a tiny community of people in the north-central part of the state off U.S. 24 near the Missouri and Grand rivers and just a ways east of Missouri 41. Walt and his many siblings grew up in the nearly all-white community. His father worked for the railroad but was injured in a horrible accident. Walt went to the University of Missouri-Columbia and often drove in to visit friends in St. Louis. It was one of the big happening places for students who wanted a break from campus life. Walt proclaimed on his first trip to St. Louis and witnessing the black businessmen and civic leaders in the 1200 block of South Jefferson Avenue that he had never seen such a thing before. All of his life he had seen black people play subservient roles, and it angered him because he knew that he and others like him could do so much better. Witnessing the self-reliance of the black folks in St. Louis and the ownership of blacks in businesses—not just in the 1200 block of South Jefferson Avenue but in other neighborhoods throughout town—gave Walt great pride. It was as if he had walked into a candy store as a kid for the first time. He couldn't get enough of what was there to patronize and he couldn't spend enough time talking with the black businessmen to see how they managed to do so much at a time when so few blacks were able to get jobs. Walt realized that the men were part of a process that enabled them to surface when so many others were held back. They were what Dr. W.E.B. Du Bois described as "the Talented Tenth." They were part of the best and the brightest that exist in any race or group of people who were destined to step into lead positions. It is what caused other blacks with ideas to knock on Doc's door to talk with an honest-to-goodness PhD and dream of other possibilities for them as emerging entrepreneurs.

The sultry St. Louis summers where no breezes blew conspired with the old brick buildings, causing people throughout the neighborhoods that draped from the 1200 block of South Jefferson Avenue to always be outside. People sat on their front porches—those who had them—or they sat on the stone stoops of their buildings or camped on the limestone front steps as long as the shade lasted. Some men and women just raised the screenless windows of their homes or apartments, kneeled on the floor and positioned their upper bodies toward the shaded outdoors hoping to catch whatever rare cool breeze that might grace their block. But people who hung out in these many summertime ways also got to watch, enjoy, interact and instruct the theater of kids, cars and adults who constantly happened by.

It was phenomenally entertaining reality TV before television was invented and certainly before television ended up in nearly every home in America. Unlike TV, it was not a one-way form of communication.

Women—particularly older women—kept tabs on every child issuing cautions about kids running, skating or biking too fast, worrying about kids who stayed out too late or skipped school and admonishing boys about getting into fights or taking what didn't belong to them. The women were exceptional, too, about calling the kids' parents and letting the moms and dads know what transpired. Summer ensured that no one had privacy; everyone stayed in everyone's business. One day, Doc's two sons got away from their mother and wandered off. The older one, David, couldn't have been more than 3, and he was leading the younger one, Lewis, who was 2 and in diapers. David was determined to get them both to the corner store to get some candy. They had gotten about two blocks away from home but had walked in the wrong direction. Mrs. Jones, who stayed in her second-story window, saw those babies, and she called them. She asked them where they were going. Lewis was crying. David was turned around and hopelessly lost. Neither answered. Mrs. Jones kept the boys standing under her window while she called their mother, Nancy, who ran from her house with the youngest, Renee, in her arms. Nancy was eternally grateful to Mrs. Jones for saving her wayward sons, whom she kept a closer watch on from then on.

The watchfulness occurred in the shops and businesses in the 1200 block of South Jefferson Avenue, too. Doc knew that boys horsed around. Their playfulness quickly got out of hand, and valuables were broken. During down time at work, the boys would get a game of softball or basketball going in the loading area. Doc, who used to play basketball, had put up a basketball goal and backboard on a tree. Doc had been an incredible athlete in high school, where he played football and ran track until an ankle injury sidelined him. But Doc continued to play on school basketball teams even after he started teaching college. Those games pitted the faculty against the students. So Doc enjoyed shooting hoops with the kids in the neighborhood in the loading area of his company. He also would see whether any of the boys had similar athletic abilities to what he had. He would tell them that he was able to run a mile in under five minutes when doing such a thing was unheard of among the general population. Doc also liked to demonstrate his athleticism by holding a broomstick with both of his very large hands and then jumping over it—forward and then backward with great ease. Several of the boys who worked at Du-Good Chemical over the years tried it. But many often landed on their faces. What Doc didn't tell them was he had unusually long arms, a long torso and short legs.

The loading area also enabled the boys to create a small diamond and bases that they would run. Too often, a ball hit too hard would break a window.

Broken glass made an unmistakable, telltale sound, and it always brought Doc running regardless of where he was in his building. He knew that broken glass left unattended invited more broken glass and like a cancer spread the look of decay throughout his property and the community. Doc would admonish the boys in the most vociferously loud voice and language he could muster to get them to tell him what happened and who was responsible. Often no one wanted to speak up. Doc always had a way of coaxing the truth out of the young offenders. He would hold them all accountable for the expense of the damage. That always got someone in the group to finger the culprit. It worked with broken lab equipment at the college when no students wanted to tell what happened and who was responsible, and it worked with the boys at Doc's company. Doc then would take the cost of the window out of the boy's salary for that week or month until the debt was paid. The experience, though tough, taught the boys the value of being responsible for the damage they caused, and it taught them honesty. It also taught them to be more careful so that accidents didn't occur because the cost of any mishap was more than the person responsible wanted to pay. Doc used the same types of hard lessons with the boys when they left on lights at his company. He wanted them to learn the value of thrift and to understand that their wastefulness had a cost that everyone had to bear. For lights that were left on where no people were working, Doc charged the boys and even his own kids a 10-cent fine. He was absolutely inflexible about it. Doc was the one who had to pay the light bill, but he wanted the boys to know that they had to assume some responsibility—for the good of the company—to keep the costs low. That enabled them to get paid in the manner and in the amount that was worthy of their work and thrift, benefiting the company and all of the workers. Jobs that were done poorly at Du-Good Chemical also had to be done over but without compensation. The boys then learned the value of doing a job right the first time. They also learned that their work was their signature in life. Doc wanted them to know that they only got one chance to make a good first impression, and often that was through the quality of the work that they did. It was a particularly important lesson for young black boys because it helped them refute the stereotypes about black men.

For his own children, Doc would only dole out a teaspoon of ice cream at a time if they were able to recite the correct formulas for chemical compounds such as table salt, sugar, lye or water. Eventually it would add up to a full bowl of dessert, but sometimes the process was painful to watch. Doc and his wife, Nancy, insisted on intellectual independence from their children. When David,

Lewis, Renee or Vincent asked how to spell a word or wanted to know an answer to other questions, each was told by both parents to "Look it up!" Encyclopedias, dictionaries, atlases and other reference books were neatly stored for anyone's quick use. Never was there an excuse not to acquire knowledge.

Whether the boys in the 1200 block of South Jefferson Avenue landed at Greasy Earl's, Shorty shoeshine shop, Sam the tailor's, Jeff's grocery store, Rev. Nance's church or Du-Good Chemical looking for some quick cash for work, they always got interrogated about their work in school. The men in the 1200 block of South Jefferson Avenue wanted to know whether the boys were making good grades. Adults had quizzed and harassed the businessmen and preacher when they were kids, voicing concerns about whether they were keeping up with their studies. Those adults and the black grown-ups on back to the times of slavery knew that education was of the utmost importance. Heck, slaves could be whipped or killed for reading. That was the unwavering law of the land. White people knew that reading gave slaves some power and that eventually they'd no longer accept being slaves. The slaves also knew that without an education, blacks would never be free. The enslavement and the exploitation of 20th century blacks would be different from the peculiar institution of slavery in 16th-, 17th-, 18th- and 19th-century America. But the degradation would be much the same. None of the younger generation seemed to get it. The boys who roamed the 1200 block of South Jefferson Avenue were no different from previous kids. School always got in the way of having fun. It kept them from getting a job and earning enough money to afford a car or have a place of their own. To many of the boys, the teachers were all seeking something the youths did not want to give. Not understanding and not caring about the lessons in math, science, English and social studies always made the boys feel bad. Having the men in the 1200 block of South Jefferson Avenue constantly ask them about school made the boys feel bad. These kids had a conscience. All kids do. They wanted to do well in school as well as just about everything they took on. But usually the juice for it just wasn't in them. They often stayed up too late watching television. Staying awake in class was a struggle the next day. Putting their head down and sleeping on the desk while the teacher droned on and on was the easy way out. The boys would brag about it when they got outside. Paying attention in school took too much energy. The lessons never got easier. Each built on the other lessons, which made picking up the follow-up studies impossible.

The men in the 1200 block of Jefferson Avenue tried to explain that to the boys when the boys finally confessed that their grades were far less than stellar—C's, D's and F's, actually. That would make Shorty shake his head. "You boys know ain't no good going to come from having grades like that, don't you?"

Doc also tried to help the boys see that they could repair things instead of just throwing broken appliances away. Doc showed the boys how to take the backs off of radios and televisions that weren't working. Doc diagrammed the insides, which were full of many tubes. He removed each tube taking care to write down the number of each one in the diagram so he could replace them. He then took the boys to Nash Rexall Drug store at 1601 S. Jefferson Ave. near Zoller Bakery at 1613 S. Jefferson Ave. They were about a half-mile from Du-Good Chemical. Doc went to the tube testing machine and tested each of the tubes. Always, one, two or three of the tubes showed themselves to be weak or bad. Doc would buy replacement tubes, take them back to the lab, replace all of the tubes and show the boys how the radio or TV worked like new with a little initiative and ingenuity. Such lessons were worth more than the coins the boys got from doing odd jobs at Doc's lab.

John McSwine was a difficult case for the men in the 1200 block of South Jefferson Avenue. John liked to box at a nearby community center and wasn't too interested in school. He also wasn't bashful about telling the men who were trying to school him when he thought they were preaching what they hadn't practiced.

"You didn't finish school," 16-year-old John shot back when one of the men was asking him about his classwork and why he wasn't doing better. "I'm no good at school just like you."

"But your life is supposed to be different, son," Shorty said with the other men in his shoeshine shop who chimed in with many, "uh-hums" and "amen's" and "You tell 'em, Shorty."

"It supposed to be different for you boys," one man said. "That's why we work with you so you can do better than we ever did."

"That's right," another affirmed.

"Can't be nobody that anybody want to be around unless you got some education—some paper that mean somethin'," a third man around a checker board in the dimly lighted room said.

The other boys with John saw how he was getting grilled. It made them feel as uncomfortable as John did.

"What are we supposed to do if the teacher don't like us?" John asked.

"Boy, like ain't got nothing to do with it," Shorty shot back. "What you need to like is getting good grades. Your momma don't buy you good clothes and send you to school expecting you to come home with D's and F's. You need to start doing right before it's too late."

"I don't want to be in that school no way," John said. "Teacher don't respect me."

"Boy, that don't make no difference whether the teacher respects you or not," said Shorty, wearing his classic suspenders and checkered shirt. "You need to get good grades—plain and simple—or you will be sweeping this here floor the rest of your life for pennies."

John picked up the broom to do some sweeping. He was upset. But deep down, he knew Shorty was right.

Doc tried to impress the boys who came into Du-Good Chemical that the fast change they made at his company or with the other black business-men in the 1200 block of South Jefferson Avenue was nothing compared with the big money they could make if they did well in school and earned college degrees. Doc always told them the story about his father, who worked more than 40 years as a brakeman for the Norfolk & Western Railway Co. "Papa started as a brakeman, and he left as a brakeman," Doc said. "He ended up training a lot of white guys who were promoted over him and became his boss.

"I was right upset with Papa for years, and so were my brothers because Papa would not help us get those good-paying jobs down on the railroad," Doc said while adding ingredients into a drum for the production of Du-Good Dry Shampoo.

"Why wouldn't he help you get a railroad job, Doc?" Jesse asked as he put labels on the gallon bottles that lined the tables.

"Papa saw that those jobs were going nowhere for blacks, and he thought his children could do better if they had college degrees," Doc said. "So Papa pushed us all to do well in school and provided us with the money to go to college. It was the best thing he could have done even way back then. You have to understand that there are at least two ways you can make money to support yourself and a family. You can use your back, which is what you do when you are doing this manual labor. There is nothing wrong with that. But you also can make money by using your head. Now here's the secret. Your head will last a lot longer than your back will. Your back—as strong as you might think you are—will give out after about 20 to 30 years.

"But if you are using your head to make a living, you will be able to work indefinitely as long as you take care of yourself. So I suggest that you start thinking about that. All of you do well in school so you can go to college and make good money. People who use their heads to make money don't get their hands dirty. They also are less likely to get all banged up and hurt."

Doc had sent Tommy to the store to get some bread and bologna for lunch. He had given Tommy $5 and knew how much change to expect back. Lunch was never exotic. It was just something to fill the empty spot that comes from working hard at Du-Good Chemical. Doc thought the least he could do for the boys who came to work was to provide them with a sandwich — albeit it meager—and some milk for nutrition.

Tommy was not necessarily the most trustworthy kid in the neighborhood. He also never went straight to the store or returned as quickly as the other boys waiting for lunch might have hoped. Jeff had to fire him when the register came up short at the end of a workday. Shorty chased Tommy away. Greasy Earl kept a close watch on him, suspecting that some of his tools went out the door when Tommy left the garage one day. Doc wanted to test Tommy's honesty and sent him to the store.

Tommy never could seem to help himself. The do unto others before they do unto you rule of the black neighborhood was too ingrained in him. Tommy returned an hour after he was sent to the store—a trip that should have taken no more than 15 minutes. He had the cheaper white bread that Doc insisted that he buy. He also had the cheap bologna. But he only gave Doc back 52 cents in change from a five-dollar bill.

"Where's the rest of it?" Doc asked.

"That's all there was, Doc," Tommy said fidgeting.

"You know that's not right!" Doc exclaimed. "Don't give me that. That bread at most cost 25 cents, and the bologna was no more than 95 cents. The tax was another 3 cents. That means you should have given me back $3.77. That also means you owe me $3.25 more than what you gave me."

Doc had an incredible mind for math and numbers. Tommy was not counting on that.

"Tommy, where's the rest of my money?" Doc demanded. Sweat poured from Doc's brow. The veins in his forehead jumped out. They always did when Doc was angry, and nothing made him angrier than when Doc thought he was being cheated by the kids he was trying to help.

Tommy fidgeted some more, and felt terribly uncomfortable as Doc crowded Tommy's personal space. It is the zone everyone has around his or her body—space that people never violated unless it was to express love or to confront someone. And this was not about love. Doc got in Tommy's face demanding that Tommy pay him back the $3.25 that Tommy took.

It was not a lot of money, and certainly Doc's life would not end if he did not get it back. But Doc made Tommy think the end of time was upon him for having misappropriated Doc's money. Doc and the other men in the 1200 block of South Jefferson Avenue could be terribly intimidating toward the boys when they had to be. But they did it to try to teach the kids the better principles of life. The boys had to know what real honesty was and integrity. They had to be about those things and more if they were to be successful as men themselves. Just as Tommy was struggling in school to make good grades, he was failing as he stood with his head down sheepishly in front of Doc. The other boys in the company normally would have laughed. But they didn't dare. They knew the wrath of Doc would turn on them if they did.

"Boy, until you come up with my $3.25 you are not welcomed back in this company, and don't expect to get a job here again," Doc said. "I want you to think long and hard about what you did. You blew $3.25 of my money, which will now cost you the $5 in pay that you would have gotten at the end of this week and the pay in future weeks that you could have earned here from working. Now I don't know about you, boy, but the math involved with what you did adds up against you.

"You get out of here, and don't come back, you hear? One of you boys let him out, and make sure the door is locked behind him."

There was a great finality to Doc's words, and Tommy felt the shame. That was hard for Tommy to do because he had grown up all of his life in the area. The streets were completely about getting over on everyone. Trust was not in the picture. Suddenly Tommy got a different view of what was right and what was wrong. He went home. To Doc's surprise, Tommy returned the next morning with the $3.25 he owed. Tommy hung his head in shame and told Doc he was sorry for what he did. Tommy promised that it would never happen again. Doc accepted Tommy's apology but added that he was going to be watching Tommy more closely. Doc got Tommy to understand that trust was a fleeting quality. It was difficult to earn and terribly easy to lose. Tommy got the message—loud and clear. So did the other boys in the 1200 block of South Jefferson Avenue.

◆　◆　◆　◆　◆

The 55-gallon drums rested silently inside Du-Good Chemical. They were the drums of chemicals delivered, used, taken away for refill and delivered again by 18-wheel tractor-trailers that dropped them off in the alley at the sliding door entrance to the manufacturing area of the company.

Doc was still in the hospital, still recovering, still unconscious. He was the last of the powerhouse of black men who took in kids in the neighborhood, gave them jobs and taught them in the process what they needed to know to be successful. No lessons in schools or in books could do the same. Fast-food and big-box jobs fall short. They want older teens who already have the skills. The vital, intermediate education about life was what Doc and the other now long dead men who dominated the 1200 block of South Jefferson Avenue provided. Doc, who tried to help a Hurricane Katrina victim, was now paying for doing what he had always done. He was in a fight for his life, a fight to go back as the last holdout of the black businesses in the neighborhood he had been part of for more than 60 years. If nothing else, Doc's will to reconnect with the life he loved would pull him back into the conscious world, where he would resume as he always had, being the African-American anchor in the 1200 block of South Jefferson Avenue.

CHAPTER 7

UP FROM SLAVERY, AMERICA'S STREETS

The boys who entered the black businesses in the 1200 block of South Jefferson Avenue all looked like street urchins straight out of a Dickens novel. None wore nice clothes. Certainly none had business suits or briefcases. They were rough-hewn, and nearly all of them behaved similarly. The black businessmen and Rev. Nance never gave the boys a chance to show their worst side—the hardness that the unforgiving concrete and merciless asphalt streets created in them. What the men saw in each of the boys was an opportunity for the youths to be better than the youth thought they ever could be. The men knew from personal experience and from seeing each new generation of boys roaming the neighborhood that each possessed an inner core of goodness. It is what many of the police and white passers-by chose not to notice. But the black men in the 1200 block of South Jefferson Avenue could sense that inner light. They saw it because each man had that core of goodness in himself. Many other, older, caring individuals had pulled it out of these black businessmen years before. It was a community tradition. The cost, however, of those black men being saved was extremely high. It is the cost that the slaves passed on to each successively free generation. The cost was that they had to detect the inner glow in every new generation, enlarge it and make it shine above the kids' worst inclinations. The boys had to be made to lose the rough edges of being boys and take on the responsibility of being men. They did it through learning the virtues of hard work and the lessons that go with each sweep of a broom, each shovel of coal, each weed pulled, each blade of grass cut, each thrust of a saw blade and each bundle or box lifted or stroke of paint applied until the coat was complete and good-looking. The money that the boys were paid was irrelevant—although none of them would say that. The lessons that shaped them into men were invaluable as were their teachers—the older black men themselves.

Regardless of how hard the black businessmen in the 1200 block of South Jefferson Avenue tried, the boys would still find ways to be mischievous—if they were lucky—or fall into deep, law-breaking trouble at the very worst. Sometimes trouble just found them. Doc would send the most trustworthy boys on sales routes telling them to go door to door peddling his products. He would give them 8-ounce bottles of Du-Good Hand Cleaner and Du-Good Cannonball Liniment, 4-ounce jars of Du-Good Lolo Pin Curl Cream and Du-Good Kreation face cream, a 2-ounce bottle of Du-Good Bull's Eye Mosquito Repellant, a 4-ounce bottle of Du-Good After Shave Lotion and an 8-ounce bottle of Du-Good Dry Shampoo. The briefcase the boys used contained about $20 worth of products. Doc promised each kid a 40 percent commission on what the boy sold. If the boy sold out that could mean at least $8 in commission on the products in addition to $5 at the end of the week for working every day at Du-Good Chemical. The boys, whom Doc trusted unless they proved otherwise, all lived for that kind of big payday. A few actually accomplished the goal and would always set back out on the sales route to try to peddle more products. People in the surrounding neighborhood were poor black folks. They didn't have much money, but they all wanted the kids to feel a sense of pride and a sense of accomplishment. When the urchins came to their door with Doc's products, and the adults knew Doc, they felt a need to buy something from the kids. Many would ask for the cheapest thing they could get, and the boys were eager to sell it to them. Older people wanted the liniment. It really did help relieve arthritis. The shade tree mechanics liked the Hand Cleaner. It did an exceptional job of cutting away grease, tar, paint and stains. Women who had hair or skin problems would get the Lolo or Kreation. Those products were not cheap, but they worked better than any other products on the market. Lolo set curls without the damage that pressing combs or lye-based products cause. Kreation helped deep clean the skin and relieve unwanted, uneven skin tones and blemishes. Doc always said he could have been a millionaire many times over as well as the boys who were his sales force if he had just had enough money to advertise his products and if his company were large enough to protect him from the big, white corporations, which were shameless about corporate espionage, enabling them to steal Doc's formulas. This was a recurring problem for Doc.

One summer's day, Doc sent his son Lewis out with Sam, one of the neighborhood boys who lived on Hickory Street. They were to scour the community for sales. The two of them did pretty well going door to door. They sold more than $10 worth of products. Sam was a good talker, and people believed him. He knew a lot of people in the neighborhood, and they knew and trusted him. It helped to have one of Doc's kids along. The two boys stopped to rest at Buder Park to get some water. It was hot out. But that did not compare with the heat of a big conflict that the two young salesmen encountered. They were quickly surrounded by a crowd of boys. The kids were not friendly. They wanted the money that Sam and Lewis had made from the sales, and they wanted the Du-Good products in the briefcase. Sam and Lewis refused to give up the goods. The boys in the park started to close the circle as they surrounded the two. Sam was always full of surprises. Faster than anyone could say his name, Sam pulled out a box cutter and struck menacingly at the loudest of the kids trying to take what the two had earned on that hot summer day. The circle around Sam and Lewis suddenly swung large as the eight to 10 boys jumped back. Sam had a wild look in his eyes. He would have cut any of the boys who tried to take what he had earned. He was looking forward to the special payday at Du-Good Chemical. Sam swung and cursed wildly at the boys who yelled incomprehensible things back at him. "Come on, Lewis! Run!" Sam took off toward an open gate on the other side of the park. Lewis followed, wondering why they should run when the box cutter clearly had the other kids backing up. Sam knew that the cutter could be taken away easily by the gang of other kids and would be used on him and Lewis. Sam hit the gate of the fence and sprinted along the top of the wall just outside the chain-link fence. The wall was about 2 feet wide and 10 feet high and ran parallel to the sidewalk on Hickory Street below. The wall got higher as Sam ran toward the corner at California Avenue. Lewis followed as fast as he could with the pack of boys close on his heels. There was a lot of yelling and screaming. A lot of profanity was hurled at Sam and Lewis. Sam suddenly disappeared off the wall. He had jumped and landed on the sidewalk at Hickory and California. He screamed from there for Lewis to jump. Lewis stopped and hesitated. The boys were close to grabbing him. Just before the first hand reached him, Lewis jumped. The force of the landing caused his knees to strike him in the face. The briefcase emptied onto the pavement. A bottle of Dry Shampoo broke. Sam scooped up the contents of the briefcase, collected Lewis and off they ran with the boys screaming from atop the wall. Those kids were not stupid. At that point, it was a 15-foot drop to the pavement, and they wanted no part of it. They were not the ones running, not the ones who were afraid for their lives. Sam and Lewis were. Sam and Lewis got back to Du-Good Chemical and explained the mishap. Doc was not pleased, and he became less assured about sending any boys on sales routes after that. Sam and Lewis had to pay for the broken bottle out of their commission. On balance they still made money. They just had less to share and to spend.

Sam seemed to change afterward. He knew that a mere box cutter would not deter the kids he encountered. He decided to take some of the metal that Doc had around Du-Good Chemical and use a grindstone to fashion the metal into knives. Lewis helped him. Together they made throwing knives, folding knives and hunting knives. The metal was not hardened steel like one finds in store-bought knives, but it was sufficient to do great damage. The boys would spend great amounts of time throwing the knives they had made into a door from the loading area into the furnace room. Thunk, thunk went the homemade knives as they hit the old wood. It was a miracle that no one opened that door and found a knife hurling at them. For many years to follow, Sam and Lewis always carried on them knives they had made.

Sam also had a serious temper and would not back down from any confrontation. One night, it proved nearly fatal. A man who worked as an attendant at a Clark service station on South Jefferson Avenue near Chouteau thought it was great fun to push and bully around the younger boys. It was his sport, and he loved it. Doc and the other black men in the neighborhood tried to get the kids not to walk to the station because they surely would be abused. The black businessmen and minister tried to get the boys to avoid places where the attendant hung out—especially the filling station itself. There were two on South Jefferson Avenue near Chouteau. On the west side of Jefferson was Les Jones Phillips 66 station. On the east side of the street was the Clark Oil and Refinery Corp. gas station. Many of the boys didn't listen—especially Sam. He went to the Clark service station one evening to buy candy. When the other stores had closed, candy at the filling station was a big night-time draw for the boys. The man grabbed and beat Sam just for sport. Sam went home, got a rifle and laid up in a vacant building across Jefferson Avenue from where the filling station was on the corner of South Jefferson Avenue and LaSalle Street. When the attendant came out, Sam shot him. The man collapsed. The police were called by someone who had stopped at the station for gas. An ambulance came. Police canvassed the area and arrested Sam. After many surgeries, the man Sam shot did live. But he would never walk again.

Some months passed before Sam showed up again at the large, sliding door entering from the alley to Du-Good Chemical. Doc was adding ingredients to a drum to prepare it to mix up more Dry Shampoo. "Look, Doc. It's Sam," one of the boys said pointing to Sam in the doorway. The bright sunshine in the alley made Sam into a silhouette. Doc squinted and realized that it was Sam, one of his best workers. "Sam! You've been gone so long I thought you were in jail!" Doc said, laughing. Sam looked down at the concrete floor. The sounds of the street and the alley filled the silence of the large room as the other workers looked up expecting a response from Sam just as Doc was. To Doc's and everyone else's surprise, Sam said, "I was." Sam had been locked up accused of shooting the man at the Clark station. He shared the painful story of those months with Doc and others in the big room. It was like a confessional. Doc told Sam he was welcomed to work at the company to stay out of trouble. He told Sam he would help and support him through the ordeal, and Doc did. The man whom Sam shot recovered but used a wheelchair the rest of his life. Sam recovered, too, eventually becoming a security guard.

John McSwine happened into Du-Good Chemical on the advice of his parents. John wasn't the brightest kid in the neighborhood. But he was a good person. He worked hard, he respected his elders and he took instruction well. John's folks thought that if he hung around Doc, he might have a better future. The future John was creating for himself wasn't the best in the neighborhood of pothole-filled streets and cracked and uneven sidewalks, and gap-toothed with missing houses and weed-strewn vacant lots. John was a big, muscular teenager, and he wanted to be a prize-fighter. He hung out at the community center gym, where he trained with a lot of other big kids. John, like a lot of black kids, had Olympic dreams. It was how they planned to sprint, dribble or fight their way out of the degradation of the ghetto and into a better life. Sure, they watched the Rev. Martin Luther King Jr. talk on TV. They heard him on the radio, telling of black people getting to the promise land here on Earth, but there was America's unpaid promissory note owed black people. King and all others marching with him hoped it would finally be made good. It was the hope that King and civil rights marchers worked for. Civil rights workers anticipated that their efforts would one day pay off. The boys hoped that the news they saw on television was true. Their reality, however, was very different. The boys witnessed daily the black men in their lives working in hard, dirty, dangerous, low-wage jobs. The black men were treated like less than dirt by whites. With the little money they made, the men would buy booze and often shoot craps against curbs and in alleys with other men hoping for easy, big money. Often they would only lose and be even worse off when they finally landed home. John wanted better, and so did many others living around the 1200 block of South Jefferson Avenue. So John followed his parents' advice and in the summer of 1967, rang the doorbell at Doc's company.

From the moment Doc poked his head from the middle arched window on the second floor of Du-Good Chemical, John instantly liked Doc. Doc was working in the lab. It was hot, and Doc had his shirt off and only a tank-top-like T-shirt covering his torso. Doc's muscular arms showed as he put one hand down on the windowsill to look out at John. "Be right down," Doc said. He ran down the winding, industrial steps and opened the arched front door. One had to climb onto the white limestone step from the street to walk inside. But John's frame was so large, he stood eye-to-eye with Doc, who was 5 feet 11 inches tall and wore a size 48 suit jacket. "What can I do for you, young man?" Doc asked.

"My parents sent me to see you," John said looking at the ground. "I was wanting to know if I could work for you."

"Come on inside," Doc said. "What's your name?"

"I'm John, John McSwine," John said. "My folks live just across the alley from you on Hickory."

"Oh yes," Doc replied. "I can see a family resemblance. You used to be a real little fella. Not anymore."

They both laughed. "Have you had something to eat?" Doc asked. "I am running a titration up in the lab. Can I make you a sandwich?"

"Sure," said John, who was never much for long conversations and was always hungry.

Doc stepped out of the office and into the kitchen. John followed. Doc took the bread and bologna from the old refrigerator. An old industrial-size freezer that held ether and other volatile chemicals substituted as a table. Doc put some brown paper napkins on the deep freeze and laid out the bread. He put one piece of bologna on the bread and topped it with another slice of bread. He handed the sandwich to John. They ate and talked. John told Doc he was in high school and was hoping to be a prizefighter someday. Doc asked how well John was doing in school. John said he mostly made C's. Doc asked whether that was acceptable. John said it would have to do. Doc promised John that he would do what he could to help John improve his grades. Meanwhile, John was welcome to come to Du-Good Chemical to work.

That began a friendship and working relationship that lasted a couple of years. When John wasn't at school or at the gym boxing he was at Du-Good Chemical. He liked it there. Doc always had a sandwich for him, a Coke to wash it down when times were good and there was a lot of work. John didn't mind the work. He also enjoyed getting Doc's dogs agitated. John would pretend to box the big black dog that Doc had. The dog, Blackie, would fight back trying to bite John's big hands. John would pull them back with a snap just out of Blackie's grasp. Occasionally a punch landed, and the dog became aggressive, barking and snapping. It was fun to watch, and John always laughed at the big dog. John could also tussle around the 55-gallon drums as easily as Doc could, and loading five and six boxes on a two-wheel dolly to put in the warehouse area was a snap for John. He was that big and strong. He was good with repairs, too. Doc was happy to teach John roofing, masonry work, carpentry, plumbing and electrical work. John wasn't the best student in school. But he took seriously all of the lessons Doc was willing to teach. Sometimes Doc took John to his home, which was in the Central West End at that time by Gaslight Square. They ate supper together, and then Doc drove John back to his home. They had become close. So it came as a surprise one day when John announced that he was joining the Marine Corps in 1969 to go fight in the Vietnam War. It was a four-year commitment. Doc wasn't happy. John explained that boxing wasn't really working out the way he wanted. He was fourth-rate, at best. John could take a punch, but he was slow, and the other heavyweight boxers were trying to emulate Muhammad Ali with a fast dance and hit-and-run style. John never boxed like that. Going into the Marine Corps was his only ticket to a good life. It saddened Doc to see such a good kid do that. Doc remembered what the military had done to his brothers. It killed one and left the other more than a little mentally unstable. Black men had a difficult time in the military, which was dominated by whites. Doc recalled that it was a lot like blacks from the Negro Leagues Baseball being drafted into the white National and American leagues. It was great to cross the color line and play ball for big money. Doc remembered the difficulties and racial slurs that black ball players faced from 1947, when Jackie Robinson went to play for the Brooklyn Dodgers well into the 1960s. In one instance, Doc recalled someone in a ball stadium calling a black player "nigger." That caused the incensed black player to charge the seats with a baseball bat. He had to be pulled down and held back until he calmed down. Racism was everywhere, and it was difficult for some blacks not to strike back. Doc often described to the boys how radio announcers who were calling the fight between Joe Louis and James J. Braddock for the heavyweight boxing title on June 22, 1937, made it sound as if Louis were losing badly. It wasn't until Louis knocked out Braddock in round eight that people knew that the fight had been called against the first black man in competition to become the Heavyweight Champion of the world since Jack Johnson did it at the turn of the century.

After John landed in Vietnam, he would write to Doc frequently. Then one day, the letters stopped. Doc learned from John's family that he had been killed by a grenade in Vietnam on April 23, 1969. Born April 9, 1947, he was only 22 years old when he died in Quang Tri, South Vietnam. The other details of his death remain unclear. Doc, who hated attending funerals, took his family to John's service when John's remains were returned to St. Louis. In Doc's own way, it spoke volumes of how he felt about John and his personal sense of loss over a hard-working young man who had tremendous potential. John Henry McSwine's name is on the wall of the Vietnam Veterans Memorial in Washington, D.C., with more than 50,000 other American soldiers killed in that senseless war. He is buried at Jefferson Barrack's National Cemetery.

Doc not only helped the boys in the neighborhood see that there was more to life than what they could touch, see, smell, hear and taste in their community. He told them stories to help illustrate it. One was "The Grasshopper and the Ant." Doc hoped the boys would be more like the ant, living frugally instead of like the grasshopper, who frittered away his resources so that he had nothing to live on when times got bad. Doc constantly shared with the boys stories about doing what's right, honest and just. He told the boys constantly that there was the easy way to learn such lessons, and that was through listening to advice from others and following good examples. Then there was the hard way to go through life and that was through acting impulsively and emotionally instead of thoughtfully, and never learning from the mistakes of oneself or others.

Doc also helped members of his own family. Ross Newsome Jr. was the oldest child of his sister, Sherley, and her husband, Ross Sr. Ross was a kid of middle-class upbringing and was not at all used to the rust-and-steel, bricks-and-mortar work often associated with Du-Good Chemical. Sherley was a librarian, and Big Ross worked as an agricultural extension agent in Virginia. They lived in Ettrick, Va., outside of Petersburg. Little Ross spent a summer with Doc. They traveled the country in one of Doc's old, barely working cars. The metal floorboards were mostly rusted out and passengers would see the pavement speed by from inside the car and feel the air on cold winter days. The tires were often either old or threadbare. With Doc, Ross had to do a lot of manual labor, and getting dirty was unavoidable. Tuck-pointing one of the back walls in Doc's company was one of the tasks Doc gave to Ross. Ross also needed to study under Doc to get a science course he needed out of the way so he could enter the Massachusetts Institute of Technology. Ross didn't have the ragged edge borne from street life that the other boys, who frequented Doc's place had. He dripped with great intelligence. Doc was happy to provide the science course that Ross needed to get into MIT in Boston. The lessons amid the hard work came naturally at Du-Good Chemical. Doc was a demanding teacher. That often meant Ross had to stay up exceedingly late to get the tutelage from Doc as Doc stood over Bunsen burners running analysis while doing other lab work. In the evening, Doc assigned homework, which Doc graded the next day. More lectures occurred amid the tuck-pointing of the masonry at the company. The building was constructed in the late 1800s and often required a lot of maintenance. First the streetcars and then the heavy trucks and buses provided a merciless pounding in the street that vibrated through the bricks and mortar of every building on South Jefferson Avenue. Ross had to help with other maintenance on Doc's building. When the summer was over amid all of the work, Ross was able to pass the tests at MIT, showing he had received the needed instruction from Doc for the science class he lacked. Ross entered the elite college majoring in nuclear physics. He graduated with his PhD and later went on to work in the nuclear technology industry and teach at Rutgers University.

Life at Du-Good Chemical wasn't all work for Doc and the youths who wandered in from the street. Doc had put up a basketball hoop on a large oak tree in the loading area so the guys could shoot a few hoops when they were taking a break. Doc's favorite sport was golf, especially when the sun was shining and the weather was good. Doc and one of his brothers, William Sherwood "Shingy" Diuguid, would play every Sunday, and during the week they would sneak away from work to get in nine holes of golf. There was a friendly sibling rivalry. The two would bet each other something nominal such as a nickel a hole for the person who won the round and a nickel for the player first on the green and a nickel for whoever ended up with the lowest score. It seemed kind of senseless, but those two fought over those nickels as if they were thousand-dollar bets. Doc would accuse Shingy of cheating such as marking a ball on the green with a coin, taking care to place the marker in front of the ball. Then when it was Shingy's shot, he would place the ball in front of the marker giving himself a few inches' advantage. Doc would yawl as if someone had poked a pin in him as he complained that Shingy was cheating. Shingy and Doc accused each other of using their putters to make tracks from their balls to the holes on the green. The goal was so the ball could follow the track right to the pin. Each brother, of course, denied the accusation

Ross' cousin, William "Bill" McDaniel, was just as smart as Ross was, but a lot more gregarious. Doc called him Crazy Bill. Bill was the only child of Doc's other sister, Elwyza, and her husband, Mac. Elwyza was a librarian, and Mac was a school principal in Washington, N.C. Doc and Bill often got into great debates, and laughed outrageously. Bill ended up working one summer at Du-Good Chemical, too. He worked harder, however, to get out of doing hard work. Doc was relentless in making sure that the labor got done, and Bill did his part. Bill also had to help tuck-point a back wall one hot summer. Doc promised him a $100 if the work got done. The back room was tremendously hot in the St. Louis heat and humidity. Doc laughed about how the summer shrank Bill's appetite for that money. Bill sniffed that no one in his right mind could do the work in that heat. But Butch, a boy who lived near Du-Good Chemical, took on the task and completed it quite neatly in a few weeks. Doc never let Bill forget that. No job is too great for any man to do especially if it originally was done by a man. Bill went to college and studied to be a doctor. Doc recalled how Bill fell asleep behind the wheel of a car one night. Bill was driving a Renault, and he tore up the little car. Bill, however, survived. He played basketball in college, and after getting his medical degree, Bill did his residency in St. Louis at Homer G. Phillips Hospital. He studied to be a psychiatrist, and moved back to Washington, D.C., to establish his practice.

Jesse Talley started coming by Du-Good Chemical alone initially. He lived in the apartment building over Jeff's grocery store with his mother and sisters. Jesse was from a large family. He was a boisterous kid with a string-bean-thin body and sported a big square head hidden partly by an oversized Afro. Jesse constantly combed his hair with a pick, however, his hair stood uneven most of the time, instead of being well-shaped. Jesse's Afro only looked good after he had come from the barbershop having gotten a neat trim. Jesse had a quick comeback for every suggestion or lecture that Doc offered, and Doc offered them liberally. But Doc saw something important in Jesse. Here was a bright kid who had a good future. Jesse just needed guidance and a direction. He wasn't the best student in school, but Jesse had tremendous potential. The key was to ensure that his vast talents—particularly for talking—got steered in the right direction. Doc wanted to do that. He put Jesse to work in the manufacturing plant and taught him to do the hard, nasty work of repairing property that Doc owned.

Jesse had a keen interest in mischief. Doc's sister-in-law, Martha, spotted that when she met Jesse on a trip Doc took to her house to pick up some things in his old red-panel 1952 Dodge truck. Martha said Jesse had roving eyes that tracked everything of value in her home, and she didn't trust him. Jesse also enjoyed causing discontent among the workers at Du-Good Chemical and elsewhere. A lot of people talk about "pissing contests." Jesse actually started one among the males at Doc's company. The boys lined up at the trough, which had been used for surgeries on large animals when the place was a veterinarian hospital. The boys then would see who could urinate the farthest in the 15-foot-long, 5-foot-wide and foot deep concrete area. Jesse had everyone beat with a stream that literally shot out 10 feet. That is until Doc's son, Vincent, stepped forward, unzipped and let his natural water flow. Vincent bore down, and literally pissed out the window that was on the far wall of the trough and 6 feet above the ground. Jesse, who loved to brag, tried mightily to extend his stream. He got it to go an additional 2 feet before he doubled over in pain. Vincent easily won.

Jesse enjoyed going to one apartment building to do repairs—especially for Mrs. Jones. She had to have been well into her 90s, if not 100 years old. Jesse said if Mrs. Jones wasn't born a slave herself, she had to have been the daughter of slaves. Her frame was bent and her feet were flat and twisted with arthritis. Her gray hair was short, tightly curled and nearly all of it was gone. She wore a house robe, slippers and a bandana on her head. Her English was the broken dialect of the South. She was always friendly and kind. Doc treated her with the respect that elders deserved, and he insisted that his kids and the boys from the neighborhood who worked with him treat Mrs. Jones likewise. That was part of the lesson that the boys picked up from black businessmen in the 1200 block of South Jefferson Avenue. Everyone merited respect until that person proved that he or she was unworthy of such treatment. Jesse, however, did enjoy mimicking the deepness of Mrs. Jones voice and the way in which she talked.

After a few weeks of earning some pay from Du-Good Chemical, Jesse started showing up at Doc's door with a friend from school named Tommy. Tommy was a brooding boy who was half white. His father was black. Tommy lived with his mother. He looked either Jewish or Italian. His hair was a dark brown and straight. Black kids he knew teased him, saying he was white when he wasn't. Tommy mumbled when he bothered to talk at all. Jesse enjoyed teasing Tommy, who often would push or punch Jesse. Jesse had a quick wit, which Tommy was ill-equipped to handle. Tommy also wasn't the best worker. He did his best to try to arrive at Du-Good Chemical after all of the work had been completed. Often the tasks that Doc had the boys take on went longer than expected. Tommy would arrive, thinking everything was done, but he would get drawn into working, too. Jesse enjoyed proving that Tommy was a thief who was always shirking work.

Hanging out with Doc, the boys got to learn how to do plumbing, electrical work, carpentry, fence building and mending, outdoor tree trimming, auto mechanics, roofing and masonry among other things. No repair was too great for Doc to take on. He instilled in the boys that the work they did helped them to save money and to be proud of themselves as black men. One onerous task involved rebuilding the 6-foot-high wood fence at Du-Good Chemical. Doc used railroad ties for posts, which required the holes—dug by hand with post-hole diggers—to go down 5 feet in the ground. That was no easy task because they had to be planted exactly where the old ones were anchored. Doc always put broken bricks and rocks into the hole to more firmly hold the railroad ties in place instead of pouring concrete around the posts. That was more costly. Jesse and Tommy happened to arrive to help. The work was not going at all well, and then it started to rain. Doc got a little cross with the boys and his own children when they wanted to go inside. "We've got work to do!" Doc demanded, asking for tools to be handed to him as he worked to get the new posts level. "If this fence isn't put back up today, those dogs will get out."

Tommy wasn't at all concerned. Doc continued to work with Jesse's help and assistance from his own kids. Tommy wandered off. Doc told him not to bother to come back. The fence got repaired despite Tommy's negligence. Tommy did return to Du-Good Chemical, however, it was not to work or to help. Tommy left abruptly and let Doc's dogs go in the alley. They ran away. Doc and some of the other boys managed to find the big dog, Blackie. That dog loved to eat, and he never wanted to miss any meals. He wandered back to Du-Good Chemical when he got hungry, which was at night when he normally got his supper. The other dog, Mutt, never returned. That dog had been abused before Doc got him, therefore he was easily frightened. He was a smaller, cream-colored, long-haired, good-looking pooch.

Doc sent boys who had worked at his company throughout the Southside community looking for that dog. Doc did not like losing anything. He had Lewis drive the company truck with some of the older boys to the St. Louis dog pound. It was there that the boys encountered something they were not prepared to experience and something none would ever forget. The person at the counter motioned the boys toward a door behind the counter. The boys had to enter so they could determine whether any of the dozens of incessantly barking dogs in the kennel belonged to Du-Good Chemical. The white worker at the front desk couldn't have cared less about his job or those dogs. He just didn't want to be around them or any of the people seeking help. The boys understood why when they opened the soundproof door. A cacophony of barking beat their eardrums. It got louder as the boys walked down the long poorly lighted corridor, which was filled floor to ceiling with dog pins on both sides. It was scary watching the many dogs lunge at the gates as if they would bite the boys if any one of the boys ventured too closely to the chain-link fences that held the dogs back. The boys walked with great trepidation, concerned that one of the gates might have been left open. What was worse than the barking and the attacking motions of the dogs was the incredible odor of dog manure, urine, canine halitosis and funk. It made it difficult for the boys to breathe and even see, and the odor got stronger with each step the boys made toward the end of the long corridor. The boys' eyes started to water from the stench. It was as oppressive as anything they had ever experienced in their young lives. They struggled to make it to the end of the building still looking for Mutt, cursing Tommy and holding on to each other for strength. They got toward the back without seeing Mutt among the many dogs. As they neared the end of the cages, they noticed something coming into focus. It was a rail-thin, older black man sitting in an old wooden, white chair, which he had tipped back on two legs as he reclined. In the man's hands was a bologna sandwich on white bread. He was enjoying his lunch. The noise and the horrible odor, which greatly offended the senses of the boys and the white man at the front desk, were of no consequence to the black man in the back who was enjoying his sandwich. It was an object lesson, and the boys could not stop talking about it long after they left empty-handed in their quest for Doc's dog

The boys never did find Mutt, but the unforgettable scene of that old black man eating a sandwich was a testament to what human beings can endure once their senses adapt. The worst conditions were what slaves had to live and work in. They had to put up with environments like no other in this country. It was what has been black people's hallmark of experiences and why they have managed to triumph over adversity despite forces set to defeat them. It is why Doc and the other black men in the 1200 block of South Jefferson Avenue never surrendered their dreams of being independent business owners and tried to instill in the boys who landed at their doors the same steadfast virtues that propelled them.

One young man was Rubin Crenshaw. Doc called him Crawfish Crenshaw because despite being a very bright kid, Crenshaw would work mightily to get out of doing hard work. Doc said Crenshaw had an excuse for everything and wiggled free of manual labor. Crenshaw was good at math and science and hung out a lot in the lab with Doc assisting with computations and lending an ear to Doc's 50,000-foot-elevation talk about chemistry. That left a lot of the boys flat-footed, but Crenshaw loved it. Crenshaw eventually became an electrical engineer.

Charlie Thomas was the opposite of Crenshaw. He loved hard work and took on jobs at Du-Good Chemical with gusto. The kid was strong, too. Doc enjoyed working with Charlie. Charlie, who enjoyed farming some acreage outside of St. Louis, went on to a career in chemistry. Doc helped him get on with a big company, and that is where he stayed until he retired.

Another young guy who worked for Doc was Nathan Johnson. He was a big man. Nathan became a salesman for Du-Good Chemical, and he put his heart into that work just as much as any other job he took on around the company. Nathan sold Du-Good products throughout the South, keeping delivery trucks coming to the side door for product pickups. Because of Nathan's work, younger boys labeled bottles, filled orders, boxed goods and kept the inventory up. When Nathan Johnson returned to Du-Good Chemical to collect his 40 percent commission he would grab the nearest boy working at the company, lift the kid up in his big arms and give the kid the fiercest "bear hug" imaginable. He literally would squeeze the breath out of the boys. But they loved it. No one had ever hugged them like that—particularly a black man. It was the kind of hands-on love that the kids needed. Sure they knew that the black men in the 1200 block of South Jefferson Avenue cared about them, but the bear hugs made it incredibly real. The bear hugs made Doc laugh. Nathan Johnson did, too. The promise or just the possibility of bear hugs happening again when Nathan Johnson was back in town was enough to keep the boys returning to Doc's door.

◆ ◆ ◆ ◆ ◆

The nurses in the intensive-care unit weren't particularly friendly. They weren't hostile either. They simply had work to do, tending to many patients like Doc. There were infinite needs and precious little time. The bed space on the institutional tile floor was scarce. When the electronic doors to the area swung open, they always hoped it was just family members coming to see a loved one who had befallen some unexpected trauma. Car accidents happened too often. Gunplay as well, landing the unlucky ones in the ICU. They were always messy. Assaults like Doc's weren't good either. People could go either way. It depended on their will to live and their physical strength. Age played a role, too. Doc was 89 years old. Because of his age, the nurses didn't hold out much hope. But he had vital signs of a man half his age, and the longer he lasted—though unconscious—the more hope they gave his worried family for his recovery. While Doc's middle-age children were away, someone came through and dropped off a framed photograph of Doc in a suit. It was merely a head shot, but he looked engaged in a discussion and full of life and joy for the sciences. Doc's kids marveled over the picture and wondered who had taken the time to share such a wonderful photograph with Doc. It captured the person his adult kids wanted Doc to return to being.

CHAPTER 8

NEVER ENDING—CONSTANT REPAIR

The old buildings that Doc owned needed constant repair. Doc kept the 1952 red panel Dodge truck for making deliveries of his products to beauty stores, drugstore and filling stations. He also used it to drive through old neighborhoods looking for demolition crews tearing down old buildings. St. Louis is an old, eastern-style, red-brick city. Nearly all of the buildings had been made of brick, giving the town a uniform, drab, dried-blood color. Unfortunately, even brick buildings go bad. A lot of the old structures, suffered deferred maintenance and no tuck-pointing. Many had old electrical wiring and fixtures. In addition, the buildings had deteriorating roofing or corroded, leaky plumbing. The neighborhoods were filled with houses and commercial buildings with such problems.

White flight during the blockbusting of the 1950s, 1960s and 1970s compounded the deterioration. Federal urban renewal programs then enabled many low-income families to buy homes that they couldn't afford and didn't know how to maintain. Vacancies were inevitable, and then the always eager and waiting criminal element moved in, stripping the homes of salvageable plumbing, copper wire and fixtures. Water gushing from the disconnected plumbing would fill the interiors, irreparably damaging the structures. That pattern was repeated throughout the South Side of St. Louis. Many homes had to be demolished, leaving communities looking as if a war had been waged in them, and the people lost the battle. It was as if aerial bombings had destroyed both the residences and the community. It was part of a plan to move the wealth, the white people and the businesses from the city to the suburbs. It was meant to leave whites in newer, better homes and blacks isolated in despair, hopelessness and deterioration with poor schools, unsafe conditions, few opportunities, and few businesses or jobs.

The teardowns taking place were nearly all done by black men. They were lean fellows. Many wore dirty jeans, T-shirts and ball caps in the summer. They were mostly guys who had little education, few marketable skills and were happy to get the jobs doing the dirty work. They called it construction, but it was really destruction. The men were dusty from the tops of their tightly curled hair to the soles of their thick shoes, which were meant to protect them from rusty nails. Part of their job was to pull the boards and bricks from the buildings. They also had to remove all of the nails from the salvageable boards and using a flat piece of steel, which they held in their thickly calloused hands, the men would beat any stubborn mortar from the bricks and then stack the bricks on pallets. The bricks and boards were resold for newer homes.

Doc knew that the demolition sites were great locations to get bargains on building material—particularly if the foreman and the owner of the company doing the work were not there. For a few bucks, the black men doing the dirty work would let Doc and the boys he had with him load the Dodge truck with whatever Doc could haul away. They would let him take the boards and the bricks that still needed to be stripped of rusty nails and cleaned of mortar. A lot of the mortar just crumbled to the touch. But some of it held to the bricks as if they were made to be inseparable. Many of the nails in the old wood were square indicating they perhaps had been forged by a blacksmith nearly a century ago.

Doc needed boards for a fence repair. He pulled up to a place on Park Avenue near the Compton Heights neighborhood where some black men in a crew were working. The names of the streets spoke to the luxury homes, businesses and churches that the area long ago showcased. Doc pulled up to the driveway of a business that was being pried apart by a team of black men. The sun was already out, casting long, distorted, morning shadows into the street. Most of the back of the 1½-story building had been dismantled, leaving only the white-brick façade with its knocked out windows and doors. From the street Doc could see stacks of good-looking lumber and pallets of brick ready to be loaded onto large flatbed trucks sitting in the driveway. The men at this site had worked hard all week.

Overall black men were the undervalued, underappreciated workhorses of America. They carried the country on their backs when its economy was agrarian-based and the wealth in the South was in land, crops and black people as human property. Black men built the halls of power in the United States from its White House to the Capitol and other buildings of government including the Supreme Court and more. They worked with Chinese, Mexican and European immigrants to build the railroads and industries coast to coast. They often did the most dangerous, dirtiest work imaginable usually because it was all that was available for them. Black men fought valiantly in every war in this country in addition to being the workhorses, moving people, providing meals and equipment and even carrying out the dead. And in the 1950s and 1960s when cities had to come down—one house and one business at a time—black men did that dirty work, too. Yet they continued to have to put up with racism and be the butt of so-called humor.

After sharing the story, Doc stepped from his truck, which had "Du-Good Chemical" and some of his products' names painted on the side. Doc walked toward the black men working at the demolition site. The boys in the truck could hear some of the conversation. The Dodge truck had only the front driver's and passenger's seats. The four boys inside sat on the wheel wells in the back. Doc came back to the truck and opened the back doors. The boys hopped out. Doc had them grab several long 4-by-4-inch, 8-foot-long posts, 2-by-4-inch, 8-foot-long studs, several planks that made up the floor of the buildings' roofs and 2-by-8-inch and 2-by-6-inch rafters—each more than 12 feet long. The boys filled the truck with the boards. Doc had them throw in several dozen bricks, which he also needed for work on his old buildings. Nails in the boards snagged the boys' shirts and pants, tearing some of them. Doc cautioned them to be careful. None of the bricks was cleaned of mortar. A lot of work remained to get the $5 truckload of building materials ready for use. The black men at the demolition site thought they had struck gold collecting $5, which the company responsible for the demolition would never see. The money would help buy the men a grand lunch, which would go nicely with the five watermelons they had sitting in the shade under the flatbed truck they were loading.

After filling his truck, Doc told the boys with him to get inside. He then roped the back doors together to secure the wood. Doc also tied a red flag to the end of the boards, which hung far out into the street. The law required the warning flag for other cars' safety. The back end of the truck hung low and the end of the boards was even lower. The truck—with its 6-volt battery, three-on-the-tree gearshift and separate starter pedal—fired up. Doc struggled to get the gearshift to go into first, shoving the stick high into reverse first with the clutch fully depressed and then throwing the thing hard into first gear. He succeeded, letting the clutch out slowly while giving gas to the old truck. It inched forward struggling with its load. Doc suddenly had to stop as the flatbed truck, with its load of lumber and bricks, drove into Doc's path. The driver apparently forgot that the watermelons were under his truck. He ran over all of them. The noise of the bursting melons sent a wave of anguish and anger through the team of black workers on the demolition crew. They could not believe that the treat they had savored was gone. They had anticipated eating the sweet fruit from the moment they bought the watermelons from a farmer selling them that morning from the back of a pickup truck. All work stopped at the demolition site as the men cursed the loss. Doc explained to the boys, who were laughing as they all strained to look out the front and passenger windows, that despite watermelon being a stereotypical food for black people, that it actually was filled with nutrients such as potassium, calcium, water and fiber. Eating watermelon actually was good for anyone. The stereotype was a takeaway meant to get black people to shun something that would be of great benefit to them. But the boys still thought the scene was hilarious, the black men screaming and raising their hands to the heavens as they walked in agony around the flatbed truck, cursing the driver as if they had just lost their best friend.

If Norman Rockwell painted pictures from what might have been characterized as Negro-Americana, he would have captured many of the everyday scenes in the 1200 block of South Jefferson Avenue. They would have been pictures of black men dressed in everything from business suits to overalls and in every possible hue working with sleeves rolled up and sweat dripping down, trying to grow their businesses and earn a living to feed their families, keep a roof over their heads, pay their taxes and be good citizens. They were a never-give-up, never-give-in lot. Sweating to get things done was a way of life. It couldn't be helped in St. Louis, where the humidity in the summer matched and often exceeded the high temperature, and the air stayed as still as thieves, waiting and looking for any opportunity to pounce. Cooler weather always seemed to blow elsewhere. Perspiration dripped from the men's brows and stayed on their chests. When his brother, William Sherwood Diuguid, also known as "Shingy," would come over they would take turns giving each other haircuts in the manufacturing area, where the lighting made it easier to see. Their father, Lewis Walter Diuguid, had taught them and his other sons to cut each other's hair. Doc had the boys at Du-Good Chemical sweep up the growing pile of gray hairs as each follicle succumbed to the sharp scissors that the amateur barbers wielded. Cutting hair was a way to save money and to discuss politics and family and community concerns. Shingy was a Howard University graduate with a law degree. He became the first elected black magistrate judge in St. Louis. When the two Diuguid brothers got together, the talk was often about golf—each was fiercely competitive. They also discussed business and race relations during the height of the Civil Rights Movement. Each envisioned better times ahead for young people. The boys who hustled for change at Du-Good Chemical got to see how real black men interacted. They learned about serious conversations. They picked up the dreams and hopes black men had for their children and the high standards of performance that Doc and Shingy insisted on from young people. The boys learned how real black men could joke about shots missed playing golf, who was best at the game and who was forever bluffing. The boys also witnessed that disputes and arguments could end amicably. No gunshots were fired; no one got hurt. Everyone walked away whole. Coming back together again out of need and family was never a doubt.

During office hours at Du-Good Chemical, the boys were prone to mischief. Doc knew that so he interested them in building go-karts like the ones they saw other kids on the street riding. The boys functioned as engines as they ran and pushed the driver. The carts went as fast as the boys could run. Other kids on South Jefferson Avenue would use nails for axles and a larger nail to connect the front wheels to the one-board frame. The kids who worked at Du-Good Chemical had access to tools, bolts, real axles and wheels. The other kids in the neighborhood mostly got their wheels from cannibalizing shopping carts. Those wheels were not the best, but they rolled fairly fast. The wheels at Doc's company had ball bearings, enabling them to fly in comparison. The real go-carts axles helped, too, allowing the hub of the wheel to fit securely to the frame providing stability and speed. None of the go-karts had steering mechanisms beyond the basic rope, bolts and wheels. The boys with their calloused hands were formidable adversaries. When Doc was finished in the manufacturing area for the evening and went upstairs to do lab work, the boys would slip out to sit on the limestone step leading into the company. They would watch the other go-karts go down the hill in front of Du-Good Chemical. The course ran from Rutger Street at the south end of the block to the north at Hickory Street, where a fireplug stood as a road hazard at the end of the block. That also was where every go-kart driver had to lean radically to the left and turn hard to get safely around the corner. There were no brakes to slow the vehicle down. Most of the competitors managed to steer around the hydrant. Bouncing off the curb and into the street meant bent axles for sure and possibly a run-in with a car if the street wasn't clear.

Only a few of boys plowed into the fire hydrant. Those kids have scars to this day from the crushing encounters. When the boys were not racing and trying to just be boys, they had chores to perform at Du-Good Chemical. That was how they earned the pay that brought them to Doc's door. The go-karts they built often got pressed into service. Doc had one set of boys go to a demolition site nearby, load some bricks on the go-kart and haul them back to Du-Good Chemical. On another occasion the boys had to load the go-kart with long planks. That was quite a sight to see for passing motorists. There was hardly a need to tie the wood down to warn people of the hazard on the road. The boys just pushed harder to get the wood and bricks back to Doc's company. Those boards and bricks also had to be cleaned of construction debris so they could be used on projects that Doc had planned. Surprisingly, the boys never got stopped by the police and asked where they were going. It was understood that they were working for Doc.

The black men who governed life in the 1200 block of South Jefferson Avenue knew that there was no fast, easy way to make a living. No one was going to strike it rich overnight and outdo everyone else. They knew that they had to proceed at a slow, steady pace and account for every penny that they spent and that they took in. By being mindful of their pennies, they could make gains by inching ahead. Extending themselves beyond that would leave them open to trouble. Too many people landed on those rocks. It was an ages-old story that dates back to black farmers after slavery. They quickly learned that neither the federal government nor bankers were their friends. They had to make it on their own or they would be in trouble.

The men in the 1200 block of South Jefferson Avenue believed that the only way they could make it was to run the race of life like mules—strong, certain and steady. They had to pull their wagonload—past the prejudices and the stereotypes—and they did it well. Sometimes they got to step onto life's racetrack and really show how well they could perform. Sometimes they even got to enter the winner's circle. But mostly they had to stay strapped to their wagon—often pulling a load no one else would haul. However, the work had the greater purpose of helping others. The black men instilled in the boys a strong sense of business and ethics and added a sense of unmistakable pride, so the boys would feel it for who they were as African Americans. They also instilled in the boys a sense of pride in who they were as African Americans.

They helped the boys realize that they would grow to be men sooner than the boys realized. They helped the boys understand that a lot of whites would never accept them as men. To some white folks, they would always be boys.

The black men in the 1200 block of South Jefferson Avenue made the boys aware of a more subtle form of prejudice. Black men, regardless of age, rank or title, would be referred to by their first names only—never "Mister." This was why black men like Doc always used their first and middle initials only when signing their name. Doc was always Dr. L.I. Diuguid—never Lincoln Diuguid. Doc hated his middle name, Isaiah, because he was named after an uncle who Doc and other family members recalled was particularly lazy. That characterization didn't fit Doc. The use of first and middle initials prevented whites from calling blacks by their first names. It was a well-practiced habit by many older African Americans in post-slavery generations in every region of the country. The habit appears to have died out in the post-Civil Rights Era as more blacks have assimilated into the mainstream. Doc also hated being called the "baby" of his family even though he was the youngest of nine children. Doc didn't like being viewed as less than anyone. A lot of those African American survival practices have vanished.

When Doc had to do masonry repairs at Du-Good Chemical or at the apartment buildings he owned, he mixed the cement with sand himself rather than pay for sacks of ready-mix. It was cheaper, and cheap was how the black men in the 1200 block of South Jefferson Avenue were able to survive. The mantra among blacks dating back to slavery was, "We can do so much with so little so often that we've finally gotten it into our heads that we can do just about anything with nothing at all." Doc would send one of the boys at his company down to Atlas Hardware Store on Chouteau and Ohio avenues. It was an old, two-story building with a large plate-glass window in front. At one time it had a stately purpose, and no doubt was surrounded by other similarly elegant buildings with ornate ironwork and decorative wood carvings and stones. Time has not been friendly to the block. LaSalle Plumbing and Atlas Hardware were two of the few buildings left standing on the north side of Chouteau. In back of Atlas was a new, heavy machinery equipment storage yard and behind that were railroad yards. The old, unfinished, dirty planks that made up the floorboards at Atlas creaked when people—mostly men and boys—walked across them. At LaSalle Plumbing, over the then-ancient cash register was a picture of two babies holding out their diapers and looking into them. The caption read, "Plumbing, just like with males and females, there's a difference." It seemed to generate laughs from newcomers. Atlas had just about everything for repairs on old property—in that community there was an abundance of need for repairs. Some of the boys whom Doc sent to Atlas for cement, often tried to walk back with the load. However, each sack weighed 90 pounds. Doc would tell them to take a two-wheeled dolly to haul back the material. Stupidly, one of Doc's sons thought 90 pounds wasn't a lot of weight. Over short distances, he was right. However, carried a half-mile or more, the load becomes nearly impossible. Yet, Lewie, as Doc called him, managed to soldier the bag back to Du-Good Chemical, even though it was only 40 pounds lighter than he was.

Doc made trips to the Mississippi River to get sand. That was also a strenuous haul. The river channel was constantly being dredged for sand by a company whose job was to keep barge traffic flowing. Doc knew just where to drive his truck to get a load. Never mind that some of the sand would sift through the gaps in the wood floorboards of the truck on the drive back to Du-Good Chemical. Doc would get enough sand to still have plenty for his uses with the cement. Doc would pay a few bucks to some guy at the gate to the river dredging company. Then he'd have the boys shovel sand into the truck—not so much that the weight would blow the old tires. Once, no one was around so Doc got the boys to shovel sand into his truck, figuring that someone would come by eventually. No one ever did. Doc and the boys drove off with the truck loaded with a mound of sand assuming he would return later and give someone at the company a couple of bucks. Honesty matters. However, honesty is one of those virtues that becomes a character flaw growing up in too many poor, inner-city neighborhoods. It was how the men in the 1200 block of South Jefferson Avenue helped demonstrate human virtues to the boys. These were invaluable traits that the boys otherwise might not have acquire. On the street, they learned well how to cuss, spit, lie, cheat, steal, fight, and take advantage of girls and women. Among their peers, those traits were rewarded in the inner city, which was pocked with massive cavities of need and want. Getting over on others was embraced as the smart and only thing to do in ghetto communities. The kids learned too well to fight for everything even if it meant taking things from others and feeling justified if they had to kill or seriously hurt someone. They learned quickly after stepping from under the protective umbrella of their parents that when they got tossed to the wolves, they had two choices and not a lot of time to decide: They could either be victims and prey for the other wolves, or they must develop a taste for wolf meat and fight back.

Doc and the other black businessmen in the 1200 block of South Jefferson Avenue would try to teach the boys differently. They would often send the boys outside to pull the grass and weeds growing in the cracks of the side-walk. It taught them cleanliness and the value of hard work even if the weeds grew back the next week and had to be pulled all over again. Doc told the other businessmen that the roots of the unwanted plants would exert a force on the concrete greater than having a tractor-trailer driving over the side-walk. As the plants grew, the force would destroy the walkway, leaving it a cracked mess, which would then be a great city-forced expense for the men when the sidewalk had to be replaced. The boys would be sent outside with small screwdrivers. They had to use the tools to dig into the cracks of the sidewalk and pry the grass and weeds up by the roots so the plants would not return. The dirty, painful chore seemed almost impossible. The boys would sit on the pavement to keep from having the unforgiving concrete grind into their hands and knees. They would chat with each other as they did the work, throwing the uprooted plants into the street. It was a thankless job. The sidewalk in front of the black businesses seemed to stretch forever. It seemed so easy to walk, faster to run but impossible to dig out one unwanted weed. The boys did their best, usually taking out the bigger weeds. Sometimes they would scrape the tops from the rest just to make the sidewalk look clean and weed- and grass-free. But inevitably, a crappy job with the crabgrass meant that the boys would be back the following week after a rainfall doing the work over again. They cussed the Sisyphean chore. However, the men in the 1200 block of South Jefferson Avenue were relentless in forcing them to do the work "until it was done right." Often the boys didn't appreciate the lessons of diligence and thoroughness until years later. Some would return to curse the work anew. Yet, each said such work helped mold them into men.

Doc and the other men in the 1200 block of South Jefferson Avenue tried to instruct the boys to think beyond their immediate needs. That included getting the boys to see beyond their hunger and craving for money. "Use your head for something besides a hat rack," both Doc and Sam, the tailor, would tell the boys. That phrase fit the era of the black men as young adults. By the 1960s, many young men had stopped wearing hats as a matter of completing their dress. The boys would look quizzically at either Doc or Sam. They essentially understood that they had neglected to think before acting. Doc would say: "You can't just worry about filling your belly. Life has to be more than that. If all you're thinking about is what you can eat or drink then you will miss out on some of life's best opportunities."

In an infamous incident, Doc caught one of his kids, Vincent, playing a pinball machine. Vince was exceptional and was on his way to beating the machine when Doc walked in, saying, "What the hell are you doing?" Vince and his other kids who were watching the excitement explained. Doc told them that the next time they wanted to waste money, they could put the coins in his pocket. He would gladly ring a red cowbell for them and shine a flashlight in their faces to give them the same effect as the machine. They would be happy and so would he because he would be better off with the coins in his pocket that otherwise would be shamelessly spent on nothing.

Often discussions about thinking would come up when Doc would ask the boys at his company how they were doing in school. When the boys responded honestly that their grades weren't good, Doc would press them. "John, what did you get in math?" Doc asked. John was putting Du-Good Dry Shampoo into boxes. Rows of about 50, 1-gallon glass jugs had just been labeled, filled and capped. The shiny, black metal caps and the yellow labels neatly placed made them look like soldiers lined up in rows on the table—six abreast—marching off to some noble campaign. These "soldiers" were intended to make money for black businesses catering to the hair-care needs of black women. John filled the brown, heavy cardboard boxes, closed them and then stacked the boxes six high on a two-wheel dolly. "I didn't do so good in math, Doc," John answered.

Doc corrected him, saying, "I didn't do so *WELL* in math!"

John replied, "Yeah, that, too."

"What does that mean, John?" Doc asked, also putting the bottles into boxes to be wheeled to the back in the warehouse.

"Well, I think I am working on a 'D,'" John said.

"A 'D'!?" Doc exclaimed. "John, I think you can do better than that. Math is your ticket to anywhere and everywhere. You don't want to be like the man from Gotham."

"What do you mean, man from Gotham, Doc?" John asked.

"The man from Gotham was the fellow whose house was broken into so do you know what he did to solve the problem?" Doc asked.

"No, Doc, what did he do?" John responded.

"The man from Gotham decided that the only way to keep his front door from being kicked in again was to carry the door around with him at all times," Doc said. "He protected his door, but he left his house completely open to burglars. You don't want to be shortsighted like the man from Gotham, do you, John?"

"No sir," John said. "But this math is so hard. How can someone like me learn this stuff?"

"Unfortunately, the schools have handicapped people like you by not giving you the lessons you needed to be able to succeed in math, science, spelling and English," Doc said. "It's as if they don't care about our black children and never have. They are being shortsighted. They need to train you and others for jobs of the future. White people may not think so today, but they will need us. They always have. It's just that in the future, they will need us more. So it makes no sense that they would cut black children out of a good education today. It is like the woman going into the backyard where the dog does its business, scooping up a pile of manure and carrying it into the living room to get rid of the flies in the kitchen. All that does is create even more problems throughout the house. The flies are still inside, plus you have a nasty smelly mess in the living room, too. I am afraid that ole Maude, the mule, will have to kick white people hard to get them to realize that they need to educate children like you in all of our schools if the white people want to have a good quality of life. If they let our children down, we will all be on the same sinking ship. Now on that schoolwork, John, you bring your books to the lab each day after school, and I will work with you to get your grades up."

The men in the 1200 block of South Jefferson Avenue always tried to feed the dreams of the boys who came looking for a handout or work. They also offered them hard-core lessons in reality to help them see the folly of their shortsightedness. Another boy, Jesse, would ride his bike to Du-Good Chemical, having tooled around the neighborhood before landing at Doc's door. Jesse loved to brag about what he could do and would do. Doc helped keep Jesse anchored. Jesse thought he played basketball well. He told Doc he planned to be a professional ballplayer. Doc had built a basketball hoop in the loading area so the boys could burn off excessive energy when times were slow at the company. Jesse was smaller than the others, but he had a high assessment of himself. He took several shots at the basket nailed with a homemade backboard to an oak tree in the loading area of Du-Good Chemical, announcing to Doc and others that he planned to play professional ball someday. With each missed shot, Doc said Jesse should leave those basketball dreams alone. He added one of his famous Doc sayings, "A bullfrog has to bump its own ass before it learns it can't fly." Jesse had neither the height, speed, agility nor accuracy in shooting to be a professional ballplayer. Doc encouraged Jesse to concentrate on his schoolwork. It was the surest way to success even though it would never put Jesse on the path of fame or fast, big money. Jesse insisted that wouldn't work for him. That was never what the boys wanted to hear, but it was what they needed to know.

Praise came hard from the men in the 1200 block of South Jefferson Avenue. The boys who landed at their door sought it as much as the few coins for their work. The men in the 1200 block of South Jefferson Avenue knew the black boys would have to demonstrate that they could work twice as hard as white people because they would have a tougher time getting and keeping any job in white America—just as the black men did. If the men praised the kids too much, they believed it would make them soft, thinking they were already talented enough. The men knew that being black in America instantly meant they would have to overcome nearly insurmountable stereotypes once the boys left the protective bosom of the black community. These stereotypes included black people being lazy, criminal no-accounts. If the kids had fire in their bellies, the will and determination to persevere and were able to do good work on simple and complex tasks, that would carry over into whatever job they took on. The men knew they had to be the ever-present, quiet voices in the kids' ears and the strong, relentless hand on their backs, propelling the boys to sweep the floor more thoroughly, clean lab glassware, dust the items so that no white glove could detect a speck of dirt and to manufacture products with precise specifications to ensure quality. Nothing less than perfection was acceptable. The men were determined that the boys would not be stereotypes.

The property that Doc rented to families wasn't the best. He had two, two-story flats in St. Louis—each floor contained one apartment. The units were clean, freshly painted and well-maintained. The rent was low because that was all people in the community could afford. Doc did nearly all of the repairs and painting. It was the way he saved money and made owning the rental property worthwhile. Doc was from the South, where property ownership meant a lot. "Money will come and go," Doc told the boys who worked for him. "But there is only so much land. If you can own some of it without being property poor, then you should do well."

"What's property poor mean?" one kid asked, as Doc had the boys loading tools in his red Dodge truck to do repairs on the house on Rutger Street.

"It's when you own a house or some land, but you don't have enough money to pay the taxes on it or do the maintenance or take care of other emergencies that might come up," Doc replied as he stepped on the truck's running board and pulled himself into the driver's seat. "Get in! We have to fix the drainpipe at the house on Rutger Street."

Three boys—Jesse, Lewis and David—climbed in the truck. There was only the single passenger seat, and its springs and haylike stuffing were exposed. The space between the seats gave one access to the back. Most of the boys sat on the wheel wells in the back with the tools, paint and supplies for repairs. The ride was bumpy but short. The building was where Doc's family had lived until they moved to the Gaslight Square area, another inner-city St. Louis neighborhood. Doc rented the first floor of that building and lived on the top floor. On Rutger Street, Doc rented each floor for $50 a month in the 1960s. On this day, the drainpipe leading to the alley in back had broken.

The pipe was 6 inches in diameter. It was elevated above the basement floor, which Doc had dug out years earlier with one of the boys he had hired at the lab. They had also laid the concrete floor. The cast iron pipe had somehow cracked underground in the yard. Doc traced the line from the house to where he thought the break was outside. The sunken area of the ground revealed the location. He got out of the truck with the pick and started digging. It was a hot summer day. Doc wasn't trying to do more damage by bashing the pick into the drain pipe. He would loosen up the dirt and then have one of the boys enter the hole with a shovel and scoop out the claylike soil. Doc would get back in the hole and loosen up more dirt. The soil got heavy, sticky and smelly with the building's sewage. Doc kept digging and insisted that the boys do the same even though the mess they had encountered got worse. The hole was more than 5 feet deep when they finished. It had to be dug out in such a fashion so the pipe was fully exposed. Doc was the king of jackleg fixes. He had the boys combine some tar with paraffin on rags. Doc's sister, Sherley, always shipped him rags from her Virginia home in a big box each year as his Christmas "gift."

Doc first cleaned and then carefully and tightly wrapped the cracked cast iron pipe with the treated rags. He had the boys gently shovel the dirt around the pipe. Doc packed it around the fix to ensure support. They mounded the dirt back up over the hole. Doc and the boys were covered with dirt from head to toe, and their shoes were heavy with the mud and filth. They cleaned off with Du-Good Hand Cleaner and a garden hose. They also cleaned what they could with bleach to kill germs that were in the sewage-filled mud. The fix held for decades afterward. Doc showed the boys what it took to make things work and how he had saved hiring a plumber for hundreds of dollars to replace about 50 yards of drainpipe from the house to the alley, where it connected to the city's sewer system.

Whether the work was digging a trench to repair an underground sewer line, painting a wooden fence, shining shoes, cleaning glassware in the lab, or sweeping, mopping and waxing floors the boys who wandered into black businesses looking for an easy coin found the work to be excruciatingly difficult and compliments were more rare than a 50-degree summer day in St. Louis. The black men in the 1200 block of South Jefferson Avenue were tough taskmasters. They were stern with the boys because they knew that once the kids left the bosom of the black community, which comparatively was very forgiving, they would face the harsh realities of racism, the electrified fence of law enforcement, the beat-down gauntlet of the job market and the hangman's noose of the judicial and penal systems. The boys had to be forged like steel in the smelting furnace of high expectations. They had to develop asbestos hides and they had to emerge bulletproof if they had any hope of succeeding. The task of getting those kids to rise like phoenixes from the ashes of slavery, black codes and Jim Crow fell to the black men in the 1200 block of South Jefferson Avenue.

Generally the boys thought the men were being cruel, unrealistic or picking on them. The black men knew that for the boys to be successful in America they had to always be at their best. The adults knew that the boys were sheltered as long as they stayed in the black community. Many of the men who had to venture out into the rest of the city encountered the unfriendliness of racism. Greasy Earl explained to Doc during one of their visits that he had driven his old wrecker into St. Louis County on a call to tow a man's car for repairs. Greasy Earl got lost and ended up driving around Ladue. The police pounced on him, interrogating him on why he was in their community. Greasy Earl explained to the police what had happened. Eventually they let him go with explicit directions on how he could get back to the 1200 block of South Jefferson Avenue.

Doc and the other men constantly corrected the boys on their use of the language. Bad language habits—often reinforced by the boys' peers and left uncorrected by the schools and teachers—are difficult to break and can endure a lifetime unless there is intervention from people who understand that such little things could greatly impair the possibility of the boys being successful in the future. The black businessmen hoped that the boys would pass the good habits on to their friends, family members and children. Unrelenting, purposeful and consistent intervention was the key.

Doc never stopped holding children to high standards even after they became adults with kids of their own. When Doc took his son, Lewis, to college, he shook his hand for the first time ever and said as he left, "I'm expecting great things from you." Lewis had worked as a journalist for nearly 15 years when he mailed to his parents a column he had written.

It was well-received by readers of The Kansas City Star. But when Lewis arrived a few weeks later in St. Louis to visit his parents, his mother looked down, knowing Doc was going to lower a boom. Doc's first words were not "Hello," not "How are you" and not "How are my grandchildren?" but, "You misspelled a word." Indeed, one word out of more than 600 words that comprised Lewis' column was misspelled. It also happened to be the word "equation," which Doc was infinitely familiar with. Lewis felt awful, yet he knew that Doc wanted him and the other boys to be excellent in everything they attempted. It was no different when Lewis was among the boys at Du-Good Chemical in the 1950s and 1960s and working under Doc's tutelage, and excellence was the only mark of achievement worth having. Even so, in Doc's eyes, and the eyes of the other men in the 1200 block of South Jefferson Avenue, excellence was merely a mark of average performance because excellence was what they expected.

The black men in the 1200 block of South Jefferson Avenue always encouraged the boys who came to their door to go to the Barr branch library, which was about a mile away at South Jefferson and Lafayette avenues. It was an old structure, built about 60 years earlier. It was a sturdy brick building with a red tile roof. Inside were books of every type and reference books, too. The boys liked to go to the library on Saturdays and during the summer. It was cool there when the weather was unbearable outside. The library also showed films in the basement. None was a recent release, however, they were all fun to watch. But the black men on South Jefferson Avenue wanted the boys to go to the library to check out books and read them, learn about their history and their heritage, and learn more about the subjects they were supposed to be studying in school. The library was a great opportunity for the boys to not "get stupid" during the summer when they were out of school, as Doc frequently admonished the teens. Some listened. Many didn't. When Doc was asked about those who didn't listen and how they were doing, Doc often replied, "Well, he's still scuffing and scratching along." That meant the young man was doing the best he could, but often ended up going in the wrong direction.

The boys often entered Du-Good Chemical complaining like Doc's own kids did about what they didn't have. Doc had little patience for such "bellyaching" as he called it. The other black men in the 1200 block of South Jefferson Avenue were equally unsympathetic. They all seemed to view life for African Americans as being the best it had ever been. They never thought about what they didn't have because as children and young men, they had a lot less. Certainly there was no doubt that what they and the boys had to endure was far less than what white people just a few blocks away enjoyed overall. Everything is relative. So when Butch and other boys entering Du-Good Chemical complained that they had no bicycles, Doc told them that if they went up and down the alleys in the neighborhood, they would find the parts they needed to build the bicycles they wanted. A bike store near the corner of Chouteau and South Jefferson could supply whatever tires, inner tubes or other parts the boys weren't able to get—provided the boys saved the money they earned rather than "squander it on junk to fill your bellies," Doc told them. So after sweeping and mopping up, the boys set out to scour the alleys for bicycle parts. They quickly found frames, rims, handlebars and a front fork—all discarded from bicycles that had been stolen and stripped. They picked up sprockets, a crank and pedals along with ball bearing rings needed for the fluid movement of the parts. The more diligent boys pooled their money and bought new tires and inner tubes at the bike shop. With Doc's help, they assembled their first bike. It wasn't much to look at—a big heavy, clunky, ugly thing that looked like a Frankenstein bike with parts dating to the 1930s. It pedaled nicely, and the boys loved what they had pieced together through their own innovativeness and ingenuity. They took turns riding the bike. Then they built another and another and another—realizing that if one worked, they could assemble others so everyone would have a bike. It gave them the freedom they otherwise would not have and the ability to stretch even farther the places they could visit for odd jobs. The boys had picked up the lifelong skill of inventiveness and self-reliance from the men in the 1200 block of South Jefferson Avenue. The black youths had learned from these men that they should never wait for something to be handed to them. They could also see that the discards of others could be gold for them. That was what African Americans going back to slavery relied on. The boys had acquired the know-how and the will to make opportunity happen for them.

◆　◆　◆　◆　◆

More people arrived at Barnes-Jewish Hospital and gathered around Doc's bed. He was still unconscious. The monitors made intermittent, irritating noises piercing people's conversations like radio waves, yet altering not a word or any of the memories that were shared. People wanted Doc to magically rise from the fetal position in the bed and get back to work. Of all of the black men who dominated the 1200 block of South Jefferson Avenue and hand-tooled the lives of hundreds of boys, Doc was the sole holdout. The boys, now men, had come to pray that he get well. The visitors to Du-Good Chemical, now visitors to Doc's hospital bed, brought with them pictures of Doc when he was a younger man and of Du-Good Chemical when it was Doc's growing dream. Explosive laughter followed the many recalled memories. The men shared stories. One was about Doc mixing a batch of Du-Good Hand Cleaner in the big tank to be put up in gallon bottles. The boys working there and Doc's own children had put the jugs on the long manufacturing table in the big room and labeled each bottle, making sure the labels were on straight. Quality control was essential. Rows of about 24 drums were neatly arranged running four deep and six abreast. It was as if they were marching from the sliding door by the alley to the area near the manufacturing tables. The drums sat on the concrete floor. The people at the hospital remembered Doc yelled pointing toward Renee over the deafening noise of two motors stirring the Hand Cleaner and two large, filling-station-size compressors building up air pressure to pump the product into the gallon jugs. "Get that bug!" On the concrete floor near one of the 55-gallon drums was a black "water bug." It had crawled from under the drum from a floor drain to explore. Nothing enraged Doc more than bugs, mice and rats. They carried germs and were a threat to everyone. Unfortunately the neighborhood had massive quantities of each. Nothing petrified Renee, Doc's only daughter, more than bugs, mice and rats. She froze. Her face instantly frowned, and she started to cry unable to move or run. Doc yelled again for her to get the bug, which was only inches from her foot. Renee still could not move, and she was in tears now. In a fraction of a second, the boys saw Doc leap from one side of the table near the tank over the bottles, toppling not one of them. He looked like a comic book super hero or ninja. The well-worn leather sole of his shoe was all the boys on the ground could see. It seared downward to the floor like a meteor toward the black water bug. The bug must have sensed it was in danger. It scurried away from Renee darting back under the drum just before Doc's right foot came down with the force of a kung-fu master. "Damn!" Doc cursed. "Renee, why didn't you step on that bug like I told you?"

All Renee could do was continue to cry. She was only about 7 years old. Like a madman, Doc grabbed the first 55-gallon drum and tossed it aside as if it were made of only Styrofoam instead of weighing hundreds of pounds with chemicals. The wily water bug darted under a second drum. Doc saw him, and seemingly effortlessly flipped that drum aside, too. Doc pushed aside four drums before cursing more and giving up going after that one water bug. The performance and rage-fueled strength astounded the boys who were there. Yet, they also knew that Doc had the delicate hands of a surgeon when handling costly laboratory glassware. It became legend at Du-Good Chemical. The retelling of the water bug story in Doc's hospital room by men now older than Doc had been back then brought tears of laughter and greater wishes for his recovery.

It was getting dark outside. The moon had what looked like a halo around it. People in the hospital room who were seated and standing around Doc's bed remembered the science lessons Doc always shared about the moon having that kind of glow. It meant, they recalled Doc saying in his deep southern-salted voice, that rain was inevitable. Great, the people in the hospital room laughed, more humidity was just what the sultry St. Louis summer needed.

Doc's middle-age children knew they should have gone to the bank before it closed. Now they had to use an ATM to get some cash to be able to cover their expenses while waiting for Doc to emerge from unconsciousness. Banking always brought back lessons that Doc instilled in the boys who frequented the black businesses in the 1200 block of South Jefferson Avenue. Doc always hammered into the boys' heads the value of thrift. "It's important to save your money instead of giving it away for something that will only keep your belly full for a little while," Doc admonished. "It's the difference between wealth and income. Most black folks ain't got no wealth," Doc said speaking the vernacular the boys understood. "Wealth is where you have money in the bank. It only gets there if you put it there. You have to make a conscious, disciplined effort to put aside at least 10 percent of what you make—preferably more—so that you create wealth for yourself. Nobody else is going to do it for you. Unless you create that wealth, you won't have squat when you need money for an emergency or for an opportunity that will fly right by you unless you have the funds to take advantage of it. It takes money to make money to lift yourself to those things that will get you more money the hard, honest way. If you don't have that cash reserve in the bank—and you always have to have it and keep it growing—you will be dependent on begging for loans, borrowing from others or stealing. The cost of each is way too high." Doc always offered to take the boys to whom he gave that lecture to the nearby bank so they could open an account, where each boy could keep his money. Doc did that for his own kids when they were barely old enough to walk. He wanted their first steps to be to the bank. He wanted to show each at an early age how he was saving a little at a time for them to go to college. There was never a doubt that they would go to college or that their way would be paid, leaving them debt-free. Doc instilled in each of his kids a strong desire to be financially independent, and that was only possible through wealth creation. Often the Doc lecture would begin with one of the boys asking for money. Doc always responded: "Do you think money grows on trees and that I can just go outside and pick some and give it to you?" Doc then would try to get the boys to see the true value of money. He would say, "It's not what you make that counts; it's what you spend." That meant curbing unnecessary purchases and putting the money in the bank. It meant not using banks that charged people fees to gain access to their money as ATM machines did. It meant banks that offered interest without fees for services. Doc tried to get that across to the boys in the 1200 block of South Jefferson Avenue. He took those who had an interest into banks so they could get comfortable with the clean, businesslike interior and the well-dressed personnel. Doc wanted the boys to abandon the cash economy of the inner city. Cash kept people handcuffed as losers. Money unsecured and exposed to individuals' infinite wants would always disappear quickly. Doc tried to teach the boys to slow down their spending so that they could put more money in the bank. It would always be there if the boys needed it. Doc wanted the boys to watch their money grow in their bank books. But few of the boys actually took him up on the life-changing offer. The magic of money and high demand for instant gratification, which came from spending money, was often too great. Doc never gave up trying.

As good as Doc was, people in the neighborhood knew he was far from perfect. Folks who had been around for a while remembered Doc had more than a few experiments blow up in his lab. In one instance, Doc had to literally jump into the iron sink by the set of stairs winding their way to the three aisles in his lab. Something blew up in the place, and Doc had to quickly drench his whole body with water because of the chemical burns he would have suffered otherwise. In another instance, Doc's secretary and lab assistant, Ida Phillips, was injured and nearly lost an eye when a reaction in the controlled, fireproof area of the lab called "the hood," exploded. In the early 1970s, Doc was working in the hood, which had an exhaust fan that carried toxic fumes outside, when a reaction with ether exploded dousing Doc's head and shoulders with intense blue flames. Doc soaked his body with water, but not before all of the hair on his head was burned off and he had suffered second-degree burns. However, Doc refused to go to the hospital, preferring instead to treat himself. In another instance, he was repairing the roof on an apartment building that he owned when a ladder that he had perched poorly on a porch roof gave way as he was about to step onto the second-story roof. Doc fell onto the slanted porch roof and rolled off of it onto the concrete path below. Doc's tenants helped him up and revived him in their home. He refused to go to the hospital and then climbed back on the ladder and finished the roof repair before limping home. He limped for several months afterward but never went to see a doctor for the injuries he suffered. Doc just complained about the fall for the next several weeks, saying it ruined his golf game.

In the hospital after the assault, Doc's kids hoped he wouldn't give up trying to pull out of unconsciousness. Doc's kids and the boys—now men—from the 1200 block of South Jefferson Avenue refused to give up hope just as Doc wouldn't give up on them.

CHAPTER 9

DETERMINATION V. DETERIORATION

By 1977 the neighborhood surrounding Du-Good Chemical looked terrible. Sam's dry cleaners and tailoring was gone. So was Shorty's shoeshine shop. The buildings that housed each business had been torn down. Jeff Johnson had moved his grocery store two blocks away to Ohio and Rutger streets, and his old building was demolished. Doc and the Rev. Nance's church across the street were the sole survivors of the black businessmen in the 1200 block of South Jefferson Avenue. Everyone was hurt by the recession of the early 1970s. A redeveloper moved into the area, promising to put infill housing between the structures that had survived and build homes on blocks that had been long vacant and overgrown with weeds. However, that wasn't enough for the developers. They wanted key properties in the community that had visible locations. Doc's company was one of them. With the other buildings gone, Doc's company was rumored to be a prime site for a McDonald's restaurant. Doc bristled at the thought of losing the company he had built. However, he already had sustained a one-two punch from the recession and changing demographics. The Arab oil embargo had raised the cost of the chemicals and bottles that he used for most of his products. The Civil Rights Movement had also caused many black families to leave what had been a clearly defined black community. That made black newspapers' job of delivering news and advertising to the black community difficult. Doc depended on black newspapers to advertise his products. The new, post-segregation "freedom" also stripped away people who had frequented black businesses. Abandoned were the grocery stores, drugstores, filling stations, barbershops, beauty salons and other companies that carried Doc's products.

African Americans were taking advantage of the opportunity to live and to conduct business in areas that offered better homes and better schools for their children.

Integration began with the 1954 Brown vs. Topeka Board of Education Supreme Court decision. Young, militant black people also demanded an end to segregation, forever changing the status quo of the United States. It was a good thing, but it devastated black businesses. The push for redevelopment was yet another blow to always struggling black businessmen. The St. Louis Board of Aldermen landed on Doc's doorstep with developers insisting that he sell his company to the businessmen favored by the city at what would have been a fire-sale price. Doc cursed them and threw them out of his office. He learned later from lawyers that his company was "grandfathered" into the neighborhood. Du-Good Chemical had been there so long that the city couldn't dislodge it or Doc without a court fight that the city was destined to lose. Doc's southern temperament toward land ownership and his boiling temper kicked in. He wasn't about to surrender to the city or anyone.

One night in November 1977, the unexpected happened. A fire mysteriously started at Du-Good Chemical. After the fire, Doc found containers and materials inside Du-Good Chemical that he had never seen before. He then knew that despite the dogs being on guard, someone had broken into his company and poured a flammable liquid around the place and set it ablaze. The St. Louis Fire Department, which had a station two blocks away arrived quickly and put the fire out. However, both the fire and the firefighters did a lot of damage to the company. Doc, his wife, Nancy, some neighborhood boys Doc hired and Doc's own kids spent the better part of a year rebuilding. Doc became more committed to the company that he had homesteaded in the wilderness of segregation. The fire helped to sear into Doc the need to steel himself, his children and other African Americans against the forces of racism. Racism, prejudice and discrimination overpower many black people in America. The only way children and adults can withstand them is to have a core of inner strength and a support network to get them through the worst of the ostracism, hatred and jealousy toward blacks by whites and by some blacks, too.

Many fires seemed to be set after the developer targeted the area with "new plans." So many dreams of African Americans went up in smoke. They were dreams of being able to move into a neighborhood that had been long closed to them. Dreams of sending their children to the once stellar Chouteau Elementary School. Dreams of going to Buder Park and having a good time with family and friends. Dreams of starting a business and being one's own boss. Fire, partly fueled by the oxygen of greed and hard times, made rubble of those dreams. Like Doc, several holdouts remained.

The strife, however, made liquor stores and taverns in the area even more popular. The dripping window air conditioners hanging over the sidewalks on the first floor of many of the places along South Jefferson Avenue belched the stench of stale beer into the faces of passers-by. The boys who frequented the businesses that once lined the broad street with its equally wide side-walks hated to walk by the taverns because of the odor. Sometimes late at night after the work was done at Du-Good Chemical, the boys would stand along the locking crossbar of the wooden gate to the loading area. Some boys would balance on stilts they had made and look over the 6-foot-high fence. They would look south toward the taverns on the west side of the street near Park Avenue. Often bar doors would suddenly fly open, and a mob of people would run into the street. In an argument over service, a love interest, disrespect or any number of things, someone would unexpectedly pull a gun. No one ever waited to see whether bullets would fly. People scattered out the door. That generally was the beginning of the end for a number of joints. But demand would dictate that others would follow in their place.

As more black businesses folded or moved, the neighborhood continu-ally coarsened with kids growing up and turning to criminal behavior. Fewer black business owners were around for the kids to seek change and guidance doing odd jobs as kids before them had done. It also meant that fewer boys were picking up training in how to do jobs well and learning what really went into becoming a man. The virtues and character traits that were taught outside of families went begging. The black businessmen who provided it had been eliminated. The cost to the community was enormous. Street life replaced those lessons, and on the street, kids learned they must choose to be a victim or predator. Often they were each taking from others when the opportunity arose or being pimped when someone got the jump on them. That hard-hearted environment etched a mean, hungry look on the faces of even the youngest children. They learned to wholesale use others or else they knew they would be used themselves. While working on his car on South Jefferson Avenue directly in front of Du-Good Chemical, Doc went inside to get a tool. Someone then went into his office, just inside the front door, and took his answering machine, fax machine and copier. Doc was furious and couldn't believe that the office equipment had been taken so quickly. Doc told some people he knew and trusted in the neighborhood. In a few days, the equipment was returned by some shady characters who working in the best interest of Doc, went and stole the material back. The good virtues, such as right and wrong, honor and integrity, and the value of hard work, though taught in many of the homes, were gone now.

Doc got caught up in that whirlwind. He had just returned from taking his family on a vacation to Detroit. They were to go on to Canada, but Doc's enlarged prostate in 1972 forced him into an emergency room in an Ann Arbor, Mich., hospital. His kids hastily drove him and the family back to St. Louis, where he had surgery to allow him to live a more normal life. Doc's father had prostate cancer when he died in 1955 at age 75. It is an "old black man's disease." African American men have the highest incidence of prostate cancer in the world. Doc's father's death from cancer was a leading reason Doc devoted his chemistry talents to doing anti-cancer research. In recovery after he was released from the hospital, Doc was unable to go to Du-Good Chemical. However, his doctor required him to go on walks around the neighborhood to exercise in the aftermath of the surgery. Doc was 55 years old at the time. While walking one day, he was confronted by two teenagers who demanded that he hand over his wallet. Doc refused. They rushed him. But they didn't know how strong Doc was despite the abdominal surgery, and how quick his reflexes were from years of working in the lab, from being an athlete and from how wildly angry he could get seeing everything he had tried to do for young people turn on him. The teens also were not prepared for Doc to fight back. Fighting back was the alpha to the omega of Doc's life.

Doc quickly went in his pocket, pulled out a pocket knife and unfolded it with a fast flick of his thumb. The blade locked, and Doc swung the knife strategically at his attackers before they could get too close to him. However, the teens kept trying to get at Doc's wallet. Doc kept spinning around to continue to face his two attackers so neither could get their hands on Doc's wallet in his hip pocket. The teens eventually became frustrated and fled. Doc, who was cursing angrily at that point, half ran back to the lab as fast as the postoperative and draining scar in his abdomen would allow. He called Greasy Earl, who was a couple of years older than Doc. Earl went to Doc's company and picked him up in Earl's old wrecker. Doc also grabbed his father's gun, a .45-caliber, six-shooter made in the 1800s, which his father carried daily to his job on the railroad in case he was accosted. Doc and Greasy Earl rolled through the neighborhood in Greasy Earl's wrecker looking for the thugs who jumped Doc. "Is that them?" Greasy Earl asked Doc. "No," Doc said. "Keep driving." They drove along a number of blocks several times. Fortunately for Doc, Greasy Earl and the teens, fate kept them apart. The forever changed community provoked that kind of action and response from people constantly, and it wasn't good. Bad and criminal behavior only accelerated as more of the black businesses in the 1200 block of South Jefferson Avenue and elsewhere folded, adding to the deteriorating community and the people struggling in hard times.

Doc had a lively spirit. It showed in his face and particularly in his eyes. They were impish. It came from the joy of life, which he embraced. Part of that was driven by his purpose. Du-Good Chemical gave Doc that purpose. It was his reason for rising in the morning and for going to sleep at night, and every bit of work in between went into keeping the dream of his company going, which he had unrelentingly maintained since 1947. Anyone would do well to be as fortunate. Years later, Doc's son, Lewis, explained that perseverance in his commencement speeches to college graduates, telling the young adults that they needed to find that one thing—be it physical, mental or spiritual—that they could depend on to keep them going even in the worst of times.

The men in the 1200 block of South Jefferson Avenue weren't the only ones guiding boys in the neighborhood. When they saw mischievous boys going astray, the women did their part, too. On one occasion, Nancy Diuguid saw her sons and some other kids in the neighborhood lose a ball they had been playing with. A swung bat in a pickup game of softball in a nearby red-brick-paved alley sent an errant ball down a sewer. The preteen boys managed to pry the heavy caste iron lid off the opening to the sewer. They had tied a rope to a bucket and were prepared to lower the smallest kid among them into the sewer to retrieve the ball. Nancy just happened to look out of her window of their home. She yelled at the boys just before her son Lewis was lowered into the hole and possibly oblivion. For years, Nancy talked about that incident and boys having little common sense. Children had to constantly be watched, she would say.

Doc liked to travel. He had been all over the country in cars, driving on two-lane highways, traveling from New York City to San Francisco, when open-road trips weren't the thing to do. He kept his cars—no matter how old—in good condition so they could get him where he wanted to go safely. After Doc settled in St. Louis running Du-Good Chemical, he made frequent trips each year to Virginia, his family home. Doc also took his immediate family on vacation camping trips to Denver, Detroit, Canada and the Grand Canyon. The Grand Canyon trip was in a 1968 Chevy van Doc had purchased for $300 in 1971. The van was to replace the red 1952 Dodge panel truck, which had long been a fixture at Du-Good Chemical with its white lettering on the outside to advertise the company and some of its products. Doc had some work done on the van to get it road-worthy. Then he and three of his kids—Lewis, Renee and Vincent—rode with him. Doc had owned several cars over the years, including a 1955 Lincoln Mercury, a 1962 Pontiac Catalina, a 1968 Pontiac Catalina and then a 1972 Dodge Coronet. That was the last new car that Doc bought. Afterward, Doc bought used Fords. In each vehicle, Doc had stashed a pair of wire sunglasses that all of the boys at his company over the years thought were really cool. Doc also had a pair of enduring black leather mittens that were lined with fur.

On this particular Southwest trip, Doc also took Jesse Talley, one of the boys in the 1200 block of South Jefferson Avenue. Like many of the black people in that area, it was Jesse's first time traveling west. The world beyond the confines of their black community didn't exist except for what people saw on television, and even that didn't seem real. There were very few blacks on TV. Those they did see didn't act or talk like them or any blacks they knew. Interstate 44 had just been completed. Doc wanted to see how it compared with the famous Route 66, which many travelers like him had driven to California. The Chevy van had no hood in front like traditional vehicles at that time. The engine sat between the two front seats, which made it easy for Doc to work on it when there was trouble. Doc told Lewis, who at age 16, helped with the driving, not to take the vehicle over 60 mph. Doc didn't want to push his luck with the six-cylinder van. No one wanted to get stuck hundreds of miles from home. The diagonal trip to the Southwest was uneventful. The van ran like a champ.

Lewis rigged sleeping quarters in the van for everyone, so those who were not driving or navigating for the driver were able to sleep if they wanted to while the vehicle was in motion. The trip south went quickly with the family stopping mostly for gas, and sometimes to get out, stretch their legs at rest stops and throw a softball around. Doc enjoyed doing that.

Doc's plan was to see as much of the Southwest as he could and expose his children and Jesse to the area's wonders. Doc got road maps at AAA. He made sure that everyone on the trip was well-versed on how to read the maps, follow the road signs and navigate to help ensure that they didn't get lost. That, of course, would be a waste of gasoline. Doc drove most of the way, letting Lewis give him some relief when Doc felt sleepy. The drive didn't get interesting until after the van left Missouri and dropped into Oklahoma. The initial stretch was mostly a drive through farming communities. Doc stopped the van only to fill up. They picked up Interstate 40 in Oklahoma City and took that west into Albuquerque, N.M. They stopped before that in Texas to rest for the night. The stop was at a filling station. Everyone slept in his or her assigned spots in the crowded Du-Good Chemical van. In the morning, the group ate breakfast, which they had packed in the family ice chest and then pressed on to cover new territory.

This travel pattern was typical of older black people. During segregation, blacks could not eat at most restaurants in either small towns or big cities. They would never be served, or if they were served, it was out of the back door because no blacks were allowed in dining areas. It was an odd practice because most of the cooks and the people who bused the tables were black. Nothing about racism made sense. Racism and discrimination backed by violence forced blacks who traveled the highways to drive at night, which minimized the likelihood that law enforcement officers would stop them. Black people also packed enough food to eat while they were on the road, and when they did get tired, they'd pull off the road for a nap unless someone else was able to drive. That way they would get to their destination more quickly minimizing the likelihood of being degraded as human beings or worse.

Doc would also pull off at rest stops and insist that the kids get out a softball and gloves to toss the ball around so they could get a bit of exercise and blow off steam after being in the van for so long. The kids were always in a hurry to get to see the sights. Doc advised them that being in a hurry would cause them to miss important things. Traveling would ensure that all of their senses be excited. Doc explained that folks in a hurry were more prone to making mistakes. It is best whenever possible for all individuals to take their time, enjoy the beauty of the land and the time that we have on Earth. Everything goes too quickly, and slowing things down when possible is the key to enjoying life. Tossing the ball around was a way to slow down the pace of life. It also was a good trick for keeping peace in the van. When they arrived in New Mexico, Doc stayed true to his word, taking the crew to the Indian pueblos built along cliffs. As they drove west into Arizona, they saw the famed Painted Desert, a fascinating artistry of sand of many colors. As they pressed toward Flagstaff, Ariz., the interstates were nice. Once off of them, the state roads became narrow and treacherous, with little or no shoulders for travelers to pull off on during emergencies.

Doc let Lewis drive on one narrow road in Arizona. Doc and the others went to sleep in the van. Doc always admonished his children and the boys who worked for him to keep their eyes on what their hands were doing to reduce the likelihood of mistakes. That skill was critically important when working in the lab with expensive laboratory glassware and dangerous chemicals and to ensure the quality of Doc's analytical work. It could be a lifesaver. But there was no way for Lewis to tell what was ahead as he drove while the others slept. The six-cylinder van ran well, but it struggled at higher speeds. Doc said to keep it at 60 mph and no more, even though the speed limit was 70 mph. On the two-lane state highway, Lewis tried to pass a slow-moving tractor-trailer. But when Lewis pulled into the oncoming lane, the truck sped up, matching the speed of the van. No cars had been in the oncoming traffic lane. However, one appeared suddenly on the horizon. In addition, an old pickup truck closed off the space behind the tractor-trailer, leaving Lewis with no place to retreat. The driver in the big truck, who had been toying with Lewis, suddenly realized that he was about to cause a head-on collision. He slammed on his brakes so Lewis could scoot in front of him. But it was too late. Lewis remembered seeing the man and woman in the oncoming car, with their eyes widening and their mouths opened as if they were screaming and frozen in terror. Without hesitation, Lewis pulled quickly to the left, lurching the van onto the dusty shoulder for oncoming traffic. The car that would have been in the head-on crash sped by as did the tractor-trailer and the pickup truck behind it. Doc's van, however, bumped violently along the dirt shoulder of the Arizona highway, abruptly awakening all of the passengers in the vehicle. Doc woke up, cursing. He demanded an explanation of what had happened. Lewis, though shaken, explained. Doc added, "Lewie almost had all of us waking up in hell!" Fortunately, the only damage done to the van was a missing hubcap. Somewhat refreshed from the brief nap, Doc took over driving.

After the Painted Desert, Doc drove the kids to the Petrified Forest National Park. It was fascinating to see so many rocks lying on the high desert floor that had actually been trees millions of years ago. Doc explained, as he had to his many physical science classes, that the cellular tissue of the fallen trees had absorbed the calcium and other minerals from the water, and under pressure that caused the cellular material to turn to a stonelike form. The many colors of reds, purples, gold and greens merely showed how the tissue had retained its own coloring and picked up different minerals. Signs throughout the national park clearly advised tourists not to pick up samples from the desert floor. However, the kids in the van were following the rules of their St. Louis neighborhood, which compelled them to take what they could stuff in their pockets. Fortunately for the Petrified Forest, they didn't have many pockets and their pockets weren't very deep. Jesse laughed when they got back to the van. He said, "Mr. Do-Good's pants were about to fall off because his pockets were so full of rocks." Everyone laughed except Doc.

Doc replied, "All right, Jesse. Enough of that."

Doc drove the odd crew to the Meteor Crater. They got out of the white Chevy van and started to climb up the side of the tall hill that was left from the impact of the meteor, which had fallen to Earth millions of years ago. The group had climbed a good way up the side of the mound when Doc stopped everyone saying about $200 in cash had come out of his sock and shoe, where he had stashed the money for safe keeping. It apparently had wiggled out during the soft, hillside climb. Doc demanded that everyone head back down the hill to look for the cash. The group would have to turn around and head back to St. Louis unless they were able to find the money. The kids responded looking along the area where they had walked. They were about halfway down the hillside when Doc yelled, "Here it is!" That was a relief. The kids started to climb back up the grassless hill, but Doc turned them around to head back to the van and the road. He had had enough excitement from that money-robbing Meteor Crater. Doc told the kids that it didn't pay to overextend themselves or do anything foolish. Doc wanted to get the kids to think about the consequences of their actions and whether there were unintended effects that they had not considered. It was why he cut short the continued climb up the hill. He did not want any additional unintended mishaps to result so far from home and with so many kids.

The group walked back to the 1968 white Chevy van a little disappointed but unwilling to argue with Doc. They knew they couldn't win. They decided instead to get lunch. They made sandwiches from bread that was stored where it wouldn't get smashed. The meat and cheese were in the ice chest. Although it was 1971, three years after the Civil Rights Movement had ended with the assassination of the Rev. Dr. Martin Luther King Jr., Doc still religiously followed an old black tradition of carrying all of the food needed for a trip. It helped minimize the possibility of encountering the discriminatory trouble of racism. People along the highways—particularly in small towns and on back roads—never have been too kind, friendly or welcoming to black people. And it wasn't just a phenomenon of the South. A lot of towns throughout the country still had signs posted telling any black workers or visitors to be gone by sundown, or else. The signs were colorfully phrased to say, "Don't let the sun set on you, nigger," or "Nigger, don't let the sun set on you."

Experiencing the geological history of the Southwest plus its Native American past and present seemed different from traversing the Midwest and South. The kids and Doc loved every minute. After having sandwiches, chips, fruit and something to drink, the kids played catch with Doc and then hopped back in the van. Doc loved the idea of never tarrying too long in one place. He enjoyed seeing one tourist sight and moving on to the next. He drove the crew to the Grand Canyon.

They arrived by way of Flagstaff. Once there, they walked around the South Rim of the canyon. It was an incredible view. A lot of people were also visiting from throughout the world. Doc and the kids just walked around the top of the Grand Canyon. Doc explained the details of the rock formations and how the Colorado River was thought to have carved the canyon many millennia ago, long before man appeared on Earth. It was hard for the kids to comprehend it. To Doc, explaining the Earth science was second nature. The group spent the night in a parking lot near the South Rim. Doc wasn't willing to pay for a campground. It was too expensive. Doing vacations on the cheap was Doc's specialty. The group took pictures—a lot of them, using Doc's old Kodak with its twin lens and 2-inch-square, black-and-white negatives.

The next morning the group awakened in a gas station parking lot, and everyone was ready to hit the road again. Doc drove them to a fenced in area where a meteor had landed on Earth millions of years ago. In the center was a mine shaft where prospectors decades ago had tried to extract rare minerals from the huge outer-space rock. What they found were no rare minerals — just known elements like those on Earth. Doc explained all of that when the group got to the crater. The massive bowl-shaped hole in the ground was quite the sight. The crater was three miles in circumference and a mile in diameter. It was nearly a mile deep. Doc, Lewis and Jesse climbed down in the hole from the visitors' center, which was constructed on the edge. For a price, climbing down in the hole was permitted. Doc bought everyone a ticket. Renee and Vincent decided to stay at the top. The climb down along the rocks was a bit more than Renee and Vincent were willing to tackle. The guys made their way down the dusty, rocky slope. They got to the bottom about 4 p.m. and walked over to the mine shaft. Doc explained that from what he read in the lobby, the area was used as a training site for astronauts. Jesse put his fingers to his lips to whistle. Normally his whistles were ear-piercing and long. However, the dusty trail down, the high altitude and the aridness left him with little spit to wet his whistle. When Jesse went to blow, no noise came out. Doc responded, "Jesse, I could fart louder than that." Everyone in the group roared with laughter.

No one heard Jesse's attempt at whistling to get people's attention. Doc looked around and noticed that he and the boys were the only ones at the bottom of the meteor pit. Doc decided that they had better start the long, pathless climb over the rocks to the top. The sun was starting to set. There was no activity around the visitor center. When the St. Louis group got to the top, they saw that the gate tourists took to get inside the area had been locked. Renee and Vincent were on the other side, worried sick. "I tried to tell them that you all were down there still, but they wouldn't listen. They didn't say anything. They just locked the gate and left," Renee said. She was only 14 years old then. "I kept saying, 'How are my dad and brother going to get out of there?' But they didn't pay any attention to me." The "ranger" was old and white. He never responded when Renee spoke to him about her family members who were still inside the hole. He only looked at her with disdain and disgust. Then he asked Renee whether she wanted to be locked inside the building.

Doc was furious, threatening to get a tow chain out of the van, attach it to the bumper and pull the gate down, chain and all. He looked up at the fence, which was about 8 feet tall, and cursed. Not only was the chain link fence high, but it was topped with barbed wire. Doc had Renee get a thick blanket from the truck. He climbed to the top of the fence and positioned the blanket over the barbed wire. He then helped each of the boys get to the top of the fence and safely over the barbed wire without getting cut. Then Doc climbed the fence, too, still fuming about what the park crew had done. "Those people are extremely callous," Doc exclaimed. "What if we had gotten hurt in that hole? We'd still be down there trying to get help. Someone could have gotten bitten by a snake. I should sue these people for what they did to us today." Instead, the kids got back into the van, and they left as the sun set and nightfall came. Doc drove off muttering to himself as he searched for a place to park for the night.

The group stopped again at an all-night gas station and restaurant frequented by truckers. Doc knew that would be safe. The kids pulled out food from the ice chest, made sandwiches and had some soft drinks and then crawled back in the van to sleep. Big 18-wheel trucks rolled in and out of the massive desert parking lot throughout the night. Doc's group hardly noticed. They were very tired from the busy day. The rising sun easily cut through the curtains covering the windows of the van, awakening its occupants. As the kids got up, they went into the restrooms of the service station and washed up. The group had hard-boiled eggs for breakfast. Doc's propane-powered camp stove enabled them to cook eggs, which they would either buy at roadside stands or at grocery stores. During breakfast, Doc told the kids that they were not too far from California. With just a little more driving they could easily get there. The kids had never been to California. The thought of crossing into the state where movies were made excited them. Doc, however, wasn't so sure that going that far in the old van and then driving all the way back to St. Louis was a good idea. Doc mulled it all over while the kids cheered and tried to convince Doc to go the extra miles. Doc's group also wasn't that far from Mexico, but Doc was even less enthused about taking his kids and Jesse into another country. After breakfast, they cleaned the dishes and drove west as if they were on the road to California. Around noon, Doc pulled off the road for lunch. Sandwiches were made and potato chips and Fritos were passed around, along with more soft drinks. Then Doc finally decided to dodge the trip to California. He got the group to get back in the van. He pulled into a Dairy Queen in a small town. The kids got out. They didn't have anything like it in the black neighborhoods in St. Louis. Doc ordered an ice cream cone for everyone. He also had the ice cream dipped in chocolate, so that the chocolate froze hard against the frosty ice cream, which had been pumped in swirls from the machine. The kids loved the feel of the crunchy chocolate. They loved its taste and the sweet goodness of the ice cream when they put the mixture of chocolate and ice cream in their mouths. It was a rich treat unlike any other they had ever had, and they noted it as a culinary highlight from the trip to Arizona.

Doc and his wife, Nancy, subscribed to the belief that if the kids were cranky they must be constipated. Doc caught Lewis and Jesse bickering about something in the van. Doc's usual response was: "All right now! Stop all that horseplay!" The road trip had been long, and it was easy to see how the kids would get on one another's nerves. It had happened before, with David and Renee fighting during a trip to Canada, and boiling water got tipped over in the battle nearly scalding them. Fortunately, no one had been injured, but dinner certainly had been ruined. David did not make the trip to Arizona. He was working that summer at Washington University while on break from his studies at Harvard University. But Jesse and Lewis, who normally got along were verbally sparring now. Doc reached into his pocket and pulled out a red box of NR, or Nature's Remedy, tablets. That was the laxative that

Doc favored. He gave Lewis one of the pills and insisted that Lewis take it. That seemed like a mighty risky thing to do on a road trip. But Doc insisted that if Lewis had to go he would pull over to the side of the road and let Lewis run to the nearest bush. But this was the desert in the Southwest where bushes were rare and roadsides were almost nonexistent. Lewis told Doc that he would take the tablet. Doc was satisfied, but Lewis never took the pill. Jesse watched the entire episode. Jesse was one of the boys who frequented Du-Good Chemical. Doc didn't have as much sway over him. Jesse loved to agitate. So after Doc walked away, Jesse went to Lewis saying: "You didn't take that tablet. I saw you toss it away." Lewis insisted that he had taken it. Jesse became adamant and loud. Doc turned around from where he was checking the van to make sure the oil, water and air pressure in the tires were OK. "Now what's all the commotion about?" Doc asked. Jesse explained. Doc confronted Lewis in the parking lot near the Dairy Queen. Lewis insisted that he had taken the tablet saying the proof would be evident soon enough. Doc took his word, saying that the evidence better make itself known soon. The group got into the van and, soon enough, Lewis asked for Doc to pull to the side of the road so he could go. Lewis took a roll of toilet paper from the van and ran far away and down a gully so he could take care of his bodily function. He came back none too happy.

Everyone got back into the white van afterward and started the long drive to St. Louis. Doc told the kids many stories along the way. They often parked at rest stops to sleep for the night and drove during the day after getting breakfast. Doc stayed on the interstates, marveling at how level and smooth they were compared with the old two-lane black top pavement that carried Route 66 mostly along the path that Interstate 44 now travels. It was a remarkable achievement, owed in part to what President Dwight Eisenhower found in Europe during World War II. The road system there was far superior to the one in the United States, enabling the safe and efficient movement of supplies and troops to places they were needed. Eisenhower knew the same could not be said of the roads in the United States. Doc explained that to the boys and his daughter as he drove on the new interstate. Construction started on the interstate highway system during Eisenhower's presidency in the 1950s and continued for decades afterward. The interstate system's essential purpose was for the military to efficiently and quickly move troops and supplies in a time of crisis or war. Since 1946, the nation had been immersed in what was called the Cold War with the Soviet Union in which nuclear annihilation was a very real threat. Children had "duck and cover" drills in schools. Bomb and air-raid shelter signs were posted on some buildings with subbasements and in limestone caves. It was a stressful, tense time in America, and the Cuban missile crisis during President John Kennedy's term in the White House didn't help matters. But providence and level heads prevailed, enabling people and businesses to use the interstates for personal reasons and commerce without the military taking over because of national security concerns.

Doc and the kids took Interstate 40 out of Arizona through New Mexico and Texas and into Oklahoma. They picked up Interstate 44 in Oklahoma City. Doc explained the geological attributes of each state as he drove. Uranium in New Mexico was big. Oil and gas as well as agriculture dominated in Texas and Oklahoma. Interstate 44 took the travelers north of the Arkansas/Missouri border. Doc explained that bauxite, a key ingredient in the production of aluminum, had been big in Arkansas, but that supply had essentially been depleted by constant mining.

As he drove, Doc talked constantly, feeling the need to affect and infect the kids with knowledge. Doc let the speed of the van get a little far afield sometimes. He would see a cop car and slow down. African Americans were particularly leery of being stopped by small-town police or even the highway patrol on vast stretches of rural areas. A long nasty history of black people being beaten and abused constantly replayed in their minds. Doc also told a story of black people in Lynchburg, Va., in the early 1900s demanding that city officials hire Negro police officers. The Negro leaders felt that police in Lynchburg were treating black citizens unfairly and thought that having black officers on the police force would provide some balance in treatment so that black citizens of the southern town could expect near equal treatment as white citizens if the city had black police officers watching out for their interest. The city had no black officers and neither did surrounding towns. Black people coming out of Reconstruction and freedom from slavery knew it was long past time for the city to have black officers. Folks wanted to see their sons in police uniforms so they, too, could be proud that their people were serving and protecting as fearlessly as the white officers were. Doc explained that his father told him that after a lot of debate, city authorities finally relented to the black community's demands and hired two Negro policemen. The officers had all of the equipment that the white officers did—uniforms, badges, Billy clubs and guns.

But Lynchburg was in the South, and most of the residents were white. Lynchburg had a lot of citizens who populated white supremacist groups, which then were seen as all-American, democratic, Christian men's organizations upholding the values of this country. White supremacy and keeping the darkies in their place was their chief concern. Doc explained that although the city had hired two black policemen, and that was a revolutionary step for Lynchburg, those black officers were only able to stop, arrest or use force against other blacks in town. Doc laughed out loud. The people in town got more than they had ever expected. The unintended consequence of their demands of city officials was that the black officers arrested more black people in town than the white officers ever did. Doc explained that the white people knew who held the power. There was never any doubt. The black officers, needing to prove they were just as good as the white officers, overdid it on the arrests of black people, and abused their authority. The black civic leaders in Lynchburg again complained to the city officials about the black officers going too far, prompting city officials to fire the newly hired black officers. Unfortunately, it didn't do the credibility of the Negro leaders any good in the eyes of the white community leaders because the blacks didn't seem to know what they wanted. Another stereotype was confirmed in their minds. Life in town settled back into a routine that had existed before the black officers were hired. Doc told the story to get the kids in the van to understand the dynamics of racism. They had to think three steps ahead of what they might request so that there would be no sudden surfacing of unintended consequences. Outcomes had to be as exact as science otherwise choose a different course of action, Doc said.

The drive took the van north on Interstate 44 into Missouri as the group continued back toward St. Louis. Just like the rest of the trip, Doc diverted from the usual path to take in additional sites especially when it involved science lessons that would benefit the kids. He pulled off the highway to go to the Onondaga Cave State Park in the southeastern part of the state. The group got out of the white van and walked to the ticket booth. Doc paid everyone's admission. This, he explained, would be quite the incredible treat. Doc told the kids that the cathedral-like caverns had been formed over millions of years. Multicolored stalactites and stalagmites filled the caverns. The group joined other people boarding a multicar open train that took tourists deep in the expansive cave. Lights were positioned strategically to show off the most interesting aspects of the arenalike opening and all of its beautiful colors. The interior was Mother Nature's canvas. Doc explained that most of Missouri was filled with limestone. Water from the surface made its way through the ground and over many millennia formed underground rivers, which had carved out underground caves such as the one the group was exploring. The different colors were the result of different elements of rocks that were in the ground. The Earth is ever changing. Man harnesses some of the elements using chemicals, engineering and physics to improve his environment. Some have good, long-lasting effects. Other things that humans have done to the planet have been disastrous from start to finish. Experiencing the interior of the cave was to give the kids a sense of the Earth's hidden majesty and inspire the youths' sense of awe and wonder. It was as important as the trip to the Grand Canyon, the Painted Desert, the Petrified Forest and the Meteor Crater. It was just closer to home.

When the tour ended, Doc's kids dug out the last of the food they had either brought or picked up. The interior of the van was pretty dirty from five people living in it for more than a week. But Doc explained as he had the kids sweep it out one last time that they were nearly home. Doc drove the last leg of the interstate back to St. Louis. There wasn't a lot of talking. Everyone was very tired. Doc dropped Jesse off at home. Jesse's mother was happy to see him and thanked Doc profusely for giving her son such a wonderful, broadening experience. Instead of Doc heading home, too, he did what he had always done after arriving in town from such long vacations. He stopped by the lab first to check on his company, open the mail, pay some bills, see whether any new orders for products had come in, and feed the dogs. Miss Phillips took care of the dogs and the company in Doc's absence. Doc's dogs were not too fond of the food he dished out to them. It was Purina Chow or what we know as a generic brand of Purina-style chow, but they preferred meat. Doc would always tell the joke of the man who loved to say that his dogs never liked meat. That would always prompt someone to ask, "I've never heard of a dog that didn't like meat." The man would respond, "Mine don't, because I don't give them any." That usually prompted people to laugh because of the unexpected punch line. Doc knew that, eventually, his dogs' pickiness would give way to their growling bellies. Dogs, like people, when they get hungry enough, will eat just about anything. Doc's kids knew Doc's habit of going to his company first, and they helped out to make the stay at Du-Good Chemical as short as possible so they could head home where they could sleep in their own beds at last.

◆ ◆ ◆ ◆ ◆

The memories were as vivid more than 30 years later as if they had just taken place. But Doc remained in the hospital. He stirred a bit more under the covers in the twin hospital bed. He still had on the thin hospital gown. He had been moved from the intensive care unit, though he was still not conscious. However, he seemed as if he was nearly out of the long deep period of being completely out and unaware. Doc's children and the others who came to visit were encouraged that he was recovering. The tubes were still attached to his skull draining fluid from the holes that doctors had drilled to relieve the pressure from the blunt-force trauma Doc suffered. But a lot less fluid was collecting in the bags beneath his bed. Hope was on the horizon.

CHAPTER 10

DOC'S RECOVERY...BUT

The first thing Doc said when he finally awakened after several days of being unconscious was that he wanted some water and something to eat. He was thirsty and famished. The people who knew him understood that he was working his way back to good health. Having an appetite for Doc was a positive sign—especially for an 89-year-old. Slowly, over the next few days Doc got stronger. He did not like being in the hospital at all. He had to be coaxed by the police to go to the hospital in the first place, and now Doc worked his hardest to get out, showing the doctors and nurses that he was fit and ready to leave. When he was released, the first thing he wanted to do was to go to Du-Good Chemical. Thinking about the lab was what sustained him and what brought him back from the near-death beating. Months later during an awards program at the Saint Louis Science Center, he told his longtime friend and golfing buddy Nathan Crump that the beating took something out of him that he wasn't prepared to ever give. Doc added that it would take years to regain what he had lost. That included a sense of confidence and a sense of trust in everyone who crossed the arched threshold of Du-Good Chemical.

Doc knew that the weeks he spent in the hospital would not cause the mail and bills at his company to stop piling up. Deterioration on the more than 100-year-old building also would not pause just because he had been away. When Doc got back to Du-Good Chemical, he realized that there was much that he needed to do. The battery on his Chevy delivery van had run down, the roof had sprung several leaks in different parts of the company, some of the plumbing was leaking and the fence to the loading area needed repair, and the gate was coming apart and needed rebuilding. Doc jumped back into work as if he had never been away. Du-Good Chemical was his life. It had always been his life for all the years after Cornell University. Working on the things around the plant helped Doc stay vital and young and have a sense of purpose. Doc climbed the ladder to the roof and rolled out tar paper and secured it with tar and roofing nails. He got his son Vincent to carry some of the material onto the roof. Doc pulled the rest up using a rope. Doc wore an old wide rimmed-felt hat to keep the sun off his mostly bald head. He always amazed the neighbors around the lab and his friends just by being on the roof at age 89. But Doc continued to climb onto the roof doing repairs for four years after that. People's assumptions were that folks Doc's age should be sitting on a porch, taking it easy in their golden years. Psychologist Diane Kappen, PhD, admired Doc. She said he always thumbed his nose at any suggestion that he should accept old age and its accompanying incapacity. Doc's sons Vincent and Lewis helped with the fence. Vincent assisted with the frame for the gate and the posts. Lewis helped put it together and get the hinges attached. Doc pronounced, as he often did: "Du-Good Chemical is back in business. We may doze, but we never close!" Explosive laughter followed, which is how people in his family expressed joy and a sense of accomplishment.

After the repairs, Doc went back to his cancer research. People often came to Doc's door seeking the serum he had developed to boost the body's immune system. It was nontoxic. In fact, several dozen people who had no hope for a cure came to Doc and found that his product worked beyond anyone's expectation. Doc always told them it wasn't for human use—just animals. However, he could not watch them 24-7 to make sure they didn't use it other than for its intended purpose. Doc also continued to send compounds to testing labs to see whether they were effective against tumors. He often boasted that he enjoyed a lot of success in tests on animals. But he was disappointed that his compounds never were advanced to test on humans. Doc was perennially frustrated that his small lab didn't have the funds or the clout to get the federal testing labs to take his work seriously. Doc saw it as another slight against him because he was African American. Doc didn't take that well and immediately pointed out any disparity in treatment to people when he thought it was merited. Doc had always been militant, fighting incessantly for the rights of African Americans. He seemed to become more militant as he grew older. He grew restless fighting the same battles and hearing the same excuses mouthed by different faces. Age dulled his tolerance and sharpened his verbal assaults against what he knew were injustices. People who visited, telephoned or wrote to Doc usually got an earful of what he had endured. Doc wouldn't give up. He continued to fight against the system that sought to limit opportunities for him and Du-Good Chemical. He always had hope, as he instilled in the boys who came to his door, that hard work would be rewarded handsomely, and Du-Good Chemical would become an empire, employing hundreds of workers, shipping orders worldwide. Doc never took rejection well. He let the boys who worked for him, some of his best students and others he could trust know that they, as African Americans, always had to work more than twice as hard to be considered half as qualified as white people, and then they needed to expect to be tested and challenged constantly in everything they attempted to prove and reprove and prove again that they, indeed, were that good. It is one of the greatest costs of being black in America. That and constantly having to put at ease white people who are in their presence. Doing both is more stressful than the actual work that blacks have to do. Nevertheless, African Americans have to do it and endure it, and deal with social exclusion, in order to succeed. It's part of the battle every day that black people face in America that their white colleagues don't know, don't understand, don't accept and many even deny exists. As Doc often said, "Racism is like the wind. You can't see it; but you can feel it."

Doc understood that the image of black people—filled with stereotypes—was the mountain that they had to climb. For that reason, Doc was never a fan of sitting through Hollywood depictions of black people. He hated "Amos 'n' Andy" and all of the other "characters" who played along with the degrading images of African Americans that the movies, television and radio projected to audiences. Doc refused to go to theaters in the South and sit in the colored-only balcony sections, which whites called "nigger heaven" because blacks at least were permitted to watch the shows. Doc even bristled after sitting through a comedy decades later at the home of his daughter, Renee, who had settled in Blue Springs, Mo. The film was simply titled "Friday." Doc said after watching the black film, "That movie had no socially redeeming value whatsoever."

Being older now and the last business standing of those that had existed in the 1200 block of South Jefferson Avenue has caused a lot of people to knock at the door of Du-Good Chemical, seeking Doc's wisdom. Some knock to learn about his life and the company he created. Others would arrive at the limestone doorstep to buy some of Doc's products, which always made him ecstatic. Doc's whole purpose with the company and the work he did in chemistry was to improve people's lives in a cost-effective manner. He would often say, "Better living through good chemistry." However, he wanted the credit for having helped people. After leaving Cornell University, he promised himself never again would his work be claimed as the intellectual property of others. When people came to his door seeking Du-Good products, it was as if they were buying a piece of Doc himself. His products included Bull's Eye mosquito repellant; Du-Good Hand Cleaner; Du-Good Dry Shampoo; Du-Good Kreation, to clear up blemishes, skin discoloration and acme; Du-Good Wig Cleaner; Du-Good Lolo Pin Curl Cream, to relax the hair of African Americans without the damaging effects of the lye used in other hair-straightening products; Du-Good After Shave Lotion, to prevent painful razor bumps in black men; Du-Good Cannonball Liniment, to ease aches and pains; Du-Good Rainbow Delight dishwashing detergent, which also could be used for delicate laundry; and Du-Good Gas Saver, for which Doc received a patent in 1985 to boost the efficiency of gasoline-powered engines. Doc was the best and most effective salesman for all of the things he made at Du-Good Chemical Laboratories & Manufacturers. His true passion was remaining fixated on doing the greater good for African Americans.

Some people rang the doorbell in the upper left-hand corner and entered the company building just to talk. It represented a new phase in which Doc helped to shape young African Americans. In the early years, he offered jobs to boys and taught them a strong work ethic. Doc did what other black businessmen did in the 1200 block of South Jefferson Avenue. In the later years, Doc became the sage, counseling young black men seeking advice. Race was always at the forefront of the conversation. It was never implied with Doc—just directly stated. You could not be black in America and ignore racism unless you were a fool or a Republican stooge. Doc always thought those were the worst kind of people because they would sell their souls and everyone else just to try to fit into white America. Surrendering their African American history, heritage and family was a fool's errand. Doc used the old Pullman porters' term to describe them: "handkerchief-head Negroes." People also would talk endlessly about starting businesses and how to do it. Doc would give them as much advice as he could spare. They were "Bunsen burner conversations" because Doc was usually working in his second-floor main laboratory as he talked with people who showed up at his company. Doc's first advice was to never depend on the Small Business Administration for help. Doc told many black men, "They only give you enough money to go broke." Many black businessmen and women start their companies frustrated because they are grossly undercapitalized, and they'd end up going belly up in less than a year. He advised people to make sure they had enough money to endure at least two years because it would take that long for a business to get a foothold, develop a market and then begin to turn a profit. Doc also advised visitors to be careful when dealing with people whose job was to "handle" minority contractors or manufacturers. That advice came from Doc's personal experience. A black businessman could expect one token order from such companies and government agencies, and that was to keep blacks who were seeking business quiet. Business success is always in repeat orders from loyal customers while attracting new clients in new markets. Anything less ensures failure. A lot of the people who landed at Doc's door had worked for corporations before deciding, as Doc had, that working for themselves at their own companies was the best way to maintain their dignity while making a living. Politics would often come up. Some folks had also worked for corporations for years and then found themselves out of a job. Age discrimination is real, and people in their mid-40s to 50s bear the scars, regardless of what the law says. Proving age discrimination is another matter.

An old television sat on top of a 1950s refrigerator in the middle aisle in the main lab at Du-Good Chemical. Usually a ballgame of some sort was on. When commercials came on, Doc loved laughing at them—especially those advertising pharmaceuticals. The long disclaimers always got Doc's attention. They would note the side effects, which often were worse than the ailments that the different drugs were intended to make right. Doc always said: "If someone came at you with a gun and shot you dead, that person would have to stand trial, be convicted and go to prison for what he did. But these corporations have the cover of time. You take their drug or use their product and nothing happens immediately. Over time, it may leave you debilitated or kill you. That time works on the side of the corporations, allowing them to get off free. The burden of proof is on the individuals, and they rarely have any concrete, convincing evidence or enough money to fight the big corporations in court."

Dr. John Gardner, a dentist, often dropped by or telephoned to quiz Doc about national goings-on. In 2007, when Sen. Barack Obama announced that he was running for president, Gardner wanted to know from Doc's perspective whether Obama had a chance of winning. People had seen Rep. Shirley

Chisholm run for president in 1972, and the Rev. Jesse Jackson in 1984 and 1988 and the Rev. Al Sharpton in 2004, all seeking the Democratic nomination for president. Obama, Doc said, was different. First, Obama had won election as a U.S. senator from Illinois. He also was a Harvard University law school graduate and was savvy as any politician. Doc didn't like that Obama threw his minister of 20 years under the bus for things the white press had accused the Rev. Jeremiah Wright of saying against white people. Obama's action seemed inexcusable to Doc, which is how many black people felt. However, Doc knew enough of politics to understand that people running for public office had to say and do just about anything to cut the right deal with the right people and raise more than enough funds from wealthy donors to get elected. Doc had seen his brother, Shingy, do it to get elected as the city's first black magistrate in St. Louis. He knew that other politicians had to do it. That was how the game was played. Obama, Doc realized, had to shape himself to be acceptable to mainstream, white America. It certainly didn't hurt Obama to have had a white mother from Kansas and a black father who was from Kenya. Many people in this country usually accepted a foreign black over anyone who was born and raised here with ancestors who had been slaves. Obama, Doc reasoned, had a chance of getting elected if he could put white people at ease, and if he could maintain the black vote by making people think he was working on their behalf while not upsetting whites or other races by actually doing so.

"Black men must always walk on eggshells in this country," Doc said. "One misstep and you're through."

Doc said Obama could make it to the White House if he remained mindful of every step he took. But if he got in, Doc said, he would have his hands more than full.

"First he will have to contend with the wars in Afghanistan and Iraq, which (President George W.) Bush left for him. Obama must also fix the economy because it was crippled by the Great Recession with a terrible jobs recovery. Times are rougher than they have ever been for poor people, although the rich are making out pretty good. Obama still has to repair the bad image that this country has abroad. Never before has it meant so little to be an American. You might as well paint a sign on your back if you are going overseas because you will be a target for scorn and ridicule." The people Doc talked to about Obama agreed.

When Obama's victory in the election was announced in November 2008, Doc said he was happy the new president was black. Yet, Doc said he remained skeptical about whether Obama would be able to fulfill all of the promises he had made. Doc believed Republicans and white people in general would try to thwart Obama's every move. Obama would have to be to the White House what Jackie Robinson was to Major League Baseball. Obama broke the color line getting elected to the highest office in the land. However, staying in office would mean he would have to be as cool as a cucumber as people would shoot racial hatred at him in condemnation of everything he might do. Not only that, but he would have to constantly be on the lookout for every crackpot trying to take a potshot at him. "Crackers will be lined up from coast to coast trying to take him out," Doc said. "If this one don't get him, then the racists feel that it will be up to the next one, and then the next one and then the next one to metaphorically assassinate his character." During Obama's candidacy for president, he had to have a Secret Service unit assigned to provide security for him and his family because of the hundreds of death threats Obama received. The threats continued after he entered the White House. Obama received more death threats than any president before him. Someone in November 2011 even fired shots from a high-powered rifle at the upper floors of the White House.

Doc said he was glad to have lived to see a black man and black family in the White House. Doc wondered how long the threats and verbal assaults would last. As the grandson of slaves and a struggling black business owner, Doc was no stranger to racism and its effects. He knew Obama's time as president would be both a tremendous source of pride and inspiration for black people but hell for Obama himself. Everything Obama proposed would be second-guessed or overruled. Nothing the new president did would be good enough for too many whites who would never accept that they were living in a nation being led by an African American—even though many were happy that Obama was half-white. Doc recalled a story in which he saw an interview in the 1950s of a white man with little formal education and whose job didn't afford him much in the way of luxuries except cigarettes and an occasional beer. But when asked whether he was smarter and better off than diplomat and U.S. intellectual Ralph Bunche, the first African American to win the Nobel Peace Prize, the man emphatically stated that he was the smarter, better man. The interviewer asked for the man to explain, sharing some of Bunche's credentials. The man said he knew he was better solely because he was white. "That sense of superiority only because of the continuing lie of race remains pervasive in America, and it will frustrate Obama from the moment he steps into the White House until the day he leaves," Doc said.

Race also crippled Obama's ability to be an effective president for African Americans. Even during the 50th anniversary of the March on Washington for Jobs and Freedom on Aug. 28, 2013, Obama, who spoke, said nothing of what he planned to do for African Americans. President John F. Kennedy didn't attend the 1963 march, attracting more than 250,000 people. But he welcomed the organizers in the White House afterward, and civil rights laws followed. Obama waited until 2014 to announce his five-year, $200 million, privately funded "My Brother's Keeper" program. In the summer of 2014 the president enlisted promises and commitments from urban school districts to help. But a lot more is needed to correct decades of neglect.

Doc knew that he and the other black men who had opened and run businesses in the 1200 block of South Jefferson Avenue were part of a glorious era for African Americans. At the time when they opened their companies, shops and churches, black people were as educated as white people like never before in the history of America. They had always contributed greatly to the United States. But they were moving more solidly into the middle class with more doctors, lawyers, teachers, engineers, pharmacists, chemists, nurses and other professionals, working in jobs that previously had been closed to black people. They were starting companies, and more were sending their children to college despite racism, segregation and Jim Crow laws. It was a slow seepage past discrimination, prejudices and bigotry, and every one of the blacks who were achieving knew they were advancing the cause not only for themselves and their families but the entire race. Never before had there been so many black business owners, and never before had they started to really accumulate wealth and own property.

All of that swiftly changed in the late 1960s and early 1970s, when so-called integration was achieved because of the Civil Rights Movement and accompanying laws. The black community that one could point to geographically in cities throughout America suddenly became less concentrated and more diffused as people sought better places to live. Upper- and middle-class blacks with the means moved to white areas that previously had been off-limits to African Americans. They weren't greeted with open arms. In fact, they often faced hostilities from whites who did not want blacks in their communities. The hostility included cross-burnings on their lawns, homes being egged and children harassed. The whites, because of blockbusting, sold their properties at a loss, fearing greater losses because of the black "infiltration" driving down their property values. The whites moved farther out into newer homes, at a greater expense. More black families then were sold the vacant homes in the newly busted neighborhoods but for actual market value. The real estate agents made a killing from the fear that racism generated. As the dollars and middle-class African Americans left the once stable black community, so did the businesses. Stores and shops no longer had the traffic and clientele. People could and did go to the white stores, where the prices often were lower and the selection greater. Companies like Doc's, producing cleaners, cosmetics and other products for the black community, found that orders from black filling stations, mechanics, and grocery stores and drugstores vanished. Big box stores and changing consumer trends, such as canvas instead of leather shoes and casual wear instead of suits put out of business what few there were left. Large corporations did the same thing to small businesses in rural, urban and suburban communities, too. The beat down was just felt in a more damaging way in the black community. Doc would lament that governments and companies would only give him unsustainable token orders for his products. As the economy continued to go bad, more black businesses suffered and folded. As the old saying goes, when white America has a cold, black America has a fatal case of pneumonia. Storefronts in the black community were boarded up, and then the buildings were torn down. Houses set empty until vandals stripped the fixtures and plumbing, resulting in massive damage. Buildings then had to be bulldozed. That went on in cities throughout the country. While the loss of property was enormous, the biggest deficit was the destruction in both black and white America of the community of small-business people who helped raise children beyond what families were capable of doing in the industrial age. Also lost were the history, heritage and sense of togetherness that bonded blacks since they were slaves in America, believing that, one day, African Americans would be free. Once they gained that so-called freedom, they pulled away from the unity that had delivered them. It was a mostly unrecorded tragedy of the 20th century.

Doc stayed attached to the old equipment and the old ways. One summer in the 1980s, his son Lewis bought Doc an electric typewriter that would enable Doc to store data so he could mass produce letters, price lists and other material that otherwise would have to be typed repeatedly. Doc's response was, "What do I need that damn thing for?" He gave the same response when Lewis bought Doc's company its first computer in the mid-1990s. But Doc's industry was changing, and a lot of data that Doc regularly submitted to the National Cancer Institute for testing of his anti-cancer compounds had to be done via email. Vincent, Doc's youngest son, took over doing that on the new computer. In the 2000s, Lewis thought Doc's office and lab chairs needed updating so he bought new chairs for the company, tossing the old, painfully uncomfortable chairs in the back of the building. After Lewis had gone, Doc went and got the old chairs. They might have been uncomfortable, but they had a history and memories with him, and that meant a lot.

The lab had witnessed a lot of history. It was in Du-Good Chemical that boys from the street watched the old black-and-white television atop a 1950s refrigerator in the center aisle at the lab as U.S. history unfolded. They saw a lot of the space program, including man setting foot on the moon in 1969. They saw many of the Civil Rights Movement marches of the 1960s, including police attacking black people with clubs, dogs and fire hoses. The civil rights protesters' main weapon was nonviolent resistance, which the Rev. Martin Luther King Jr. insisted African Americans use. The boys with Doc and Miss Phillips watched the aftermath of the assassination of President John F. Kennedy in 1963, his brother Robert Kennedy's assassination in 1968, Malcolm X's assassination in 1965, and the Rev. Martin Luther King Jr.'s "I Have a Dream" speech during the Aug. 28, 1963, March on Washington for Jobs and Freedom. They watched footage of Dr. King receiving the Nobel Peace Prize in 1964, and then King's assassination on April 4, 1968. With Doc, the boys saw and heard the many scenes of the Vietnam War unfold constantly on the TV and radio news. Miss Phillips brought the St. Louis Globe-Democrat to read; Doc took the St. Louis Post-Dispatch. Both brought in the black newspapers—the Argus, the American and the Sentinel. Du-Good Chemical was a library of newspapers, black magazines and scientific journals. The boys who entered wanting to read and learn had a wealth of information at their fingertips and very bright people who were only too eager to challenge and engage them. Doc was always there to help the boys decipher and analyze the news of the day, put it into context and connect it with history. When the boys had questions about the meanings of different words or asked about companies, Doc would charge, "Look it up!" and then toss them a dictionary or telephone book so they could find the information for themselves. Doc wanted the boys to be self-starters who could think their way out of problems rather than be dependent and create more problems for themselves.

Doc often worked late, paying bills and writing letters as the last chores of the day. He would give the mail that had to go out to whoever was still at the company with him. They would take it to the blue mailbox at Rutger Street and Jefferson Avenue. The mailbox was always there, always ready to accept what businesspeople and residents had to give. Decades later, the U.S. Postal

Service's billion-dollar debt and people's increasing Internet use caused mail service cutbacks. By the 2000s, the many, always dependable blue mailboxes and post offices had disappeared like pay phones and fire department call boxes that populated South Jefferson Avenue in the past. All of that went the way of the horse and buggy. It was the same progress that changed the veterinarian's hospital into Du-Good Chemical. Change is the only constant. Beautiful ideas bring new uses to buildings and the land. The Rev. Nance's church, the Second Corinthian Baptist Church at 2352 Hickory St., became a beauty salon and nail parlor. Instead of being a house of worship, ministering to the souls of black folks as they settled in the city during the Great Migration from the South, it became a place that catered to the material needs of blacks who put a premium on looking good and feeling well-polished. The salon didn't champion the need for a good education and wealth creation, which Doc and many of the other black businesspeople in the 1200 block of South Jefferson Avenue thought were important for folks seeking a better life for themselves and their children.

Doc got out front and stayed there as he aged from 89 into his 90s, surviving the terrible assault at his company. The Saint Louis Science Center at the urging of Doc's daughter, Renee, honored Doc for his work. The Science Center since it opened had set up exhibits honoring Doc and had him there as a speaker because of his research and for having trained and coached hundreds of blacks for many fields in the sciences.

What riled Doc were the organizations that for decades had shunned or diminished his work in research and chemistry. After the Science Center award, groups and people who had shunned Doc for years eagerly knocked at Du-Good Chemical's door wanting to honor Doc for his commitment, his contributions and his staying power. Doc accepted the honors, but he would never forget how they kept him down and refused to do business with Du-Good Chemical. It was only when it benefited their organizations, making it appear as if they supported the work of black scientists, that they turned to Doc to help bolster their image. Doc spoke of it often after he accepted the honors. The acknowledgements followed work Doc had done decades earlier for the National Association for the Advancement of Colored People and the Urban League to test companies that said they had hired blacks. Doc would put in applications at the urgings of the civil rights organizations only to have chemical companies where he had applied say he had never been there. Confronting companies in such lies and racism gave Doc great satisfaction.

Toward the end of Du-Good Chemical, Doc feared that young blacks had lost that sense that something was wrong in America. They had a feeling that they were just as accepted and welcomed in this country as whites were. Doc and other older African Americans feared that young blacks were being set up for a great fall and generations of continued exploitation. The question was who would help teach them the truth if the old lions of the Civil Rights era had all passed away, and all that was left were those who Dr. Carter G. Woodson feared were all too eager to feed young blacks untruths about the race. It was a vacuum as old as slavery in the Americas, and without black teachers who were aware and prepared, the lie would advance unchallenged.

Doc did commonplace things, too, especially when the boys in the neighborhood had grown up and new generations of others stopped coming to the door for work. Doc always got the neighborhood's attention by mowing the curbside grass in front of Du-Good Chemical with a push mower. He did that into his early 90s. The neighborhood had changed a lot by then, going from rundown older brick homes and apartments to newer units installed in the 1970s, 1980s and 1990s, when the area went through redevelopment. Older families were replaced by younger people, many of them barely getting by or living in units that had been converted to Section 8 subsidized housing. The neighborhood was still rough, with kids hanging out a lot. But what was different was there were no businesses run by black men who would take the youths in and provide the instruction they needed to help them navigate the world.

A lot had changed for Doc and Du-Good Chemical. Each was aging. The assault at age 89 was not Doc's first setback. His wife, Nancy, had begun to lose her memory in the late 1980s. By 1991 on a trip to New York City to visit their oldest son, David, a physician, it was clear she was suffering the effects of Alzheimer's disease. On July 17, 1994, Nancy walked away from the family home on Lafayette Avenue a half block west of Grand Avenue. Her body was found three days later in the Mississippi River near Jefferson Barracks about 30 miles downstream from downtown St. Louis. The cause of death was undetermined because of the condition of the body. She was the first of her six siblings to die. Her mother and grandmother had had Alzheimer's at the time of their deaths. Nancy had gone to college to be an educator. Her most important work was raising and adding to the education of the couple's four children.

Doc remained proud of the accomplishments of his company, and soldiered on after Nancy's death in 1994. Doc grieved the loss of his brother

Shingy in 1971 of cancer. Hubert Diuguid, the Lynchburg, Va., dentist, died in 1985, also of cancer. Doc's oldest sister, Sherley Newsome, who used to mail him old clothes which Doc used for rags at the company, died in the 1980s. His younger sister, Elwyza died in 2002 at age 90. Of the nine children of Lewis and Bettie Diuguid, Doc was the last survivor. The other brothers died years earlier.

Doc kept going focusing mostly on research after the Arab Oil Embargo of the early 1970s and the disappearance of black businesses that used to buy Du-Good products. That was part of the high cost of integration. Thanks to the Civil Rights Act of 1964 and the Voting Rights Act of 1965, African Americans with money could move into homes or apartments just about anywhere. Public accommodation laws made that possible. They could go to bars, restaurants, movie theaters, swimming pools, parks and amusement centers that previously kept them from entering. As white businesses opened up to black customers, black shoppers stopped going into black-owned businesses. Doc managed to stay afloat. The teaching job Doc held at Stowe then Harris and then Harris-Stowe State College provided a steady income. Du-Good Chemical managed often to just break even or have slight losses, all because of Doc being a tight money manager. Doc, more than anyone watched his pennies closely, figuring that if he kept close track of his pennies, he would never have to worry about the dollars. They would naturally come.

Still Doc played golf regularly for entertainment and exercise. He also regularly attended annual meetings of the American Chemical Society and sometimes went to the regional meetings as well. He often presented scientific papers on the groundbreaking work he continued to do at his company.

In his storied career, Doc after graduating magna cum laude from West Virginia State College in 1938 with degrees in chemistry and education, and then a master's degree in chemistry in 1939 from Cornell University in Ithaca, N.Y., became head of the chemistry department from 1939 to 1943 at AM&N College, Pine Bluff, Ark. In addition, Doc bought a used, beat-up truck and did light hauling to earn extra money. Doc always taught the boys who came to his door looking for work to be enterprising and assertive if they had any hope of making it in the world as young African American males. Doc lived it, and he knew it paid off.

Doc went back to Cornell University to get his doctorate and continued working there doing post-doctorate studies on malaria. While working under Nobel Prize-winning chemists, he developed a plasticizing agent using jet fuel, enabling plastics to be developed for everyday use. Doc often said that although he did the work, all he got for it was a pat on the back and a handshake. That left a bitter taste in his mouth, realizing that when he worked under others, he had no control and no ownership over his intellectual property. That became Doc's motivation for starting his own company even though decades of struggles followed to keep it going. After Cornell University, Doc did research and consulting work, finding it impossible to land a job working as a highly credentialed African American chemist. Doc said many companies wanted to hire him, however, they said he would have to completely abandon his family and any history of being black and pass as a white chemist. He also was told that because the corporate administration knew his racial background, they prohibited him from interacting with the rest of the staff. He was to do his work, associate with no one and leave when the work was done. Doc could not surrender who he was or the family he held dear. Doc tried to instill that sense of heritage and pride in all of the boys who came to work at his company and especially his own children. After starting Du-Good Chemical in 1947, Doc also worked as a consultant in science for AM&N College from 1949 to 1955. He did that in addition to running Du-Good Chemical and working at Stowe Teachers College as a professor of chemistry from 1949 to 1955. Doc stayed with the college, though the name changed, until 1982 when he retired at age 65, always insisting that the college get its staff to become published researchers. Few did. The college had been part of the St. Louis School District when Doc started, and moved under the Missouri state university system years later. Doc had served as a professor of chemistry and chairman of the physical science department from 1955 to 1982.

Doc was a stickler for perfection. He insisted that his students accept nothing less than excellence. They were future teachers, and Doc knew that they had to know science in order to teach it to children. Many of his students returned, often thanking him for being so tough on them. One nun who was in Doc's class was among them. She went to see Doc at Du-Good Chemical and told him, "I've often had very bad thoughts about you."

Doc only laughed. She followed up saying that his unyielding demand for excellence in his class helped make her a better chemistry professor. She was able to write good lesson plans each day for her students because of Doc's insistence when she was in his class. A lot of Doc's chemistry students often had to make up their lab work at his company on the weekends to get a passing grade. Many grumbled to Doc's kids about having to go that extra mile. Doc's kids often shot back: "You only have him for a semester. We have him for life." Doc's insistence prepared everyone who passed through Du-Good Chemical to be able to endure the worst that life and the corporate world had to throw at them and still be successful.

Doc served as a good example of someone who was an overachiever. He was a research associate from 1959 to 1961 at Jewish Hospital. Doc was research director for the Leukemia Guild of Missouri and Illinois from 1961 to 1963. He was a visiting professor at Washington University in St. Louis from 1966 to 1968. And after retiring from Harris-Stowe, he was professor emeritus.

Doc continued to run Du-Good Chemical until 2011. The organizations he belonged to included Sigma Xi, the American Chemical Society, the National Education Association, Phi Kappa Phi, the American Association of University Professors, the Missouri State Teachers Association, the Association of Consulting Chemists & Chemical Engineers Inc. and Omega Psi Phi Fraternity.

Doc's honors and awards included the publication of "The Use of Amalgated Aluminum as a Catalyst in the Friedel-Crafts Reaction, Journal of the American Chemical Society 63"; 1941, Ref, In Organic Reactions Vol III 1946, "Synthetic Organic Chemistry" 1953; "Benzothiazoles II Nuclear Chlorination in the Hertz Process" 1947; "Joint Symposium on Micro Chemistry & Pet Industry" 1949; "Synthesis of Long Straight Chain Dicarboxylic Acids via the Ketene Synthesis" 1952; "Methods for the Micro Determination of Mixed Halogens & Amide Group" 1952; "Synthesis of Plasticizing Agents from the Reaction of Olefins & Formaldehyde Condensation" 1957; "Micro Determination of Sulfur & Phosphorus in Organic Compounds by Perchloric Acid Digestion"; co-authored a chapter on thyoxine research in "Radiossay in Clinical Medicine," by CC Thomas, Springfield, Ill.; Man of the Year Award from Omega Psi Phi, 1960; vice president 1963 of the Leukemia Guild of Missouri and Illinois 19; Carver Civic Award, 1979; U.S. Patent 1985; Burning Efficiency Enhancement Method, Santonic Acid, Pyrazinondole and Indole 85; St. Louis American Newspaper Merit Award 1992; recipient of the American Chemical Society Award Salute to Excellence, 2000. Doc was well-known for his continuing work to discover a cure for cancer.

Doc has received lifetime achievement awards and legacy in science awards from the Saint Louis Science Center and from Harris-Stowe State University for Honorary Doctor of Humanities. Doc was also honored by Blacks in Science at its annual awards dinner in 2008 at the Science Center. Dr. Lincoln Diuguid's name is included with 16 others in the St. Louis Walk of Fame at North 21st Street and Dr. Martin Luther King Jr. Drive. Other notable St. Louis residents whose names are embedded in the sidewalk are rock 'n' roll musician Chuck Berry and musician and businessman Lloyd Arthur Smith.

Doc has accumulated many awards and honors and has spoken to science, education and community groups all over the country. His message remains simple. Never give up; never give in. There are always other answers and other solutions to problems. One just has to remain committed to finding the answer that works.

Doc's greatest legacy and his greatest reward were his children and the young men of the 1200 block of South Jefferson Avenue. Many of them went on to great careers in the sciences because of Doc and the other small black businesses of the past and the hunger those kids had for something more.

AFTERWORD

"I am only one, but still I am one. I cannot do everything, but still I can do something; and because I cannot do everything, I will not refuse to do something that I can do."

— Helen Keller

Now that you have gotten to know Doc Diuguid and his many contributions to his community and the science world, let me ask what he would ask—"What are you going to do, now?"

Doc knew the only way to truly affect change and to help improve the world around us is for individuals to engage. I know few people could start a small business in a community of color or teach science at a university. (If you can, please do.) But there is something you can do. There is something we can all do! If Doc asked you what you were going to do to contribute as he had contributed, he never would have a tolerated an answer like "I don't know" or "The problems are to big. I am not sure what I can do." As an example, Doc became estranged from his fraternity in the late 1950s, early 1960s when he sought contributions for scholarships for black students and encountered shrugs, closed doors and turned out empty pockets from fraternity brothers he approached. Doc would insist that each of us must do something! In a society with so much trauma—and blacks are subjected to the worst of it—there is always something each of us can do to contribute to improving life overall.

Having read Lewis' first two books, "A Teacher's Cry" and "Discovering the Real America" (available on Amazon), before I met Doc Diuguid, I knew

Lewis had a real passion for helping others and doing his part to improve the world condition. I only really began to understand the origins and passion for this work when I met his father, Dr. Lincoln Diuguid. Then, when I read the early drafts of the manuscript of *Our Fathers*, did I understand that the true depth of this passion and commitment were instilled in him over decades of working with and receiving a lifetime of guidance and wisdom from his father and the men of his St. Louis childhood community.

In speeches and lectures on diversity Lewis says that because of his childhood in the lab and working with Doc that he thinks in formulas. During my visits with Doc, we often had discussions about race, education and the world. He always said everyone must contribute to making things better. I would ask Doc how others could contribute as he had. He always turned to his love of science. He would say: "I love chemistry because everything is a formula. To find the answer you just have to find the right formula." The same is true in life! You have to find the right formula—the right plan—for you to have a positive influence on those around you. You don't have to reinvent the wheel, just find your formula.

That formula for you might include something as simple, yet as important, as reading to kids in your community. Or your formula might include investing in and engaging in organizations that are already doing good work. There are many churches, synagogues, mosques and temples that do great work. You can find one in your community. There are also organizations, large and small that would appreciate your involvement.

Here are just a few organizations that would welcome your involvement and contributions:

My Brother's Keeper https://www.whitehouse.gov/my-brothers-keeper
My Brother's Keeper is about "helping more of our young people stay on track. Providing the support they need to think more broadly about their future. Building on what works—when it works, in those critical life-changing moments."_ President Barack Obama

100 Black Men http://www.100blackmen.org/mentoring.aspx
Mentoring the 100 Way® *— A holistic mentoring program that addresses the social, emotional and cultural needs of children ages 8 to 18. Members of the 100 are trained and certified to become mentors, advocates, and role models for the youth within their communities. Our members forge relationships that positively impact our greatest resource: our youth. The program focuses on building essential skills needed to become productive, contributing citizens.*

National Urban League www.iamimpowered.com/programs/project-ready
Project Ready is designed to get African American youths ready for college, work and life. It helps eighth-12th-grade students make academic progress, benefit from cultural enrichment opportunities and develop important skills, attitudes and aptitudes that will aid in their transition from high school and position them for postsecondary success.

Habitat for Humanity http://www.habitat.org/getinv
Habitat for Humanity is a nonprofit Christian housing organization founded on the conviction that everyone should have a decent, safe, affordable place to live. We have more than 1,400 local U.S. affiliates and over 70 national organizations around the world. Together, we have helped 6.8 million people find strength, stability and independence through safe, decent and affordable shelter since 1976.

Big Brothers, Big Sisters http://www.bbbs.org/ (then click on the volunteer button)
Being a Big Brother or Big Sister is one of the most enjoyable things you'll ever do. Not to mention, one of the most fulfilling. You have the opportunity to help shape a child's future for the better by empowering him or her to achieve. And the best part is, it's actually a lot of fun. Whatever it is you enjoy, odds are you'll enjoy it even more with your Little (Brother/Sister)—and you'll be making a life-changing impact.

Fathers Inc. http://www.fathers-inc.com/index-1.html
Statistics show that children from single parent homes are currently more at risk of neglect, low self-esteem and behavioral issues. We work to combat these statistics by empowering families through education that will better equip them with the tools to overcome adversity. It's our way of making a lifetime investment in the community.

Girl Scouts of America http://www.girlscouts.org/content/gsusa/en/adults/volunteer.html
As a volunteer, you'll introduce girls to new experiences—and show them they're capable of more than they ever imagined. You'll be their cheerleader, guide and mentor, helping them develop skills and confidence that will last a lifetime.

Boy Scouts of America http://www.scouting.org/Volunteer.aspx
The Boy Scouts of America relies on dedicated volunteers to promote its mission of preparing young people to make ethical and moral choices over their lifetime. (Doc's sons were Boy Scouts).

Camp Fire http://campfire.org
As a Camp Fire volunteer, you will make a meaningful difference, whether your time is devoted to youth programming, fundraising, event planning, serving on a board of directors or in other ways that you help determine.

Girls Who Code http://girlswhocode.com/get-involved/
Girls Who Code is a national nonprofit organization that aims to close the gender gap in technology. Our programs inspire, educate and equip girls with the computing skills to pursue 21st century opportunities. Girls Who Code Clubs are expanding nationally to offer computer science education and tech industry exposure to sixth- to 12th-grade girls during the academic year.

Million Women Mentors http://www.millionwomenmentors.org
Million Women Mentors supports the engagement of one million Science, Technology, Engineering and Math (STEM) mentors (male and female) to increase the interest and confidence of girls and women to persist and succeed in STEM programs and careers.

The National Mentoring Partnership (MENTOR) http://www.mentoring.org/get-involved/
MENTOR's vision is that every young person has the supportive relationships they need to grow and develop into thriving, productive and engaged adults. MENTOR's mission is to fuel the quality and quantity of mentoring relationships for America's young people and to close the mentoring gap for the one in three young people growing up without this critical support.

There are many more national and local organizations that help affect positive changes in the lives of children and adults. There are also many soup kitchens and food pantries that help feed those who are struggling. This may be a part of your formula.

Our Fathers is Doc Diuguid's story. But it only tells you about the boys he mentored. He didn't restrict his mentoring to children. That was just the beginning. He mentored his students at the universities, where he taught chemistry. He also mentored many men and women who sought him out for work or wisdom. Please take the time to read the appendix and the remembrances from some of Doc's mentees, shared with the family after Doc passed in 2015. Their words help tell his story and the importance of mentoring.

Mentoring is vital to expanding the horizons for young people in your community. But if you are more comfortable with adults, you can still speak into the lives of those needing guidance.

Mentoring can help undo the damage of many types of trauma. According to The National Mentoring Partnership (MENTOR) young people who are mentored are 55 percent more likely to go to in college. They are 78 percent more likely to become regular volunteers themselves. Young people who have mentors are 130 percent more likely to become leaders as adults.

The need for mentoring crosses all barriers. Young women need to be encouraged to go into math and the sciences, as do young men of color. Young men need to be encouraged to consider nontraditional jobs like those in primary education. An important part of diversifying the teacher workforce is getting more men in the classroom. Kids also need to be encouraged and engaged in the arts. Creativity can be very healing from the effects of trauma. All young kids need to be read to and encouraged to read. Kids who are not reading at grade level by third grade account of 64 percent of the kids who do not graduate from high school. Those not reading at grade level by third grade are also far more likely end up in prison. You can help with this! Simply reading, questioning without being judgmental, listening and engaging their curiosity is important. So, whatever your interest or theirs, you can easily support the positive growth of a child (or many). It isn't rocket science—like chemistry—just find the formula that works best for you.

Whatever you do, please do something. As you learned from reading this book, Doc would never tolerate laziness, and he expected a strong work ethic from everyone. These are important attributes to have and to pass on. Doc also, managed his money well, he taught his children and mentees the importance of being fiscally responsible and other important values for good citizenship. He wasn't always easy, but he was consistent, insistent, irresistible, committed and engaged. There is so much wisdom in the pages of *Our Fathers*. Please go back through the book and find the wisdom that speaks to you. Find your "formula" to being a part of the solution and contributing in a positive way to those around you. Also, encourage others to read *Our Fathers: Making Black Men*. Enjoy Doc's story, and learn from it. In doing so you can, like Doc Diuguid, make an important difference.

Bette Tate-Beaver
Executive Director
National Association for Multicultural Education (NAME)

APPENDIX

Lincoln I. Diuguid Enriched Lives of Many

For nearly four years I have kept a set of hair-cutting tools in my car.

That way they'd be there on my monthly trips to St. Louis, where I cut my dad's hair. He adored having my partner Bette do his nails. Dad had been so fiercely independent that he did all of that and more until his memory failed in June 2011.

For his safety and others', my siblings and I had Dad evaluated against his protests, and then admitted to a nursing home. We failed to act similarly with our mom, who had Alzheimer's disease. She walked away from the family home on July 17, 1994. Her body was found days later in the Mississippi River. She was 62.

Dad in 2011 was 94. His dementia was from being beaten unconscious and robbed Aug. 5, 2006, inside his chemical company by a Hurricane Katrina evacuee. Dad was trying to help the man with a job at his chemical company doing some painting. Brain surgery followed. Miraculously Dad survived.

But stubbornness prevented him from returning to have some remaining fluid removed from his brain. He went back to his life, the company he founded in 1947 and his work. Dad had a love for science, growing up in the heyday of Thomas Edison, Lewis Latimer, Albert Einstein, Henry Ford and Garrett Morgan. It drove him to work harder than anyone I've ever known.

He graduated magna cum laude from West Virginia State College in 1938. It was there that he heard lectures from George Washington Carver, who saved American agriculture, and Carter G. Woodson, who started Negro History Week in 1926, which became Black History Month in 1976.

At Cornell University, Dad got his master's in 1939. From 1939 to 1943 he was the head of the chemistry department at AM&N College in Pine Bluff, Ark., and worked at the Pine Bluff Arsenal during World War II. He returned to Cornell University in 1945, getting his PhD and did post-doctorate studies, developing a plasticizing agent from jet fuel. If you love plastic, credit Dad. But because no one would hire a black chemist, Dad in 1947 left to start his own company, working with his dad and brothers to convert a large animal hospital into a black business.

He taught chemistry and physical science for nearly four decades at Stowe Teachers College before integration, and after at Harris-Stowe State University and Washington University. He ran his company, maintained rental property, did cancer research, microanalytical work, consulting, advised Veterans Affairs in research and annually presented scientific papers at the American Chemical Society. Dad worked from 7 a.m. to 1 a.m. He'd go home, get dinner, grade papers, sleep for four hours tops and charge again at each new day. As kids, we worked at the company, keeping Dad's hours and pace. He also loved to play golf. Dad won numerous honors and awards.

At a court hearing in 2011, where my sister Renee became Dad's guardian, the judge asked, "I'll bet that all of your life you were the smartest man in the room?" The judge was right. But Dad couldn't remember that he had seven grandchildren. When asked what year it was he said, "1950-something."

He had been in the nursing home since, where I've cut his hair, using the skills he taught me. Bette cut and filed his nails, and we'd chat about Tiger Woods, President Barack Obama, race relations and work—things Dad adored.

The nursing home became like a hotel to him after his initial hatred faded in a dementia fog. At a family reunion last year he shocked everyone, saying his end was near.

Bette and I were to go to St. Louis on Friday to get Dad dolled up for his 98th birthday. But my brother Vincent in St. Louis texted us Jan. 27, saying Dad had died. He had gotten the flu and pneumonia.

So the family will gather Saturday for Dad's memorial service with many of his former students and boys (now men) whom he pulled from the street into his company for jobs and careers in the sciences.

We'll celebrate Dad's incredible life and how this grandson of slaves enriched us all.

Lewis W. Diuguid
The Kansas City Star
Feb. 4, 2015

Museum displays familiar black history

The four desks at my dad's St. Louis chemical company stayed piled high with months of science journals, letters, his research notes and papers from his students.

But no one was to disturb any of it. Dad knew exactly where he left things, why they were there and what he intended to do with them. So it was odd to see clear space on two of those desks at the George B. Vashon African American Research Center Museum in St. Louis.

But it was also gratifying to know that key items from the company Lincoln Diuguid started in 1947 after post-doctorate studies at Cornell University had been preserved. Du-Good Chemical Laboratories and Manufacturers began in what had been a large animal hospital the Diuguid family retrofitted.

For 64 years, Dad kept the company alive, only closing for good when he went into a nursing home in 2011. He died last year. He would have been 99 this Saturday.

But Dad and the legend he became live on in the museum that Calvin Riley started in the former mansion, turned mortuary, turned church, which Riley rehabbed and has opened. For Black History Month, the museum is where people can go to research black accomplishments and culture. Riley, a retired St. Louis schoolteacher, also was one of Dad's college students.

"He was rough—good, but he was rough, " Riley said, echoing what I've heard Dad's chemistry and physical science students say for decades. Students who had to make up classwork often did it at Dad's company under his intense scrutiny. My siblings and I worked there from our earliest memories through college and beyond. Riley had products we manufactured, shipped and sold nationwide to black drugstores, mechanics, beauty salons, barbershops and distributors. Dad advertised in black newspapers and radio stations and had us mail calendars to customers. He'd hire kids off the street to help with the production, and then sell them on science careers.

Company artifacts, letters, photos and cancer research papers in Riley's museum tell the story. Some of the pictures I took for Dad to accompany scientific papers that he presented at American Chemical Society conventions. Other photos of Dad with his Cornell classmates and the men with whom he pledged Omega Psi Phi fraternity at West Virginia State College in the 1930s I'd never seen.

The museum includes Dad's laboratory glassware, scales he used to weigh compound samples down to fractions of a gram and a microscope.

"People come through, and it blows them away, " Riley said. "They say there's nothing like it in St. Louis."

He's right, but it was the everyday stuff of my youth.

The museum also houses photographs of civil rights leaders like the Rev. Martin Luther King Jr., autographed pictures of legendary black singers, musicians, sports figures and entertainers such as Jimi Hendrix, Sam Cooke, the Marvelettes, Satchel Paige, Louis Armstrong and Little Anthony and the Imperials. President Barack Obama is in the museum, too.

The museum contains black-face antique items and minstrel show images. It has a 20th century Formica top kitchen table, chairs, decorative shelves, canisters, cabinets and wall hangings. There are black beautician and barber tools, work table and mirror - some pulled from Dad's company. Dad had rented space to beauticians.

There are items from Stowe Teachers College, which before the Brown vs. Topeka Board of Education Supreme Court ruling in 1954 was where black students were forced to go. After the high court ruling, outlawing legal segregation, Stowe closed, and Dad with the black faculty and students were merged into Harris Teachers College. That's at the museum, too.

The museum is a treasure. More people need to enjoy the black history it has to offer.

Lewis W. Diuguid
The Kansas City Star
Feb. 3, 2016

Friend, Mentor, Guiding Light in Total Darkness

I like Dr. Lincoln Diuguid. He went beyond his role as mentor and became my friend, one of my best friends. The first time I met Dr. Diuguid, was the summer of 1980 or 1981. I was waiting at the door of his laboratory, at 1215 S. Jefferson Ave. I looked down the street and saw, what I thought, an old white man approaching me. When he reached the door, he asked me, "Can I help you?"

I said that I was looking for Dr. Diuguid. He said he was Dr. Diuguid. And he invited me into the outer office, where we discussed my purpose for wanting to see him.

Afterward, he invited me upstairs to the second-floor lab, where we continued our conversation.

At the time we both smoked, an ugly habit we both later gave up. But when ashes from my cigarette fell to the floor, he became very irritated, and abruptly said: "What in the hell are you doing? My daughter Renee just swept, mopped and waxed these floors."

Needlessly to say, he scared the hell out of me. And I didn't know what to think at the time. But we continued our conversation and a couple hours later I came to the conclusion that if he had a mind to do it, I thought he would be a good mentor for me.

At the time I really needed direction. And I was lucky, or blessed to be directed to him and his lab.

I was three years out of college with a degree in biology. I was working at Sigma Chemical as a chemist, and at that time this company was not very diversity-oriented. Two or three months after meeting Dr. Diuguid, I was asked to quit or be fired at Sigma Chemical. And thus began a journey that would not only transform me but also transform my life.

When I told Doc, as I called him, he immediately asked me to work for him for about $50/week until I found something else to do. I thanked him, and asked him, "Where do we start?" The first thing he did was to access how much chemistry I really knew. I hate to admit it now, but it wasn't very much.

Not only did he teach me the A,B,C's of chemistry, but he also taught me how to tar paper a roof with light and heavy tar, he taught me plumbing and some electrical work. He always said that if you own your own business, you have to know how to do everything.

Dr. Diuguid was a micro-analytical chemist. Nowadays, machines do the work he did. At that time he was the only person with a company that did that kind of work in the entire St. Louis region. He did analyses for Shell Oil, Monsanto, Mallinckrodt and a host of other medium and smaller sized companies.

Being around him lit a fire in my soul that led me to yearn for more education. I re-entered college to obtain a bachelor's degree in medical technology.

One of my first classes was organic chemistry. I aced the course, and my organic chemistry teacher asked me whether I wanted to get a master's degree in chemistry. I jumped at the opportunity. Having carried a B+ average in my master's program, for some reason I was led to take the dental admissions test. I didn't prepare for the test at all but passed with scores to rival my peers. I was accepted into four dental schools.

While working on my chemistry degree, Doc decided to teach me golf at the Forest Park golf course. We would sneak on the course around the seventh or eighth tee and play for free. And so began my lessons on life.

I was usually complaining because of the ill treatment I received from my advisers and some of the other teachers. Doc listened for a while. But he would eventually say, "Shut up, and hit the ball."

Even today when confronted with problems I am reminded to shut up, stop complaining and do what must be done to hit the ball. Golf is a complicated sport, with a complicated swing, and it's more complicated because of the obstacles. You have to first learn the game, learn what makes a good swing for you and learn how to stay out of the obstacles and/or get out of obstacles.

Life at its very best is very complicated. You have to learn the games people play, learn what works for you and learn that wherever you go, there are obstacles that have to be avoided and/or learn how to get out and away. From Doc I learned that golf is symbolic of every aspect of life.

To make a long story short, I received my master's in chemistry and my doctorate of dental medicine. I have been a dentist for more than 23 years. Would I have succeeded and accomplished all that I have without having known Dr. Diuguid? I'd like to think I would, but this I do know, it would have been a hell of a lot harder if I had never met him.

It's been said:

If I can help somebody, as I travel along

If I can cheer somebody, with a word or song

If I can show somebody, he is traveling wrong

Then my living shall not be in vain.

In my opinion the life of Dr. Lincoln Isaiah Diuguid was not in vain.

Dr. Jon Gardner
Dentist
Friend of Doc's
St. Louis

Inspirational Cancer Researcher

I taught math at Harris-Stowe Teachers College while I was still a graduate student, which is to say that I was quite young—certainly 20 years younger than Dr. Diuguid was. My most vivid memory is of a conversation we had shortly after we met when he explained his work researching the effectiveness of cancer drugs, and I was so impressed by his patience and drive. He obviously was devoted to his work.

Deborah Doyle Faust
St. Louis

Helping and Learning from Greatest of Teachers

I met Dr. Lincoln Diuguid when he was 81. I suppose that makes me one of his newer friends. I had read about him in the St. Louis Post Dispatch. Being a teacher, I feel like I have the ability to recognize individuals with great intellect and talent. And Dr. Diuguid met my criteria instantly. I wanted to help him in any way I could and learn more about cancer research, after having lost my aunt to cancer the year before.

I helped Dr. Diuguid with some of his unfinished projects, including an animal tissue extract, and his desire to see some of his compounds tested in a mouse model. In the process, he taught me a lot of chemistry and how to submit compounds to the National Cancer Institute's extramural program and about the institute's Natural Products Branch. To this day I still have a close relationship with both aspects of the institute and submit compounds to the extramural program for testing against 60 different cancer cells.

Twice a year, I teach with the St. Louis American Chemical Society Chapter at the St. Louis Science Center. Last fall there I taught two Southern Illinois University at Edwardsville chemistry students how they can submit compounds to the National Cancer Institute, keeping Dr. Diuguid's dream of finding a cancer cure alive.

Dan Newman
St. Louis

Diuguid Foundation Needed to Help Others

Doc Diuguid's impact on me was great. Doc was a mentor and father figure to me. I lost my dad 28 years ago to cancer. Doc gave me good advice and guidance when I needed it. Rudyard Kipling wrote about keeping the common touch in his poem, "If." Doc kept the common touch with all people, considering his brilliance and innovation. Doc had lot of stories. The one I liked the most was his Cornell University story. When I think about it and the way he presented it, you can't do anything but laugh. It is when Doc met this white man that went to Cornell College in Iowa, and Doc told the man that he went to Cornell University in New York. The man mused and asked him did he mean Cornell in Iowa and Doc using his sarcastic comedy told the man, "No, I mean Cornell University in New York." The man's response was, "How did you get to go to a school like that and not me?" Doc exposed the man's white privilege. This is but one of the many stories Doc would tell when making a point about white privilege and racism.

I would like to see a Diuguid Foundation created to help desiring African American students go to college or graduate school in the area of science and entrepreneurship. It would be a lasting legacy to Doc. He believed in both areas, and I am sure there would be enough support to make it regional at first, and then national especially at historically black colleges.

King L. Taylor Jr.
Florissant, Mo.

My Teacher, My Friend

From the time I was a young boy growing up in Richmond Heights, a suburb of St. Louis, one of my early boyhood interests—second only to sports and military science—was chemistry. But it wasn't until I met Dr. Lincoln Diuguid, aka "Doc" that I knew it was "cosmetic chemistry" that would occupy my latter years. I started studying under Doc in the mid-1980s off and on, and then again years later at his laboratory at 1215 South Jefferson Ave. It wasn't until his later moments, his last days on earth that I truly began to feel and appreciate the life-altering effect Doc had on me. While visiting and sitting with him at Beauvais Manor Nursing Home, I found myself thinking, childishly wishing somehow I had magical powers, the ability to communicate with him via the dark cloudy recesses of his great and resplendent intellectual mind, wishing I could somehow reverse his dementia and restore his beautiful mind.

I oftentimes played music from the 1930s and 1940s via my smartphone (Billie Holiday, Sarah Vaughan, and Duke Ellington etc.). He always recognized all of their voices especially Billie Holiday or I would mention Lynchburg, Va., or Cornell University, hoping this would help restore his memory even for a fleeting moment. At times it worked as we dove into a conversation about one of the subject matters. At first, I found myself overwhelmed with sadness looking into his bright, joyful and full-of-life eyes, thinking how unfair life was as I sat next to this genius, "Einstein-like" person, yet his mind was in a different dimension and sphere. Then joy began to overtake me as I began to reminisce of better days, happier times, mind-changing experiences that God had allowed me to have via this wonderful teacher and friend.

I recall the second or third time visiting Doc when an African American male aid/nurse, whose name I can't remember, had me in stitches laughing as he told me a story about Doc shortly after he arrived at Beauvais Manor. Doc was sitting and talking among some of the other residents when one of the nurses/aids was attempting to draw attention or point Doc out to one of the other employees for some reason and made the mistake of pointing his way and referring to him as "that little white man over there." Doc noticing and overhearing her refer to him as a little white man responded like the mighty battleship Missouri, giving her a full broadside, letting everyone know he was African American, and I'm told it took him a whole week to calm down.

After medically retiring from the U.S. Army after the first Gulf War and returning to St. Louis, I ran into one of Doc's older students and fraternity brothers who informed me Doc had passed away. I recall tears filling my eyes and the great sadness that overtook me. A few days had passed, and my soul would not let me rest. Something just didn't add up as I heard nothing of Doc's death on either TV or in the newspapers. Surely a man of his stature passing away would be covered by the local media. I recall that day in May picking up my phone to call his number, not knowing what to expect. After a few rings, an old familiar voice answered, saying "Du-Good Chemical." For a fleeting moment my mind and voice were frozen. "Doc, is that you?" "Yeah, this is Dr. Diuguid." After gathering my composure, I explained to him how I was told of his passing. In the typical Dr. Diuguid fashion he replied, "Well, didn't nobody tell me, and I feel I should have been the first one told, that's only fair." I hysterically laughed yet felt overjoyed that my mentor and friend, the man who helped me experience and do so many wonderful things in his chemistry lab, was alive. "Doc, how about lunch tomorrow?" I asked. "Sure that would be fine," he replied.

Wanting to impress my teacher, I had plans to take him to the Chase Park Plaza Hotel for a first-class lunch. Once I arrived at 1215 S. Jefferson Ave. to pick Doc up, I recall banging on the front door of the building only to receive a permeating pious voice from the roof of his two-story red-brick building. Raising my head skyward while shielding my eyes from the mid-day sun, I heard "Who is it?"

"Doc, it's me, Daryle, and what are you doing on top of that roof?"

Again, I got a typical Dr. Diuguid response: "What does it look like? I'm patching a hole, I'll be down."

Now I'm thinking to myself, what in the …. Doc was 90-something years old climbing up and down on a ladder on a two-story building to repair a hole in his roof. Oh my God, I thought, but then again it's Doc! If ever there was a man on earth who could rub two pennies together and get a dime, it's Doc!

Once down from the roof and we were face to face, I recall simply looking at him and quoted something he told me many times before, "Live everyday like it's your last day on earth" and one of his favorite responses was, "You've got that right!"

"Come on Doc, we're headed to the Chase for lunch."

His reply was: "The Chase! Man you can save that money. We can go right around the corner to Lee's Fried Chicken."

And we did. We had a great lunch and a great conversation! So many stories I could tell about Dr. Diuguid that he shared with me while teaching me cosmetic chemistry: about his days growing up in Lynchburg, Va.; his father, a railroad man putting him through college; his being the only African American in the college of chemistry at Cornell University, a man whose research and inventions were stolen; a man who I like to say was looked upon by some closed-minded people as being "too light to be black and too black to be white"; a man who truly attempted to make a difference in the lives of young African American youths growing up in the mean streets of St. Louis; a man who dedicated his life to finding a cure for cancer (and I bear witness, he did...). He was truly a man who walked among Kings, yet kept his touch with the common people. He is a man who will forever live in my heart, mind and soul—my teacher and friend, Dr. Lincoln Diuguid of Lynchburg, Cornell University and St. Louis. I leave you with one of my favorite quotations, which I feel best describe Doc's journey on earth:

"All men dream, but not equally. Those who dream by night in the dusty recesses of their minds, wake in the day to find that it was vanity: but the dreamers of the day are dangerous men, for they may act on their dreams with open eyes, to make them possible."—By Thomas Edward Lawrence aka Lawrence of Arabia

It may not be much, but 10 minutes or so before the start of Doc's Homegoing celebration, a very strong spiritual encounter happened. After viewing Doc's body, I took my seat 10 or 15 minutes before it started. As I sat there deep in thought, I became full of rage like a mad man possessed after thinking of what the Hurricane Katrina transient from New Orleans did to him, possibly bringing on his dementia and shortening his life. As my military training kicked in, I thought of all kinds of ways to bring pain to that person. As I began to sweat as the rage grew inside and obviously outward on my face, I remember being snapped out of it by Renee, Doc's daughter, as she hugged me telling me to let it go. Dad wouldn't want you grieving like this. Wow, I'm thinking to myself how did you know? I did let go and allowed the love to pour in rather than hate.

Farewell to my teacher, mentor and friend, Dr. Lincoln I. Diuguid, who, in life, made his dreams and the dreams of others possible! May his intelligence, zeal, spirit, wit and love and devotion to mankind forever dwell on earth!

Daryle E. Aitch, CEO
Zanzibar Island Trading Co, Ltd.
and The House Of Aitch
St. Louis

Incredible Times of Youth, Trust and Great Possibilities

I first met Dr. Lincoln Diuguid in June 1948, right after I graduated from Lincoln University in Jefferson City, Mo. My chemistry professor at Lincoln, a Dr. Moddie Taylor, who was from St. Louis had met Doc and knew that he was just starting up his laboratory there on South Jefferson Avenue. Dr. Taylor also told me that he had mentioned me to Lincoln as one of his promising graduating students who would be looking for work, especially because there were very few if any opportunities for blacks in the field of industrial science in the Greater St. Louis Area. And we never enjoyed the privilege of meeting with recruiters from companies needing science graduates. At that time we were not even permitted to go to the flagship state university (the University of Missouri-Columbia). Lincoln University served that purpose for black students. Dr. Taylor, who was a physical chemist and had worked on the Manhattan Project, was also leaving Lincoln University in June 1948 to teach at Howard University.

I did approach Dr. Diuguid for a job in June 1948. After looking around the laboratory seeing that it needed some expansion, I could understand when he told me that at the present time he was not in position to hire anyone else until he had built more business.

He did, however, take the time to explain to me what the business was all about, that it was a micro-analytical laboratory with an emphasis on the analyses of organic compounds for proof of structure, component parts and other chemical and physical properties.

Then he showed me some of the equipment used for analyses and the micro-balances used to weigh out the samples for analyses. As if my head wasn't swimming enough already, he showed me how to use the micro-balance. When I saw the size of a typical sample used for analysis I was almost in shock. Instead of the customary size of samples I used in my chemistry lab class at Lincoln, I was weighing out samples one thousand times smaller, and then it dawned upon me the significance of the term micro-analysis.

After that Lincoln showed me some of the cosmetic products that he had developed, hand cleaners, dry cleaning and hair shampoo, facial creams, perfumes and other hair products.

He then told me that even though he could not hire me, I could come to the laboratory and learn the procedures and techniques used there, which would help me later on in my career.

I gladly accepted this offer.

After some months, one of the assistants who was a classmate of his, left, and I was hired. I stayed with Lincoln for four years. There were many moments of recollection: I learned the procedures and techniques of the analyses we needed to do. This allowed Lincoln to continue his personal research work in developing cancer and leukemia compounds with activity for a cure. We spent some time in refining the techniques on some of the equipment. On slow days I would take a batch of the Du-Good Hand Cleaner to what used to be a large trucking company, down near the riverfront and I did not need to stay very long before selling out. The Hand Cleaner was different from most on the market at that time in that it did not contain ammonia as many others did. The truckers and mechanics liked this because it didn't sting if they had a cut or bruise on their hands. One fellow in Ohio wanted to market the cleaner under his own name.

My being at Du-Good Chemical also allowed Lincoln to teach at Stowe Teachers College during the day. Lincoln had a little old raggedy Ford car that he raced across town between classes. But, he made it.

There was this hair product that Lincoln named "Lola" named after a beautician who worked with us on demonstrations. This product could pin curl black women's hair. We patterned the demonstration after one used by Gillette when that company did two women's hair and asked, "Who's got the Toni?" This beautician was very prominent, and we had two young ladies who were in nurse training at Homer Phillips Nursing School, and they were twins. So she would do one twin with the regular process and pin curl the other twin just as they did in the Toni ad.

Lincoln had worked on synthesizing a compound that could be used in the preparation of perfumes. They are called a fixative. Its purpose was to blend the various odors used in making the perfume and to blend it into one characteristic distinct odor. After a very long process, he only had a few grams of the material. He decided to send it to one of the large perfume houses in New York to see whether it had any interest. The company was very interested and wanted to know what he wanted for the material on a pound basis.

One day on an incident involving the perfume, and I don't remember why I was even fooling with the perfume, I spilled some on me and it was nearing time for me to go home. I didn't have a car so I was riding the Jefferson streetcar. I sat down beside a lady and I could see her out the corner of my eye, she was sneaking looks at me.

Finally I realized that she was smelling the perfume and was wondering about this guy sitting next to her. I finally caught her when she was giving me a look and I told her everything was OK. I told her that I had spilled the perfume on me earlier in the day and that we make perfume. She was relieved but said that she would certainly like to have some. So I got her address and sent her a bottle.

I've always had the greatest respect for Lincoln's family. His dad, Lewis Walter Diuguid, was one of the most devoted and dedicated fathers I've known. He was determined for Lincoln to make it. When his mother, Bettie Diuguid, and other members of the family would come in the summer and Lincoln and his dad would go back with them, I was pleased that Lincoln had enough trust in me to leave the lab in my hands.

I knew Lincoln's brothers, Sherwood and Alfonso. In fact, Alfonso did a lot of retrofitting work at the lab. The night before Alfonso passed away, he drove me home, and when I got to Du-Good Chemical the next day, the ambulance and fire trucks were all there. They said that Alfonso had had a heart attack.

I'm in a social club called the Oaks. Sherwood was one of the early or founding members of the club. We were never in the club together. I did, however, play golf with Sherwood and Lincoln, which was always a classic event. Those two guys would compete with each other tooth and nail, and they were only betting each other a nickel per hole. Sherwood would even cough when Lincoln was getting ready to putt to disturb him. I also knew Hubert, the dentist.

I left Du-Good Chemical in 1952 when the Urban League had canvassed all of the companies around in the Greater St. Louis Area to hire blacks. They arranged for an interview for me with the armament Division of Universal Match Company. I was hired and worked there for seven years setting up a lab, doing government contract work with the Naval Ordnance Lab and others. My career went from there to do another couple years of government contractual work with Hanley Industries, a couple more years in medical research through Washington University cardiology section at St. Louis Children's Hospital and finally 26 years with McDonnell-Douglas working on the early space programs, including Mercury, Gemini, Apollo, Sky-Lab missions and the space shuttles. Other programs included the F-4, F-15 and F-18 as well as laboratory research and development and materials study programs. I retired in 1987.

Lincoln Diuguid helped me to find "me" and to have the courage to believe in me as he has done for many others over the years. One example of that was on one occasion a professor at one of the large universities sent us a sample of a metal-looking material for analysis. I performed the analysis and sent the results back to the professor. He sent us a scorching letter, saying that he thought that we were considerably in error for the analysis for nitrogen.

When Lincoln asked me about the results, I told him about what I had done and had checked standards before running the analysis. He then said check it again, which I did and got the same answer. So Lincoln wrote the professor and told him we had checked the sample and we stood by our results. The professor wrote us back saying that he had sent the sample to four different reputable laboratories, and they all agreed, and as he put it, we were considerably different in results. He sent us the results from the other laboratories and asked us to check our sample again. My guess is that he expected us to find some error that we made and come up with answers like the four reputable labs. I told Lincoln that I would check it again. He said no that I didn't have to because he believed in my results. So I did check it again but by an entirely different method and got an answer that agreed with the answer I got from the first method.

So when I told Lincoln what I had done he told me that he was glad that I did it, but he was satisfied with what we had done before because he had confidence in my work and in me, but this was a reassurance for me to believe in my work and to believe in me. We wrote to the professor and told him that we had rechecked the sample and got the same results that we got before and that we have only a few milligrams of the sample left. A few weeks later we heard from the professor, saying that we should feel especially proud because someone at the university had made a dilution error in getting the samples into a solution that they sent to the reputable laboratories. He also stated that the answer that we got helped them to solve a problem in their research work. He never made an attempt to apologize to us because he had sent us a solid sample for analysis and liquid samples to the other labs. In addition he realized that someone at the university had made a mistake.

The big thing out of all of that was the lesson I learned and was reinforced by Lincoln's belief in me—a lesson that I used and called upon all of my career.

Lincoln and I also played golf together for more than 30 years.

Nathan Lloyd Crump Sr.
Retired Chemist
St. Louis

In The Classroom, Always A Teacher With Good Humor

Memory has the unusual property of keeping major historical events in the forefront, be they tragic or rewarding, while subconsciously retaining snippets of events that guided one through the labyrinth of life's choices. Just as a catalyst in a chemical reaction seems to bring forth the products that are the hidden potential of the reactants, some comments made during an informal conversation extracts memories long hidden under the blanket of time. One such occasion was an informal discussion with Lewis Diuguid. It occurred to us that his father was my freshman chemistry teacher many decades ago.

There appears to be a hint of destiny in a surname. As an example, the name "Trump" suggests the desire to "take the whole trick" - especially for state delegates in the Presidential primary elections. In this regard, Professor Diuguid not only took advantage of the destiny of his name in founding Du-Good Chemical Laboratories and Manufacturers, but also wanted his students to "do good." He did this, not only in the usual way by telling students to study hard, but also a subtle way by the mention of the surname of a famous artist: Goya. This was not done in the context of a discussion on art, or even making a comment about art. The surname Goya was an acronym for "get off your ass," which was not said in reference to an animal of transportation in the biblical sense. It was a means of encouraging his students to actively engage in the art of learning throughout their lives by using a phrase that would be hard to forget.

My last contact with Professor Diuguid was a telephone conversation, several years ago, that was not very long, but it was very pleasant. It has found a peaceful place in my memory bank.

Kenneth S. Schmitz
*Emeritus Professor of Biophysical Chemistry
and Environmental Studies
Emeritus College
University of Missouri at Kansas City*

Family Ties and Du-Good Chemical

As the only surviving relative who spent several months at Du-Good Chemical Laboratories & Manufacturers within a year after Uncle Lincoln and some of his brothers opened the company in St. Louis in 1947, my perspective may add some insight about its creation and legacy.

Two principle advantages of St. Louis over their hometown of Lynchburg, Va., for the location of Du-Good Chemical were that the larger city contained easy access to more potential customers and the building sites. Racial attitudes and customs were, unfortunately, comparably backward in both cities. For example, after my uncles made a bid for a desirable building, the local realtor tried to stop the sale when he discovered that they were "colored." Fortunately, the owner of the building, an elderly German named Dr. William F. Heyde, stated that he did not care who they were as long as their money was good.

The acquired building had been an active veterinary hospital, with an extensive array of cages in a large room on the second floor of its front wing, behind which was a large enclosed area on the ground floor that was used for care and treatment of horses. My uncles decided to use the ground floor area for production of products and the second floor room for location of a laboratory to perform precision micro analysis of samples from customers in St. Louis and beyond. The latter conversion was the most demanding because it required the construction of long work benches with conveniently spaced sources of water, gas and electricity. It also had to be performed with family labor because all available funds had been used to purchase the building.

All available family members contributed to the work, but Uncle Alfonso deserves special mention because his critical contributions are often neglected. The contributing family members were my grandfather, Lewis Walter Diuguid, who had recently retired as a brakeman on the Norfolk and Western Railway; Uncle Lincoln, who had recently completed a postdoctoral appointment in the chemistry department at Cornell University; Uncle Sherwood, who had recently graduated from Law School at Howard University and had moved to St. Louis to set up a law practice with a former classmate named Bush; and Uncle Alfonso, who had recently moved to St. Louis from New York City.

Uncle Alfonso was the oldest member of the Diuguid siblings, and was also something of a black sheep because he left home while in high school and moved in with his grandmother in Lynchburg because he could not tolerate the rigid regiment of discipline demanded by his father. He subsequently drifted into bootlegging and migrated to New York City after some problems with the federal authorities. Nevertheless, he managed to acquire exceptional skills normally associated with a building contractor.

He also managed to avoid the tendency of many of his brothers, including yours truly, to become pack rats. For example, his tools were always stored in special places, and no one, including Uncle Lincoln, was permitted to violate his rules for return of borrowed items. His gray-green eyes, which appeared capable of freezing water at 40 paces, were indicative of a person with a hot temper. Nevertheless, I never experienced any conflicts with him during the few months spent in his presence as a young teenager in St. Louis. But Alfonso defensively exhibited regret for leaving home at an early age because it forfeited his opportunity for more formal education.

The laboratory component of the company remained economically viable for about 40 years until its manual operation procedures could no longer compete with large scale automated facilities. Nevertheless, the fugal business style of Uncle Lincoln enabled him to make an orderly shift into cancer-related research in a lab affiliated with a local hospital. His legacy of persistent hard work was admittedly difficult to pass on to younger generations because of the excessive amount of attention and money bestowed on the small numbers of athletes and entertainers who attain success in our current culture.

Another significant legacy from the entrepreneurial venture of the Diuguid brothers that is seldom appreciated by descendants of the family as well as the public at large is the pivotal role played by their father, Lewis Walter Diuguid. He set an example of honoring all obligations promptly without using issues of past or present discrimination to excuse shoddy work. That mantra proved to be invaluable, not only for the limited success of Du-Good Chemical, but for enhancing the education of its founders and endowing them with a productive work ethic.

Dr. Ross W. Newsome Jr.
Massachusetts Institute of Technology graduate
Class of 1957
Nuclear physicist
Oakhurst, N.J.

Michael Alexander, a videographer and former St. Louis TV cameraman, shot footage of Dr. Lincoln I. Diuguid at Du-Good Chemical Laboratories and Manufacturers in the early 2000s for an oral history of Doc's life and work at the company. It was after Doc was assaulted at Du-Good Chemical by a Hurricane Katrina evacuee whom Doc tried to help by providing the man with a job in 2006. You will see the scar on the right side of Doc's forehead. It is one of several he had to have from brain surgery to relieve the swelling from being struck on the head with a heavy object three times, robbed and left for dead. Fortunately, someone in the community surrounding the lab saw Doc's door ajar, knowing that was unusual, entered and immediately called for help. The link to Michael Alexander's video and interview by Gwen Moore is below.

https://drive.google.com/file/d/0B17Nv9FiJlSbcERfc3ZySlk3OFU/view?ts=581a2725

ABOUT THE AUTHOR

Lewis W. Diuguid is the recipient of the 2017 Louis M. Lyons Award for Conscience and Integrity in Journalism at Harvard University. With the honor, he was named a 2017 Knight Visiting Fellow, at the Nieman Foundation for Journalism at Harvard. Diuguid was an editorial board member and columnist with *The Kansas City Star* until October 2016. He started with the newspaper as a reporter/photographer in May 1977 after graduating from the University of  Missouri-Columbia School of Journalism. He is the author of *A Teacher's Cry: Expose the Truth About Education Today (2004)* and *Discovering the Real America: Toward a More Perfect Union (2007)*. He is a founding member and president of the Kansas City Association of Black Journalists. He is the winner of many awards, including the 2000 Missouri Honor Medal for Distinguished Service in Journalism.

CPSIA information can be obtained
at www.ICGtesting.com
Printed in the USA
FFOW05n1940230717